SOFTWARE QUALITY MANAGEMENT

with contributions by

W. EARL BOEBERT
Honeywell Systems and Research Laboratories

JOHN R. BROWN
Boeing Computer Services

HAROLD L. ERGOTT, Jr.
Norden Systems, Inc.

BARNEY M. KNIGHT
IBM

HORACE M. LEAVITT, Jr.
Naval Electronic Systems Command

ROBERT O. LEWIS
Science Applications, Inc.

WILLIAM R. LIGHT, Jr.
Bell Telephone Laboratories

JAMES A. McCALL
General Electric Corporation

J. GARY NELSON
U.S. Army Test & Evaluation Command

LAWRENCE J. PETERS
Boeing Computer Services

DONALD J. REIFER
TRW

NORMAN F. SCHNEIDEWIND
Naval Postgraduate School

JAMES D. STRINGER
Computer Sciences Corporation

GENE F. WALTERS
General Electric Corporation

JON A. WHITED
TRW

DENNIS L. WOOD
Software Enterprises Corporation

Software Quality Management

JOHN D. COOPER   *Commander (Ret.)*
MATTHEW J. FISHER   *Department of the Army*

editors

PBI

A PETROCELLI BOOK
new york / princeton

Library of Congress Cataloging in Publication Data

Main entry under title:

Software quality management.

    "A Petrocelli book."
    1. Computer programs — Reliability. 2. Computer
programming management. I. Cooper, John D.
II. Fisher, Matthew J.
QA76.6.S636 001.6′42   79-14172
ISBN O-89433-093-4

Contents

v

Preface

This book is an outgrowth of an earlier initiative to conduct a software reliability, availability, and maintainability (RAM) conference. The group behind that initiative consisted of several well intended hardware RAM professionals. Software had become problematic within their discipline and they realized that solutions for software did not exist. Their idea was that if a large conference could be held, maybe some solutions would result. Unfortunately, their concept of a solution was mean-time-to-repair (MTTR) for software.

The ensuing discussions centered around topics such as: "Why can't you have a MTTR for software?" and "There are lots of people that include in their contracts, mean-time-between-failure (MTBF) as a measure of software reliability." They felt that the software engineers were "a bunch of cultists" and were being stubborn by not seeing things their way.

In any debate one useful tactic is to always overstate the truth. Thus, the software counterargument went like this:

The subject of software reliability has been extensively researched for over twenty years. It has been conducted by thousands of knowledgeable scientists, many of whom are brilliant. Perhaps the reason they have not yet arrived at a consensus definition of "software reliability," much less any of its measures, is that it doesn't exist—in short, these scientists have been chasing a holy grail.

On the other hand, software is perfectly reliable. It works the same way each and every time. It never wears out or deteriorates; spare parts for software are inconsequential. What is preventive maintenance but further debugging and testing?

From here the software side's logic continued by admitting that there was indeed something intuitive about software reliability, but what was really being thought was that the programs should operate the way they are expected, i.e., correctly. What is correctness but one of the quality factors of software!

The eventual compromise between the two camps was that, for the time being, the RAM thrust would be dropped and the conference would concentrate on quality. This was especially appropriate since both groups espouse that reliability should be designed in up front in a software development.

This book, which is the collection of all papers presented at the conference that ultimately resulted, treats reliability, availability, and maintainability merely as subsets or factors of software quality. Many of our software development problems in the past were brought about by the blind or uninformed application of traditional hardware RAM techniques and/or procedures. A major purpose of this book is to take that issue head-on. It will be pointed out that hardware and software really are different in many important ways. It will also be shown where and why many of these hardware-oriented techniques and procedures are inappropriate for software. Finally, some of the latest proven and effective software techniques and procedures are presented. It is hoped that by the end of the book a good case will have been developed that can be used to educate and enlighten those persons not familiar with software engineering.

Another thrust of this book is in the area of management. The literature is full of articles and papers on technical issues in software quality. Conversely, very little has ever been written about the management aspects of not only software quality but all of software engineering. This void is the subject of this book. You will find management as the major theme throughout. It can then be said that this was at least one book that did not neglect coverage of software quality management.

The Editors

Software Quality Management as a Discipline

HAROLD L. ERGOTT, JR.

Programming technology is now becoming a major science. It is developing as an important physical branch of mathematics in much the same way as physics and engineering. Programming technology has much in common with engineering technology and, in particular, computer system architecture and logic design. It is sufficiently different, however, to require its own disciplines, design practices, theoretical tools, and management standards. The software that is developed as a result of the application of programming technology is of such importance to the performance of any system that significant attention should be paid to the quality of that product.

One of the significant challenges of software quality management, and certainly a challenge for overall software and program management, is the fine line between the supervision of software quality and the management of software development. If the overall software management team performs in a truly outstanding manner so that all expected outcomes are realized, then, of course, additional activity in the way of management for quality is redundant. Experience has shown, however, that the developmental pressures of schedule, technical performance, and cost are not always conducive to provide line management the continued opportunity to operate with the necessary independent discretion and judgment in order to produce a product of maximum quality. Recognizing factors such as these, software quality management must emerge as a separate and distinct element of the overall development process and should, as will be described later, be maintained in a reporting structure that is independent of the development process.

Leading toward the idea that software quality management is a discipline, I would first like to discuss some connotations of software quality. The chapters that follow will treat this subject at some length. However, I would like to start with a look at software quality in its highest form. I will not attempt to provide a detailed definition of what is meant by software quality management other than to assert that the management of software quality must provide assurance that the end product achieves the expectation of the designer or user in both short- and long-term needs. Assessing progress toward this goal requires consideration of many parameters such as core utilization, code readability, acquisition and maintenance cost, accuracy, performance speed, and general functional performance. However, I believe that the quality of the end result relies on much more than ensuring that the software product performs in a prescribed manner. I believe there is much more to quality than reliability of documentation and adherence to accepted design practices and standards. In fact, two software program modules can pass identical verification and validation testing and provide equal performance against a specification and still be considerably different in overall quality. For example, one program module, while it might meet all of the specifications and be relatively easy to maintain, might not have the structure that permits ease of expansion of functions. If this "ease of expansion" against unexpected requirements is a desirable attribute of the program module, then this must be a part of the quality assessment.

This idea might be considered obvious; however, I have often seen software quality programs that have focused only on a performance specification, a core allocation, documentation criteria, and schedule or cost criteria. Many of these programs have successfully passed all of the established management criteria but, in the field, have proved to be programs of overall poor quality. This result occurs because the initial system concept and software architecture paid too little attention to the definition of the total structure of the intended environment.

Systems concepts and software architecture should be considered in their broadest terms, with the requirements for system testing during advanced and engineering development phases playing a significant role in the overall requirement specification. System developmental requirements should be considered as well as the requirements of the system in its ultimate operational form. The type of flight testing, field testing, or sea trials must be carefully considered in structuring the system requirements that lead to the software specification. The expected longevity of the system and its ultimate interfacing requirements must be considered early in the design process. It must also be recognized that most successful weapon systems have a longevity that is well in excess of that postulated during initial development. As a result, the configuration should be defined to permit the acceptance of presently unknown technological advances as well as connection to, as yet, undefined weapons, command and control, or intelligence systems. Software architecture must consider the total breadth of software from operating systems to application software to high-order languages, software development and debug tools, general diagnostic aids, existing software libraries, and general utilities.

In short, to achieve improved software quality, more definition and structure is required earlier in a program than usually occurs. I will not elaborate on these points any further here, since the remaining chapters address in detail issues related to the management of a product for a high level of quality. This will include an ability to place a quality assessment on the total architecture of the software package.

The concept that completeness of system requirements is fundamental to the generation of quality software leads to the question of where systems analysis stops and where software development begins. There are a number of standards which define the levels of design and development specifications that must be developed and utilized during a system development program. However, the quality of this process bears on the identification, understanding, and communication of requirements which we must have in order to yield a quality product. My experience, supported by a number of authors, has been that many of the fundamental problems attributed to software are actually initiated during system analysis. Therefore, it is important to recognize at the outset that we must be assured of a high-quality, reliable set of design specifications and that these faithfully reproduce the system requirements. Then we can have a development that provides for a high-quality product at each step.

While complete data is not yet available, I have estimated that approximately 45 percent of all software problems discovered during system integration and initial testing have a genesis in an imperfect understanding of the requirements at the time that the software was initially considered. Although problems such as these constitute less than half of the difficulties that are found in tests and eventual system application, they most likely account for over 80 percent of the cost associated with software debug during integration and operational use. Errors of this nature are the most expensive to fix on a per line of code basis because, in general, more documentation is impacted when corrections must be made to conceptual problems rather than simple coding errors. These factors clearly indicate that quality management can make the greatest contribution by assuring that the initial development requirements and the development approach are of the highest quality prior to the initiation of actual software development.

One method of providing assurance of the development of a quality specification is the reduction of the system requirements to an executable format through use of executable design language. This provides a computer-based tool which supports interactive, structured, top-down development. A design language, which allows for entry and editing of structured narrative for maintenance of the conceptual-level flows associated with the early stages of the product cycle, provides a systems analyst with a technique for the examination of the design. This examination is such that a top-level test of design consistency may be achieved, thereby providing criteria against which the software can be developed so that the resulting product serves the intended use. It is also very important that this capability exist early in the development process to provide management and potential users with a clear description of what will be achieved if the software faithfully executes the system design. Very often the development process goes all the way through coding, simulation, or actual application in a system, and it is then discovered that the user has either changed his mind about the requirements or the requirements were miscommunicated. The bottom line result is that a great deal of time was spent developing software that does not perform the functions desired by the customer.

It is not my intention here to describe the total development process, but a few comments on this subject, which is conducive to development of quality software, are in order. The design language and structured top-down development should not be considered as independent elements in the design process. The total software development process should be thought of as a pyramid with the statement of requirements at the apex and the completed software package making up the lowermost strata of the pyramid. The objective is to achieve at the bottom the requirements as stated at the top. The first strata below the definition of requirements could be thought of as the level of execution of system requirements in some form of design language. If proper top-down structuring in this pyramid is obtained along with the proper set of tools, it is then possible to segment the total set of requirements into individual modules so that each module has a uniquely defined set of interfaces and a transfer function. With the total set of requirements thus segmented, it is possible to demonstrate the expected performance of these modules either singly or linked in proper combinations. Such a demonstration, if performed in a simple executable design language, provides an early and low-cost assessment of specification completeness and correctness. As each module is reduced to executable code, the design language module is replaced by its executable code successor. The total system may then be re-exercised, made up of design language modules linked to fully coded modules. Expected performance may be evaluated as each module is completed, thereby providing a significant measure of development progress. Equally important is that this method permits additional insight into the quality of the software as the program moves through the development process. By use of compatible design languages at the various strata within the pyramid, development may proceed at various levels simultaneously as long as each software module passes through the complete sequence of development from the statement of requirements to its particular level of development. This approach, then, permits the binding of the total package into a sequence that consists of many different levels of developmental completeness but should, nevertheless, provide results that are totally consistent with those achieved by execution of the system requirements at their highest level. This approach not only permits a high degree of parallel development but also provides management with an absolute go/no-go indication of the status of development for each module.

Many system and software companies currently possess the capability to generate an executable system description using high-level language. I am not trying to present this as new data; however, I would like to assert that this is the point at which software quality starts. Such capability permits a clear description of the design requirements based on an execution of the design. This allows documentation of system performance and flexibility prior to the release of the software specification. The process yields a high degree of assurance of a quality beginning for the software product.

It is true that many of the quality procedures and quality management requirements to be addressed herein require a great deal of technical and management attention and, therefore, cost. However, quality management should be viewed as an integral part of the development process and, hence, can be a significant development aid. For example, the use of an executable design language is often thought of as prohibitively expensive. However, it should be recognized that many of the errors attributable to initial design problems, found during acceptance and field trials, could have been detected earlier using the techniques described here. Early discovery of major problems can provide a significant reduction in cost per line of code.

Just as the hardware engineer would never release a new design to full production without thorough verification in the form of design reviews, breadboards, prototypes, and system integration activity within the laboratory, software quality management must ensure the adequacy of the software by imposing plans and procedures that provide for well-defined milestones that allow the evaluation of level of performance at each step. In this way, errors found during acceptance tests are minimized, and software costs are brought to their lowest level.

Current quality management methods usually treat items such as (1) verification and validation, (2) contractual controls, (3) use of unit development folders, (4) walk-throughs, and (5) documentation criteria as milestones in a software development program. There is another aspect of quality management, however, that is often overlooked and should be seriously considered as a part of the quality management discipline. This aspect concerns itself with development tools and programmer aids. For example, I am sure you would agree that, in general, it is more difficult to develop quality software as economically at an assembly level as it is using a higher-order language. Many people claim that programmer productivity is increased by a factor of four by going from assembly language to a high-order language. My experience generally supports this; however, I have seen instances in which use of a particular compiler yielded software of overall lower quality and higher cost than a specific assembly language approach due to the differences in availability of program development aids and software diagnostic tools in the two systems. I believe that software quality management as a discipline should focus not only on the development process and resulting production system but also on the programmer support tools needed for any software development system in order to provide a quality product at reasonable cost. In particular, each of us interested in software quality should do our part in assuring that the new Department of Defense Common High Order Language does not have serious shortcomings relative to programmer development aids that some of its predecessors have.

When considering the quality of the development process, one must not neglect the quality of documentation. Milestone documents such as (1) software system design criteria, (2) implementation concept and test plan, (3) software system interface specification, (4) software module design specification, (5) software module documentation, (6) system test and acceptance specification, and (7) the operating instructions and system configuration index should have specific standards of quality. Tools such as Script and Hierarchical Input Processing Output (HIPO) should be seriously considered as requirements for meeting basic quality management documentation standards.

What we have discussed thus far has related to specific areas of software development and the requirements for quality management of these areas. These activities do not, however, stand alone and must be applied within the framework of a comprehensive software development plan. This plan must establish the proper management commitment and should delineate the communications required by and the authority given to the various management elements associated with the software development process. The plan should state in unambiguous terms the organization, responsibilities and structure of the groups that will be designing, producing, and testing all of the computer programs. It is important here that adequate consideration be given to the interfaces between all these organizations and program management.

The plan must clearly delineate the management and technical controls that will be used during the development process including the controls that will ensure that all performance and design requirements have been implemented. This plan should specifically define the role of software quality management and must address the techniques that will be utilized to ensure that true status will be reported to senior management and customer organizations in a clear and concise manner. It is fundamental to the success of the program that such status reports be organized and presented so that judgments relative to the progress of the software developments may be made by management personnel who are not necessarily trained in the field of software development. These controls also must provide the proper methodology to ensure satisfactory design and testing, and complete delineation of the role of quality assurance in the process.

The software development plan must provide an overall development schedule for each computer program configuration item and should include a schedule of program milestone review points associated with each configuration item. This schedule must also show key relationships between the system development process and external influences such as system analysis, hardware/software integration, and field testing.

The phasing of resources required to support the software development and test must also be specified in the plan. These resource requirements should include not only human resources and software development facilities, but also recognition of special simulation, data reduction, or utility tools that are planned for use in the development of the software.

General procedures for reporting, monitoring, and resolving program errors and deficiencies during development and testing must be specified. Typical of the documents required by such a procedure would be:

1. *Program change request* which documents the request for and the results of analysis and evaluation of a new or changing requirement or other technical issue which requires a coordinated project response.
2. *Program trouble report* which documents the symptoms and results of analysis of observed or suspected program trouble and authorizes source code changes to the master system, both for trouble corrections and for implementation of approved functional changes.
3. *Program maintenance status report* which summarizes each reported program trouble, its current status, and the action taken to close the item.

Software quality assurance should take an active role in the review of each of these reports.

The development plan should provide the methods and procedures to be used for collecting, analyzing, monitoring, and reporting on the timing of time-critical programs as well as performance against core allocation.

A librarian system should be specified to provide for the management of computer program development master, data bases, and associated documentation, including its relationship to the configuration management plan.

Consistent with my previous assertion that software quality must also consider the future use of software, the development plan must have appropriate guidelines and check points for ensuring computer program growth, modularity, and ease of modification. The development plan is the place where the approach for the development of computer program documentation is clearly defined. Documentation must be an up-front decision and cannot be left as an additional task for the programmer after software development has been completed.

Training requirements for the deployment phase must be considered early, and the relationship of operational or maintenance needs to the architecture of the software or software development tools must be considered and firm policies adopted.

Software security controls and requirements are specified in the development plan. This is an issue that will provide severe tests for the quality assurance organization in terms of its ability to make correct judgments relative to the degree to which security requirements are being met.

Of course, no plan would be complete without the specification of standards, conventions, and rules for program design.

Thus far, several of the elements required for a quality software product have been delineated and are background for the discussion of software quality management as a discipline. We have seen that the need for breadth in software quality management is greater than the breadth required for the development of system software. It is also key that management for quality be independent of the development process. The most successful quality organizations that I have known have reported to the program manager directly, and independently of the manager of software development.

The discipline of software quality management must cover, as a minimum, (a) analysis of system requirements; (b) application software development procedures, such as top-down programming and structured programming; and (c) software quality management procedures in order to be in a position to evaluate and make recommendations for the improvement in programmer productivity. Software quality concepts should also be intimately involved in the specification of environments for software development tools and aids. For example, the concept of a software development laboratory or software factory is very useful for efficient generation of software for large systems. Software quality management should consider such a capability as an overall tool for quality improvement and, as such, the requirements for such a facility including procedures, practices, standards, and programmer measurement techniques should be an integral part of the quality program.

In summary, I have touched on several ideas regarding "software quality management." First, it should be considered a discipline as formal as that for "hardware quality management." Second, the first step in achieving an adequate quality program involves early definition of the overall structure of the software system, including design requirements as well as the usual performance specification, documentation criteria, etc. Third, requirements for computer-based tools and program development aids and, hence, programmer productivity should be an integral part of the software quality assurance program. Fourth, that strict quality standards for software documentation be required and, finally, that the management of a software quality effort be independent of the software development management.

PART ONE

Principles of Software Quality Management

CHAPTER 1

Definitions in Software Quality Management

MATTHEW J. FISHER and
WILLIAM R. LIGHT, JR.

INTRODUCTION

Meaningful discussions in any scientific area can occur only if the participants agree to structure their dialogues around a common framework. For the rapidly evolving field of software* quality management, this framework can be provided by a consistent set of definitions.

Clearly, the very attempt at such a compilation implies some selection and baselining of terminology; while the particular selection may not meet the universal agreement, it is the intent here to provide just the required framework relative to the remainder of this book.

When one examines the abundance of pertinent literature, it becomes evident that three fundamental concepts emerge as the prime structural members of our common framework. These concepts are:

1. Computer software
2. Computer software quality
3. Computer software quality management

In choosing this specific triad, we emphasize the relationships among all the concepts, functions, and terms rather than stressing the words themselves. Other desired terms can be grouped within these

*The term "software" as used throughout this book will mean computer software.

three major areas. Table 1 presents an example of such a grouping with a partial list of underlying terms. In this chapter, our approach will be to concentrate on defining the three major terms and a sufficient number of subordinate terms to support the major areas. Subsequent chapters will expand upon the base of these definitions.

This "relational" approach rather than a "glossary of terms" has been adopted for the following reasons: (1) The form of a glossary is a set of definitions related to a particular field, in the language of that field. It may be too terse, placing upon the user the burden of understanding the underlying connectivity of the terms; (2) The functional dependence implicit in the concepts of software, software quality, and software quality management represents the more important element in our understanding of software quality management.

TABLE 1. *Grouping of terms*

I. Computer Software
   A. Computer Program
      1. Applications programs
      2. Support programs
      3. Utility programs
      4. Deliverable programs
   B. Computer Data
   C. Computer Program Documentation
      1. Computer program documentation
         (a) Specifications/narratives
         (b) Listings
         (c) Manuals
      2. Other documentation
         (a) Verification cross-reference index
         (b) Program trouble reports
   D. Firmware

II. Computer Software Quality
   A. Quality Attributes/Factors
      1. Performance compliance
      2. Flexibility
      3. Testability
      4. Reliability
      5. Acceptability

III. Computer Software Quality Management
   A. Assessment
   B. Verification/Validation
   C. Certification
   D. Maintenance

The sequence our discussion takes relies upon the functional inter-relation of the three major concepts. The definition of software quality management rests upon the definition of software quality. The qualities of software are, in the same manner, dependent on the nature of software itself. Therefore, the order of definition in this chapter begins with software, proceeds to software quality, and concludes with software quality management. The concept of firmware takes its place as a special case of software.

COMPUTER SOFTWARE

From a software quality management perspective, software can be defined as: "computer programs, associated computer data and documentation" [1]. Computer software is a comprehensive term that includes both abstract and nonabstract items which encompass all the planning, rationale, design criteria, standards, and other intelligence concerned with the development, operation, and deployment of a computer program. In a broad sense, computer software represents the transfer of the problem-solving process from conceptualization to the computer equipment, documentation, or other physical representation.

Problem solving may be considered as an abstract thought process which involves: (1) Establishment or formulation of the problem, (2) a specific implementation mechanism for its solution (e.g., a series of instructions or steps required to obtain the solution).

In terms of computer software, these thought processes are usually manifested in a physical form. That portion representing the formulation of the problem, rationale behind the implementation, and the implementation itself — all in human-readable form — is called computer program documentation. That portion representing the implementation of the solution — in machine-readable form — is called the computer program and computer data (it is noted that when a computer program resides within a computer, it is still a physical representation).

It is equally important to consider the rationale supporting a specific solution as well as the solution itself. Therefore, the term computer software may be thought of as a comprehensive term including all the physical representations of the entire problem-solving process, i.e., computer program, computer data, and computer program documentation. The subordinate definitions that support this are [1]:

Computer program — A series of instructions or statements in a form acceptable to computer equipment and designed to cause the computer to execute an operation or operations.

5

Computer data — A representation of facts, concepts, or instructions in a structured form suitable for acceptance, interpretation, or processing by computer equipment. Such data can be external to (in computer-readable form) or resident within the computer equipment.

Computer program documentation — Technical data, including program listings and printouts, in human-readable form which document the requirements, design, implementation, and other details of the computer program. It also provides instructions for using and maintaining the computer program.

The above set of definitions may be clarified if one approaches them from the standpoints of the owner and the creator. The *owner* is often referred to as the *user* or *acquisition manager*. The *creator* is normally considered the *developer* or *contractor*. For both the owner and the creator a computer program represents the implementation of a set of functions in the form of a series of "instructions" or statements suitable for execution by a computer. Also common to both is the set of associated computer data consisting of constants, tabular representations of functions special to the task, or sequences of instructions that are task independent but may be particular to the hardware.

On the other hand, one finds that owners and creators have separate ideas concerning computer program documentation. Documentation stands as the formal communications among the software development community, i.e., among the users of the software, among the developers of the software, and between the user group and the developing group. From the owner's perspective, documentation can include:

1. A record of the concept formulation phase culminating in a list of functional requirements for the desired task.
2. Creator-generated records of the design, coding, and testing processes in human-readable form in sufficient detail to allow the owner or his representative to subsequently change the software as necessary.
3. Operator's manuals for the system, including instructions for effecting program changes.
4. A record of problems encountered during program operation, plus the resulting changes to the software. Interpretation of this data can facilitate the concept formulation stage of a follow-on system and can assist in determining when the task should be performed.

From the software creator's viewpoint, documentation consists of:

1. An owner-generated set of system requirements.
2. Preliminary and interim design, coding, testing reports, operating manuals, and interface parameter lists.
3. Configuration control records, including program trouble reports and change proposals for evaluation.
4. Standards for designing, coding, and testing of software. In any event, it can be seen that documentation is an integral part of computer software, and whatever quality management activities apply to computer programs and data are equally applicable to the documentation.

Firmware

Finally, one must consider the term "firmware." This term has been greatly distorted by people in the management area, sometimes from ignorance and often as an excuse for not applying good software management practices. Firmware is a blend of hardware and software consisting of software algorithms stored in relatively permanent hardware (media) [2]. Thus, *firmware* is *software* (computer programs, associated computer data, and documentation), but in a form practically unalterable except by replacement of hardware components.

The critical point is that the generation of firmware should follow precisely the same development principles as followed for all other software. The quality management and the quality factors that must be considered are the same. The only difference might be the influence of certain factors relating to the relative unalterability of the final form.

COMPUTER SOFTWARE QUALITY

Software quality may be defined as: "The composite of all attributes which describe the degree of excellence of the computer software" [1]. Computer software quality is a *composite* of the intrinsic attributes of computer software. The "quality" is not dependent upon what is desired, specified, or measured, but, rather, only upon the nature of the software. It may be noticed that the quality includes all aspects of the software: computer programs, data, and documentation. For some applications, the quality of the documentation may be as important as the quality of the computer programs and data.

It is critical to understand that one primary quality factor to be addressed for computer software is compliance with desired performance requirements (these requirements relate to the functions to be performed by the software). Many quality management activities are directed toward determining this compliance.

Software Quality: Attributes and Metrics

In contracts, and for purposes of software quality management, practical usage of terms like "degree of excellence" (in the above definition for software quality) implies a measurable quality that can be precisely specified by the prospective software "owner." This leads to the concept of software quality metrics, which themselves are the subject of several subsequent chapters [3,4,6].

Table 2 presents a brief list of qualities and the associated quality factors. Note that both of these terms are word statements of the problem, i.e., they are qualitative statements. The subsequent transformation into quantitative expressions is accomplished through metrics. To illustrate the connection among qualities, quality factors, and metrics, consider the software quality "easy to change" and its quality factor "flexibility." Flexibility of software includes "adaptability" (the ease of modifying, extending, and maintaining computer software while, at the same time, sustaining or improving performance) [3]. Criteria which affect adaptability include:

Module coupling
Time-dependent code
Data/control flow
Percent cycle time uncommitted
Percent memory uncommitted
Number of lines of code

All these attributes can be represented by separate analytical expressions which then can be combined to yield a "measure" of adaptability [1]. This measure is a metric for the quality factor of adaptability. Table 3 illustrates the analogy of this quality factor and its metric to the hardware quality factor, reliability and its metric, MTBF.

TABLE 2. *Partial list of software quality attributes*

Quality	Quality factor
Easy to change	Flexibility
Easy to use	Acceptability
Easy to test	Testability
Easy to understand	Human engineering
More efficient	Efficiency

TABLE 3. *Comparison of hardware and software quality factors*

	Quality factor	Metric	RQMT/test
Hardware	Reliability	Equation for MTBF	3000 hrs/ Test conditions for measurement
Software	Adaptability	Expressions for coupling, etc.	95% Test conditions for measurement

Software Reliability

A current fallacy is that the terms software quality and software reliability are synonymous. This equivalence is perhaps the result of the traditional quality assurance syndrome — trying to force software definitions into existing hardware components. Based upon the fact that quality is a composite of many attributes, one may conclude that reliability does not constitute all of software quality but is only a subset of total quality. The term software reliability has received considerable attention in the literature. (For this reason it will be expanded upon later in this book.) Past efforts have centered about predicting the probability that software will fail to perform as expected [6,7]. In the name of software reliability, estimates have sometimes been made of mean-time-between-failure as if software "wore out" like a shoe or "burned out" like a vacuum tube.

Clearly, software development is a new process involved in implementing a human intellectual endeavor. It is the norm in any human endeavor to commit errors. Thus, errors are implanted in the software. This is the true source of software failures — not the fault of "wear and tear." More simply stated, the source of software failures is not related to time as it is with the physics of hardware failures. Time only comes into play if one considers that detecting software failures indirectly involves a period of testing and use. However, this relationship is far from being direct. Therefore, for software, reliability becomes a question of correctness, confidence, accuracy, and precision rather than the time to the next failure.

COMPUTER SOFTWARE QUALITY MANAGEMENT

Computer software quality management may be defined as: "A program of planned and systematic activities to determine, achieve and maintain required computer software quality" [1]. Quality management activities include all actions performed to assure the quality of the software. These activities are not restricted to quality assurance functions. Quality management (QM) and quality assurance (QA) are not synonymous. Quality management includes QA but is a more comprehensive entity. Table 4 gives a partial list of functions which can be considered as quality management actions. Note that verification and validation, the subject of a subsequent chapter, is a subset of the total span of quality management activities.

By using functional rather than organizational definitions for software quality management, our discussion has attempted to eliminate prejudices introduced by traditional quality control activities and their organizational boundaries. Hardware quality activities fall into an established discipline with the associated organizational boundaries and responsibilities being well defined. Conversely, software quality management is a new discipline entitled to different organizational boundaries and responsibilities (rather than arbitrarily assigning these responsibilities to existing hardware organizations).

Consider, for example, hardware quality control which relies heavily upon product inspection for evaluating workmanship. Technical understanding of the design of the product is not required for this inspection. When trying to impose the same approach on software, one quickly learns that most of the quality problems lie in the design, not in the final code per se. More technical competence is therefore required when "inspecting" the design of software. When responsibilities for software quality have been assigned to established hardware organizations, the typical result has been that the inspection-type

TABLE 4. *Partial list of quality management actions*

1. Preparation of software quality management program plan
2. Development of policies/procedures/standards
3. Software quality assurance audits of documentation, design, configuration management, testing
4. Analysis/evaluation/enforcement
5. Certification/testing
6. Verification/validation
7. Education/training
8. Participation in design reviews and configuration audits
9. Subcontractor control
10. Preservation/handling
11. Program management support
12. Identification and certification of tools, techniques, and methodologies

functions for software were relegated to hardware QA groups, while software quality evaluations (which required higher technical ability) were assigned to other organizations within the quality management sphere.

Software quality management activities may be broadly classified into two categories: quality control and quality design [8]. Both of these areas are functionally interdependent. Table 5 shows these categories and the general functions related to these categories.

Quality Control

Quality control activities for software and hardware are, in general, similar. They differ primarily in the detail of their implementation. Such activities may be grouped into three broad categories — planning, procedural assessments, and product assessments.

PLANNING. The control of software quality requires the ability to specify and measure the attributes desired. Similarly, controlling quality management activities requires specification of milestones, procedures, desired or expected results, etc. This specification constitutes a plan. Such a plan must answer: Who is doing "how much" of "what" for "whom" by "when" at what "cost"? Such a plan should be established early in the acquisition process and continually updated over the life of the project. Both the owner and the creator must be part of the planning process and their actions unified under the plan.

Many developers are opposed to generating a software quality management plan because of the status of their development, small size of their computer program, use of firmware, or a variety of other reasons. Contrary to this perspective, it is felt that a software quality management plan is useful for all software developments whether firmware is being acquired, microprocessors are being used, the computer program is 10 lines of code or 10^6 lines of code. While the plan should be tailored to the size and complexity of the project, it is

TABLE 5. *Software quality management*

Quality control
    Planning
    Assessment of Procedural Aspects
    Assessment of Product Quality Compliance

Quality design
    Implementation of Quality Criteria

---

critical that a plan exist. The opposition is usually based upon short-term cost savings. In the long term, however, such a plan tends to save significant amounts of resources in terms of money and manpower. A typical format for a software quality management plan is given in Table 6.

PROCEDURAL ASSESSMENTS. Software quality management encompasses assessment of the procedures and disciplines used in the development, acquisition, management, and maintenance of the software product. This concept is reflected in the phrase "program of planned and systematic activities" in the definition for software quality management given earlier. Quality management may be characterized by the regulations to be obeyed in structuring a software life cycle program. It provides a framework of laws within which the software community operates, thereby introducing engineering discipline to the software effort. Once such a framework has been established, it is a function of quality management to monitor and enforce compliance by the software community members to the policies, regulations, guidelines, and standards constituting this framework. One example of a procedural assessment is the enforcement of drawing standards during the creation of software flow diagrams.

PRODUCT ASSESSMENTS. In addition to the examination of procedures, quality management also includes assessment of the software product

TABLE 6. *Format for a software quality management plan*

1.0 Management Overview
    1.1 Objectives of plan
    1.2 Schedule
    1.3 System overview
    1.4 Management control procedures
    1.5 Organization/resources

2.0 System Functional Summary
    2.1 Information required
    2.2 Software development process

3.0 Software Quality Requirements
    3.1 Software quality factors
    3.2 Software quality metrics

4.0 Life Cycle Tasks
    4.1 Software quality management flowchart
    4.2 Task descriptions

5.0 Documentation Requirements

itself. Through continuous review, analysis, verification, validation, etc., of the software as it is being developed, deficiencies may be found which have two sources. First, such deficiencies may be indicative of procedural problems as discussed above. For example, by performing trend analysis of software deficiencies, quality personnel may trace these deficiencies to the failure of a programmer to follow stated interface standards. Thus, product assessments can lead to the discovery of procedural infractions.

Second, the deficiencies may be in the software product itself. Independently finding these deficiencies assures compliance of the product with stated requirements. Checking product compliance in this case is akin to but not the same as the quality control process for hardware fabrication. Examples of methodologies used for these assessments include design walk-throughs, code audits, evaluation of support software, analyses of test results, and review of automatic test equipment performance.

Quality Design

Software quality design relates to the approach used in designing quality into the software product. Here, one is explicitly concerned with precisely defining what level of quality is desired, how higher-quality products are designed, and how the level of quality is determined through testing. While the quality control function elicits an external or "independent" role, in terms of software development, quality design involves more of a participation in the actual design.

The first step in quality design is to specify and quantify the quality factors or attributes desired in the final product. For example, one might desire to have "85 percent flexibility" and a "reliability measure of .99" (these are hypothetical measures). Then, practices, tools, and methodologies must be implemented to help assure that the product will exhibit the desired qualities and to the degree specified. Such items may include the use of HIPO, chief programmer teams, top-down design, or, minimally, standards for naming subroutines.

In addition to these procedural approaches, quality personnel may then require that the software be designed or structured to yield the required "85 percent flexibility" and ".99 reliability." For example, they may require each subroutine to have single entry-single exit, or they may forbid time-dependent code, or they may set down other design regulations which increase the flexibility and reliability.

Finally, quality personnel must develop and implement test scenarios which validate that the quality levels desired have been achieved.

13

SUMMARY

The definitions presented here are offered in the spirit of guidelines only. Further expansion of the terminology is deferred to subsequent chapters. We highlight below some of the basic points:

1. Definitions for computer software quality management can be grouped under three fundamental concepts: software, software quality, software quality management.
2. Computer software consists not only of computer programs and associated data, but also of computer program documentation.
3. Firmware is a special case of software; thus, its development requires the use of the same quality management practices used for other software.
4. Software quality contains many attributes including those for performance and reliability, i.e., these two are interrelated with but not synonymous with the total software quality.
5. The physics of software reliability is not related to time, and attempts to measure this attribute using time-oriented hardware techniques such as MTBF are inappropriate.
6. Hardware management perspectives of software quality are only partially viable. New management perspectives need to be developed.
7. Software quality management consists of quality control, the assessment of procedural and product compliance; and quality design, the insertion of quality attributes into the software design and development.

References

1. Fisher, M. J., et al. "Software Quality Assurance and Reliability as it Relates to Configuration Management," *Report of the Eleventh Annual EIA Data and Configuration Management Workshop, Panel No. 7*, San Diego, CA, October 17–21, 1977.
2. Klingman, Edwin E. *Microprocessor Systems Design.* Englewood Cliffs, N.J.: Prentice-Hall, Inc., 1977.
3. Light, William R. "Software Reliability/Quality Assurance Practices," *Software Management Symposium*, Washington, D.C., March 1976.
4. McCall, Jim A., et al. "Factors in Software Quality," *Volumes I, II and III, RADC-TR-77-369, Final Technical Report*, November 1977.
5. Boehm, B. W., et al. "Quantitative Evaluation of Software Quality," *Software Engineering Conference*, August 1976.
6. *Proceedings of International Conference on Reliable Software*, Los Angeles, CA, 1975.

7. Musa, J. P. "A Theory of Software Reliability and its Application," *IEEE Transactions on Software Engineering,* vol. SE-1, no. 3, September 1975.
8. Fisher, M. J. "Software Quality Assurance Practices," *Proceedings of the American Society of Quality Control,* Bethpage, L.I., April 1976.
9. Barricelli, F., Fisher, M.J., and Light, W.R. "Software Quality Assurance," Fort Monmouth, N.J., December 1976.

CHAPTER 2

Software Quality Through Software Management

W. EARL BOEBERT

INTRODUCTION

There exists at the present time a large and growing body of embedded computer systems, computers which perform some controlling function in a larger system such as a factory or a warship. These embedded computer systems are typically developed by project teams whose upper management levels have a predominate or exclusive hardware engineering background; software-trained managers seldom have the seniority to achieve these positions in other than a "software house" atmosphere.

This predominate management background was consistent with the technical nature of embedded computer system development when that development had a relatively small software component. The availability of cheap, general-purpose microcomputers of significant capacity, however, has served to move the system functionality from hardware into software; it takes extremely large production runs to justify the engineering cost of a special-purpose hardware device against the off-the-shelf cost of a microcomputer. As a result, the engineering which used to be conducted in a hardware design atmosphere is now being conducted in a software design and programming environment, and the skills and intuition of hardware-trained upper management may not appear relevant.

17

The irrelevance of hardware engineering background to software is more superficial than basic, and software development can benefit from many of the disciplines which have been traditionally associated with hardware. The hardware-based manager will, however, have to learn some basic facts about the nature of software projects in order to insure that these disciplines are applied. These basic facts are the substance of the remainder of this chapter.

DIFFERENCES BETWEEN HARDWARE AND SOFTWARE ENGINEERING

One of the most fundamental differences between hardware and software engineering is the attitude toward prototypes. Hardware engineers are familiar with a "breadboard/brassboard/preproduction prototype/production model" sequence, and use this sequence as a built-in source of major project milestones. Software projects have historically begun with the idea that the first version to be developed will be the version to be delivered, and this idea is often institutionalized in the staffing, financial, and calendar-time aspects of the project. Experienced project managers, however, are now beginning to recognize the value of a clearly defined software prototype phase and incorporate such a phase in their basic plans.

The various versions of a hardware device, as mentioned above, provide a natural set of milestones for a hardware project, since the design effort must stop at defined points for the various hardware versions to be physically constructed. This also provides a natural set of points at which requirements can be "frozen" and changes stopped. Software, since it has no such natural points, often tolerates changes throughout the development, and software developers who combine a lack of maturity with a desire for easy praise often actively encourage change, with a detrimental effect on the success of the project as a whole.

Hardware projects have historically been controlled by formal design reviews; software projects historically have not. This situation is changing rapidly, and project management should not hesitate to insist on substantially the same form and timing of reviews that they are accustomed to having with hardware — but with more technical depth.

Hardware engineers have long accustomed themselves to the idea that their designs will be tested by technicians, and they have therefore become used to preparing test plans. Software developers have historically relied on "debugging," or the informal test by the developer, with success being defined by the developer's engineering judgment.

18

This has made the quality of a particular piece of software highly dependent upon the judgment and personality of its developer, coupled with the degree of outside pressure to complete. As a result, quality software has historically been commonly produced by one- or two-programmer teams whose personalities were known to project management, and uncommonly produced by larger numbers of relatively anonymous programmers who were expected to perform in a more traditional engineering management environment.

Hardware is largely assembled from standard parts, and as a result the hardware engineer has a "head start" over his software counterpart: he will be dealing with parts whose characteristics are relatively stable and which may be known to him in detail; the programmer will be dealing with modules which are generally brand-new and whose characteristics must be discovered and understood as part of the development project. There has been a great deal of effort in the software community to develop tools and techniques to allow the construction of software out of standard modules. This effort has had little impact on embedded computer systems, since each of them typically has radically different requirements, and hence designs and modules, from any of their predecessors.

The final difference between hardware and software is an intrinsic one and therefore not one that project management can do a great deal about. It has to do with the manner in which software designs are documented and reviewed. It is best explained in the following way: If a project manager reviews a set of prints for a hardware device, and then distributes those prints to three different teams for implementation, the three resulting devices will be very similar if not identical. If a project manager reviews a software design (in any of the commonly used notations, such as flowcharts) and then distributes that design to three different teams, the resulting three software sets will very likely be radically different in all the essential areas of size, speed, freedom from errors, etc. This has two lessons for project management: advanced methods of design documentation should be used, and management control and visibility should be maintained well into module implementation.

PHASES OF SOFTWARE DEVELOPMENT

The software for an embedded computer system can be thought of as being developed in four general phases: requirements, functional design, module implementation, and integration/validation. We will discuss each phase separately, but before we do we would like to make some general observations about the course of a software project.

Software is a completely paper product. There are no physical brassboards or engineering prototypes whose construction provides visible milestones. The phases in a software project are accordingly marked by the documents or information which that phase produces.

Difficulties in a downstream phase will often cause recycling of the same part of the software product through a prior phase; as a consequence, a software project typically has some element of its effort in all phases at a given time. This is one of the causes of the notorious difficulty managers have in marking the progress of a software project.

Each phase has an essential leading or planning task which represents the hidden part of the project iceberg. While module implementation, for example, represents a highly visible task (programmers at their desks, programming away), the selection and validation of the tools used by those programmers is a hidden but essential prelude to that task. Failure to properly plan for the various phases of a software project is a rich source of difficulty; this is especially true of the integration/validation phase.

We will now describe each of the phases and discuss the documents which mark their successful completion.

Requirements

The development of an embedded computer system usually begins with a set of system requirements. These requirements are then partitioned between the software and whatever special-purpose hardware must be developed. The result of this partitioning should be documented in two documents. A software performance requirements document can be viewed by management as a contract between the systems engineers and the software engineers; it states the portion of the system task the software team is to perform. The interface requirements document can be thought of as a contract between the hardware and software engineers: it states that the hardware must adhere to certain key specifications (such as the value of signals or the output of analog-to-digital conversion) before the software can work. Failure to provide an interface specification document is a common source of severe software difficulty, as the software team becomes overwhelmed and demoralized by the problems of tracking a constantly changing hardware interface.

Performance requirements means just that: a statement of the required performance. A partial design is not a set of requirements; requirements are mandatory objectives whose meeting is a criterion of system success. The performance requirements document should also define the error budget for the software. It is tempting to assert that one's project is going to produce error-free software; tempting, that is, until the cost of error-free software is estimated. A more mature approach is to consciously set the error budget for the software as a requirement like any other.

Requirements should be verified and reviewed; it is impossible to spend too much management time on this phase of the project. Every effort should be made to insure that the requirements are complete, correct, and relevant. The last attribute, relevance, is often overlooked. Achieving it means that the software requirements should be reviewed in the context of overall system requirements, and excessive software functionality purged at the start.

It is very important in embedded computer system development to have software personnel involved in the early requirements stages; some truly impressive software disasters have been caused by hardware engineers imposing impossible requirements upon the software team. The feasibility of the requirements should be evaluated by management *in the context of the available tools*: it is not enough that a proposed set of requirements is implementable upon the world's finest software development facility; it must be implementable upon the facility at hand.

Functional Design and Module Implementation

In the functional design phase, the set of requirements is converted to a top-level, procedural representation of what the software system as a whole is to do. The output of this phase is a functional design, a complete description of the functional properties of the system. This has historically been done in some combination of English language and flowcharts; a more satisfactory and accurate notation is provided by the various program design languages which have recently been introduced.

After the functional design has been reviewed and approved, the system is cut into modules for the purpose of module implementation. There exists a large body of divergent opinion on the criteria that should be used to define modules; for the purposes of a project manager, it is sufficient to view a module (however established) as the basic unit of programmer work load. During module implementation the project breaks down into a series of parallel miniprojects, one per module; this is the point where project management traditionally loses visibility into the progress of the project as a whole.

A software system of any size must be modular; it must be divided into elements which are relatively independent of each other. This has an important effect upon the manageability and efficiency of the project: if the modules are relatively independent of each other, then the programmers will be. The programmers can then concentrate more on implementing their own modules than finding out what someone else's module looks like. Moreover, a management review of a module becomes a bounded activity with a defined conclusion, instead of a partial review of a multimodule subsystem whose attributes are never clearly understood. The most visible impact of modularity, however, comes in the management of change. Modular software is changeable, because the effect of change can be bounded and predicted. Nonmodular software is not changeable, because the uncontrolled interaction of software elements will cause unknown second-, third-, and fourth-order effects of change which will lead to completely obscure problems.

The best thing any project management can do to improve performance in these phases of a software project is to adopt the collection of practices and notations which go under the general heading of "structured programming." This includes such things as top-down design, chief programmer teams, programming secretaries, program development libraries, etc. There are innumerable documents and courses on this subject and therefore will not be covered here.

The single most common problem that projects have in these two phases is changes to the requirements (which preoccupies programmers with change at the expense of getting modules implemented and tested). The most common source of requirements changes is failure to impose configuration control or baseline the requirements documents.

Another prevalent problem is that which has come to be called the "software wizard syndrome." This occurs when management abdicates its responsibility to some highly trusted software specialist, whose pronouncements are viewed as correct by definition. The "software wizard syndrome" can strike anywhere in the project, but is most prevalent during functional design and module implementation, for this is traditionally where management loses visibility into the project. The trouble with the syndrome is that software wizards, unlike the mythical kind, are both fallible and mortal.

Another problem which manifests itself in these phases is the design of an unconstrained or nonmodular software structure leading to an excessive interdependency of modules, and therefore programmers. Productivity accordingly suffers as the programmers spend time asking each other what they are doing instead of doing it.

Functional design and module implementation can also suffer from the effects of a compressed schedule and an expanded staff. "Too many cooks spoil the broth" may be a cliché — but it is apropos.

Finally, these phases can be adversely impacted by the late delivery or low quality of software development tools such as compilers, text editors, or debuggers. The prevalence of this problem is due to the historical manner in which computers have been sold: as hardware with "free" software. Procurement activities have consequently worked to insure that the delivered hardware performed according to specification and ignored the software. As a result, software tools whose quality was essential to project success were accepted on faith. The solution to this problem lies in the formal validation of the necessary tools *before* they are needed by the programmers. The output of the module implementation phase is a set of debugged software modules. These are small units of software which have been shown to run correctly by themselves; there remains the problem of assembling them into a system and showing that the result conforms to the system requirements. This is the task of the integration/validation phase.

Integration/Validation

This is the phase that experienced software developers sometimes refer to as the "big bang" or the "integration orgy." It is a time of great pressure and confusion, and historically the point at which the majority of software disasters occur. The integration phase of an embedded computer system typically involves two forms of integration: software/software, in which individual modules are synthesized into subsystems and then systems; and software/hardware, in which the entire software subsystem is integrated with whatever special-purpose hardware was developed as part of the overall embedded computer system. The output of this phase is a single, validated system: one that not only works but also is shown to conform to the requirements.

The integration and validation phase occurs last, and is accordingly the one which shows the strongest schedule pressure as it attempts to absorb slippages and overcome deficiencies in previous phases. It also is the phase which receives the greatest attention to management outside the project, since it is the closest one to the delivery date. In addition, it often is technically the most difficult, since it involves the successful bringing together of all the elements of the hardware and the software development. It consequently should receive a significant amount of attention on the part of project management; some of the aspects of that attention are covered below.

Hardware is not engineered in its shipping crate; it is engineered in a laboratory, which is larger than its shipping crate and contains more equipment. Similarly, just because a given body of software is to be operational on (say) a 4K microcomputer, management should not assume for a moment that it can be developed on a 4K microcomputer.

This disparity between the operational and development hardware facilities is generally most marked during the integration/validation phase. Programs can commonly be written and compiled, and sometimes even "extensively" debugged, on machines which are only slightly larger than the operational or "target" machine; an adequate integration/verification facility may often be several *times* the size of the operational computer.

There is no single phase of embedded computer software development that requires more planning than the integration/validation phase. The integration and validation facility must be defined and constructed. The system requirements must be reviewed and a verification plan developed to show, by specific test, that each of them is satisfied by the system. The validation team must be assembled and its makeup reviewed to insure that the correct mix of systems, hardware, and software engineers are on it. The configuration control system must be reviewed to insure that it is adequate to handle an entity as large and complex as an integrated system. It is a great deal of work, and it is all too often postponed and then done incompletely, with catastrophic consequences.

Test, integration and validation represent about half of the typical software project. Unfortunately, this fact is often not incorporated into the project plan. The result is that the project is on time through functional design and module implementation and then slips badly in the last phases.

SOME GENERAL OBSERVATIONS ON SOFTWARE PROJECTS

Software Has Historically Been Developed Informally

Software is a new discipline which evolved as almost a side effect of the availability of computers. Software practitioners come from a rich variety of backgrounds: engineering, mathematics, accounting, music, etc. This had the effect of making the field very dynamic and creative during its early years, but it also meant that the software for the early embedded computer systems was developed by personnel who were generally unfamiliar and uneasy with the degree of engineering discipline that the hardware-based project management took for granted. Although the rise of computer science schools and other training establishments has worked to increase the amount of discipline in the field, there still remain traces of the practice described in the preceding paragraphs, practices which the management of an embedded computer system project must recognize and control.

More Personnel Doesn't Always Mean More Software

Increasing the size of a software team increases the amount of software produced per unit time, up to a point. Then the problems of communication among the programmers begin to dominate the project and reduce the amount of software being produced. The result is a definite valley in any curve which realistically plots team productivity as a function of team size. Historically, this valley has been relatively constant at a value of three to five programmers; that is, the fastest *rate* at which software can be produced is the rate sustainable by a three-to-five-programmer team. This is about half the team size which hardware engineers typically regard as optimal. Ten programmers then represent two teams, two team leaders, a manager over them, with a secretary, etc. — very close to a whole department. Team size is a very real indication of the risk of a software project: five programmers is manageable, ten is large, and anything over fifteen represents a major management problem.

Staffing Is Static after Functional Design

A software system is an artifact of staggering complexity, often barely within the capacity of its developers to understand or mentally internalize. The major jump in complexity occurs at the time of module implementation. As a consequence, it is generally not possible to add project personnel after the functional design is complete and module implementation begins, for it becomes prohibitively expensive to educate the new staff in the intricacies of the system.

It Pays to Catch Software Errors Early

A software system becomes progressively less flexible and modifiable as it moves through the development phases. This is because the various modules become more tightly "bound," that is, more and more dependent upon each other. As a result, the expense of making a change or correcting an error rises dramatically from phase to phase; the more tightly bound the modules, the more information that must be generated to design the change and the greater the risk of injecting an error as a consequence of making the change. The historical evidence suggests that a change during the integration/validation phase can be fifteen *times* as expensive as the equivalent change made during functional design.

Testing, Integration and Validation Is Half the Job

There is ample historical evidence to the effect that the last phase of a software project is approximately half the effort, both in calendar time and person-hours. This point has been made enough times that it is now somewhat prevalent amongst the software management community, but it still runs contrary to the intuition of many software developers or managers who have been loosely associated with software projects. There is an erroneous tradition that the module implementation phase is the principal effort of a software project. This tradition arises from the aforementioned visibility of the phase and the corresponding emphasis on programming languages and other tools associated with it. A contrary position is taken by the experienced manager, who does not ask, "How many lines of software are we going to write?" but instead asks, "How many lines of software are we going to write, integrate, and validate?"

Management Interfaces to the Project Through the Tools

Programmers are paid to program, not to pay attention to progress; good programmers will often be so involved in the problem being solved that they won't know what day of the week it is. Management should not expect to get progress or status information by asking programmers; the typical programmer doesn't know or care, and will usually give whatever answer is needed to end the meeting and get back to programming. The way to get management information is to instrument the set of tools used by the programmer so that management reports come "free," at least from the point of view of the programmer.

One important set of tools are those which impose configuration control on the software and supporting documentation. Configuration control means that changes can be made only with management permission and after management review; the placing of a document under configuration control is often referred to as "baselining" the document. In general, the documents produced by a given phase should be baselined before the next subsequent phase is begun. Thus, the software performance requirements should be baselined before the functional design is begun. This insures that the functional design will be based on a stable set of requirements, since any change to the baselined (under configuration control) requirements will require management review and the impact of the change on the design will be taken into account. Failure to impose configuration control is one of the most fundamental mistakes a project manager can make, for it is the equivalent to relinquishing control of the software subsystem entirely. After that there is nothing but luck to rely on.

SOME GENERAL OBSERVATIONS ON PROGRESS MEASUREMENT

The progress of software projects is notoriously difficult to measure. This comes from the "soft," or paper, nature of the product and the temperament of the typical programmer, who is highly motivated by technical problems and generally not motivated at all by management ones. This section discusses the problem in more detail and suggests some measures management can use.

The fact that software projects are typically estimated accurately up through functional design and module implementation also teaches a lesson for management: if the project is slipping during those phases, it is probably because the overall software task has been grossly underestimated. When module implementation is complete, management should then assume the project is half over and use the elapsed time as the value of the time required to complete. The result will generally be dismaying but accurate.

Define Measurable Milestones

A milestone is an event, not a percentage; 65 percent complete does not represent a milestone, nor, indeed, anything except a string of symbols on the page. Milestones mark the end of intervals, or phases, in the project. If the milestone is not successfully passed, then the phase is *not* "almost complete," it is not complete at all. We have already noted that the broad phases of a software project are separated by documents, whose production is the task of the phase. This is true of intermediary phases as well. Milestones in a software project are typically document reviews. If project management takes these document reviews seriously, attends them, and insures that any deficiencies uncovered in the review are corrected promptly, then management will be taking the project seriously. The converse is also true.

Track the Error Rates

If management has had the foresight to impose a set of configuration control tools and instrument the tools used by the programmer, then management will be able to determine the number of errors outstanding in the software at any given time. This figure is an extremely useful index of progress, especially in the later phases of a project.

In general, this number will follow a sawtooth curve through the life of the project: the number of errors will decrease until a stage of testing, integration, or validation is complete, and then take a step jump when the next stage begins. This is inherent in the nature of testing. Testing is a process of experimentation, and a phase of testing is a class of experiments. When a class of experiments fails to uncover any more errors, management should not assume that no more errors exist — it should initiate the next class of experiments. Thus the number of outstanding errors during informal test will drop to near zero, only to jump again when the process of testing against the requirements begins. It will then drop to an acceptable level, and jump again when predelivery field test begins.

This sawtooth effect is most prominent at the beginning of the integration phase. Prior to integration, practically any software project will show the sum of the errors in the unintegrated modules rapidly heading for zero. This is because none of the really difficult problems of intermodule interaction have been uncovered. The worst thing management can do is assume that this low error rate for the unintegrated system represents a sign that the project is close to completion, for the first thing that will happen after system integration is a frightening jump in the error rate, followed almost immediately by an increase. A naive management is then faced with a false dawn followed by a very dark night, and if it does not have confidence in its staff and the procedures it has followed up to that time, it runs a significant risk of losing its nerve. A seasoned management will recognize this phenomenon for an inevitable one, retain its composure, test and correct errors until the curve rolls over and the integrated system begins to show signs of potential acceptability.

Watch the Percentage of the Hardware Used by the Software

Another index, which mixes progress with risk assessment, is the amount of operational computer speed and memory consumed by the software. This number should be estimated at the beginning of the project. If the software is forecast to use over half the memory and speed of the operational computer, then the project should be assessed as a high-risk one, and correspondingly more stringent management controls placed upon the design and the requirements.

If the percentage of memory and speed used remains relatively stable as the project passes from phase to phase, then management can maintain a degree of confidence in the design. If the number moves upward rapidly, especially between functional design and the end of module implementation, then management has cause for alarm and should immediately review the design and the requirements as a first step in regaining control.

The penalties for pushing the limit of capacity of the operational computer are high. Practically everything a programmer does to provide modularity and make software easy to change and test is done at the expense of "efficiency" in the hardware utilization sense. If the software is pushing the limits of the computer, it may be very difficult and expensive to make necessary changes. As a result, there is some historical evidence that software which uses 85–90 percent of the operational computer is seven to ten *times* as expensive to develop than software which uses only 50 percent. With the continuing decrease in hardware prices, there is very little justification remaining for forcing programmers to squeeze their software into computers of marginal size and speed.

SUMMARY

Software is different from hardware because it has no physical manifestation except for paper products; it is similar in that it can be engineered and its development can be managed. The management of a software project requires constant attention, especially during the early phases, but it is not impossible. The principal requirements for the management of a quality software project is the discipline which has been historically associated with hardware.

ACKNOWLEDGMENTS

I would like to thank Carl Vignali and Chuck Nichols of Honeywell Avionics Division, who helped me prepare the Software Management Seminar which was the source of this chapter. I would also like to thank the multitude of attendees at the seminars, whose questions and observations have enlarged my understanding of software management for embedded computer systems.

CHAPTER 3

Current Software Quality Management Activities

JAMES D. STRINGER

INTRODUCTION

Software quality is everyone's business in the development and deployment of real-time embedded computer systems, indeed, in all computer-based systems. It is a fact that software quality, akin to hardware quality, cannot be tested-in or added-to a system or product by quality personnel during the final phases of design or manufacturing. As it is in all human endeavors, software developers and inspectors in the past have attempted to make use of established techniques and analogy when going from the known (i.e., hardware) to the unknown (i.e., software). However, chapter 11 clearly demonstrates the limitations within which analogy may be used in assessing the similarities and dissimilarities between hardware and software errors and failures. No attempt will be made to duplicate that treatise, only to set forth the following observations extending the philosophy.

Hardware failures adhere to the laws of physics and the interrelated properties of electrophysical matter in an assemblage. As such, hardware failures may occur as a result of design logic errors, poor workmanship standards or practices, improper component screening or selection, the unwitting or inadvertent discovery of laws of physics not *now* known to science, transient stresses to electronic circuitry, poor maintenance practices, and sloppy operator usage to name but a few. Hardware failures tend to become progressively worse with equipment age, and only hardware design errors have any true analog in the software realm.

Software errors, on the other hand, are mainly the visible result of omissions or commissions during the design and implementation processes, that is, software bugs are built-in. Like a nail lying on a highway awaiting the unwary motorist, both nails and software bugs are removed as they are stumbled across, thereby improving the pathway for the next user. Thus, the general rule for software is that it improves with usage (sic, age).

It is because of the amount of uncertainty ascribed to this "stumbling" process that the requirement for the engineering and management support functions of software quality assurance and software quality management arises. Before Government and industry users can have quality software, these organizations must first recognize the need for software quality management. As a corollary, most engineering organizations at least give lip service to the need for software quality assurance especially in light of recent Department of Defense directives such as DOD Directive 5000.29.*

Even after 20 or so years, the software arts are still jelling into the formal subdisciplines of design, development, test, integration, measurement, etc. Software quality assurance (SQA) has only recently, i.e., within the last four or five years, gained a place of formal status and recognition within engineering hierarchies. Software quality management (SQM) has just within the last eighteen to twenty-four months become recognized as a formal requirement—stated or unstated—in the successful accomplishment of major embedded computer systems acquisition.

The point is simply that the SQA and, more especially, SQM are new subdisciplines—but, nevertheless, fields of worthy and necessary real human endeavor—in the more general field of embedded computer systems engineering. In recognizing the need for software quality management, one must completely understand its functions, organizational structures, technology and disciplines, and all other ingredients which make up any *important* field of business endeavor. Secondly, we must act to fulfill this need.

This chapter will discuss briefly some of the most recent activities taking place throughout Government, industry, and academia concerning software quality management which show an attempt to follow this course of recognition and action.

*See Chapter 7 for a more extensive description.

BUSINESS PRACTICE VS. SQM ENGINEERING

Within this chapter it is hypothesized that the "quality" of a software product arises out of the entire process of business and engineering development beginning with the initial system concept formulation and flowing through the final customer acceptance. Like it or not, western business development is ever increasingly more complex with the passing of time. While organized engineering is a very old discipline — at least in the civil and mechanical fields — management as a professionally studied field of the applied arts — outside of the military — is quite new, dating from the time of the Hawthorne (Western Electric) experiment of the 1920s.

Software quality management (a business support function) is the professional practice of control upon the processes of assuring an acceptable, minimal standard of quality within software delivered to an end-item user. While SQM directly impacts SQA (an engineering support function), it reaches out to embrace the other engineering support functions of configuration management and control, engineering cost estimating, project management, hardware quality control, and product assurance. It also reaches deep into the engineering processes of software design, development, testing, training, and integration.

In order for all this to happen in an orderly manner, the focus must be at the top of the corporate managerial chain. Topmost management must set out as the fundamental policy of the business entity that: (a) software quality management is an essential function; (b) corporate activities are assigned to monitor and enforce a policy requiring SQA/SQM; (c) resources are actively allocated toward this objective; and (d) a model SQM plan is issued for general corporate guidelines as to minimally acceptable and measurable SQA/SQM standards. Then, and only then, can a successful SQA (engineering) or SQM organization come into being. Where corporate managements have taken the view that SQA and SQM are *only* necessary evils imposed by an unkind Government customer and that any funding to support such activities must (indeed, shall) come directly out of contract dollars, one will probably find infertile ground for nurturing good software quality. Firms creating SQA/SQM offices on such an economic basis are building disasters into their software (and subsequently their system). The fate of the *Titanic* was not foreordained by the position of an iceberg so much as it was designed-in by engineers convinced of their infallibility and a management structure that wanted just "profits." In our time, the monstrous overruns on such software-driven projects as the Army's AN/TTC-39 Switch or the FAA's Enroute System are manifestations of the lack of corporate commitment to placing SQM high enough on the scale of business practices to be believed in and followed. (There is no need to particularly pick upon those two systems — others have had such disasters; however, some have been more visible than others.)

And just saying that it (SQM) will be so by corporate and Government management won't make it magically happen. Marketing, through their pricing structure, must accept it; accounting must also accept it as a legitimate overhead or burden function; and laboratory managers, especially, must allow the requisite time, space, manpower, etc., for its successful execution. In short, the whole business structure must, first, actively plan for a quality software product (our objective in SQM), constantly refocusing on the objective, and, second, be flexible enough to modify its original plan in order to achieve the objective of quality software. Lacking this total commitment, the quality assurance organization can continue to review and inspect the software and still another debacle in the software field will be recorded.

QUALITY MANAGEMENT FUNCTIONAL REVIEW

Within this chapter, software quality activities — and here the term "activities" is used in its broadest sense to include the roles of Government, industry, professional and trade associations, and academic institutions — are reviewed primarily from a functional (what it is that we know we wish to accomplish) perspective rather than from an organizational (what each of these organizational entities is doing with regard to software quality) view. Similarities and differences between traditional hardware quality management and the newer functions of software quality management are highlighted, contrasted, and discussed. As stated earlier, SQM must be given the highest priority by corporate management in order to be effective. At no time should any of the partners in the creation of quality software be allowed to lose sight of what it is that must be accomplished, either from a traditional business or engineering role, or from the vantage of what new thing (or things) it is that should be accomplished in SQM. To begin with, once having gotten appropriate management attention, we must establish a policy that *all* software must be high-quality software. We cannot allow engineering developers to say that *some* software will have quality, i.e., be done according to minimally acceptable standards, and some will be done in a manner free from standards imposition, i.e., in the old "freebooter fashion" we have all come to love in the past. This freebooter syndrome will continue to be the case if management fails at the outset to establish the SQM functional entity at a high enough level, or fail to give it managerial clout, or treat it as an u' stepchild.

Let us return to our hardware analogy for a moment and see what quality functions the hardware creators have devised over the years. (Note that these may be *activities*, i.e., departments, sections, etc., or *individuals* in a more broadly organized entity such as product assurance.)

Value engineer: The hardware community has an engineer who does nothing but think of ways to make the same thing (functional equivalent) less expensively, better, safer, out of different materials, or with less labor. In software this is all left to the native genius of the system architect.

Workmanship and standards engineer: Through practice and evolution, hardware is constructed under rigid standards of workmanship, man-hours alloted for given functions of assembly and/or inspection, and time and motion investigations. Only since the introduction of top-down design and work breakdown structures has software engineering had any portion of this.

Inspectors: Hardware goes through many stages of inspection for both being there (in situ) and for quality of construction. These inspectors charge their work effort directly to each contract end-item. They are also tested and certified as to their skills. Although several companies have instituted code inspection, the software equivalent has yet to emerge as an industrial standard.

Configuration controller: Either on project or production management level, an individual or center is established to maintain the integrity of the baselined system. Any and all changes to that "NBS meter stick" design are coordinated and controlled by that office. This discipline has only recently been adopted by the software community and has not yet reached the same level of maturity.

Product or quality assurance (as implemented in MIL-Q-9858A): Usually a department or section exists wherein reside the skills of product inspection, vendor screening, workmanship standards and practices receiving inspection, statistical sampling, nondestructive inspection and control processes inspection. There is no *direct* software analogy since within hardware engineering, this is an "institutionalized" function, whereas in software it is usually established as a one-time organization. However, software quality assurance should definitely be institutionalized.

Quality control (Q.C.): The term Q.C. often refers to the department and procedural on-the-floor (fabricate, tool, and assembly) aspects of the broader discipline of quality assurance. It covers mainly the "buy-off" or rejection at the end of the production or engineering function and steps leading to that happening. In hardware this includes the work-in-progress inspection processes. There is no standardized software equivalent.

Engineering documentation and drawings control, vaulting, and reproduction: All major engineering shops have an entity which handles these functions for engineering designs which are considered by management to be completed, finished, and ready for fabrication or assembly. These documents include the "how to do it" and "how it works" variety as well. The data base librarian and the forcing of top-down methodology on the design organization have partially filled this void in software, but the lack of "corporate memory" from project to project is all too readily apparent.

Engineering change control board: These boards support the configuration manager and the two functions of engineering change control and engineering change control boards (ad hoc or permanent, but usually project-management directed). Usually, software change control is done ad hoc on a project basis. It is imperative the software change control be institutionalized and be fully integrated into all hardware activities.

Reliability engineering: This is a hardware engineering function which focuses on designing-in product reliability by employment of best engineering practice in parts selection and use. Corporate management historically has been unwilling to commit the requisite resources to provide this same support to software.

Reliability assurance: This is an aspect of Q.A. which is centered around testing: testing and test monitoring in the field, collection and analyses of data from tests, and the feed-back of results to engineering. Data collection in order to measure the effectiveness of software as related to its quality has not been widely accepted during project development or post-deployment.

Summed up, all of these individuals and functions taken together constitute the hardware quality management system of most development firms. The 100 percent or so overhead cost these firms apply to their engineering bids or rates goes to pay for not only the corporate "drones" but also for these vital support functions.

That being the hardware case, what about the case of software quality? Can we identify similar functions and/or skills which must be present for SQA and SQM? Software quality (in the general case), owing in part to its youth, is an amalgam of force-fitted hardware quality functions, e.g., Q.C. personnel labeling software programs as "engineering drawings" (and then finding that card decks and mag tapes don't fit nicely into this scheme), or new functions uniquely software oriented such as compiler certification. It is because of this amalgamation that most SQA/SQM projects and systems come to grief. Another contributing factor is that most Q.A. directors see that they can get *some* software quality working by patching their existing hardware system.

Just for the moment — recognizing a lack of standard definitions — let us examine what some of the SQM and/or SQA roles can or ought to be. From observation and practice, personnel engaged in SQM or SQA activities occasionally or regularly do the following kinds of tasks or things (this list is by no means all inclusive):

Prepare test plans and procedures
Prepare acceptance plans and procedures
Prepare test code generators and test scenarios
Prepare test scenario tapes and other computer media
Exercise live code using test scenarios
Write simulators to test live code
Write software problem reports (define problems)
Fix software problems (sometimes)
Establish audit trails for problem fixes
Sit as members of software change control boards (CCB)
Chair software CCBs
Review and critique Part I (A-level) specs
Review and critique Part II (B-level) specs
Vault software products
Control delivered data base and any changes
Monitor laboratory and subcontractor development processes and units
Control computer hardware configurations
Control software configurations
Handle project management office (PMO) interface to software configuration control
Fight with engineering labs
Fight with PMOs
Work long hard hours
Handle systems integration
Remain undaunted in the face of indifference
Get mad and quit (often)
Occasionally get recognized
Get to do it all over again on the next job

But the problem isn't only one of defining SQA and SQM organizational functions and individual job roles. In defining software quality functions, we also suffer terribly from a lack of standardization of nomenclature and terminology. However, that complaint is nearly universal. The following is a brief quote from a recent article entitled "The Communications Barrier of Nonstandardized Logistics Terminology," by Fred Gluck in the July 1978 issue of *Defense Management Journal* [1]:

> Because of the failure to standardize and centrally control the generation of logistics terms, the size and scope of the total language of logistics are currently unknown. In addition, this failure has allowed the originators of as many as ten thousand military source documents (i.e., regulations, manuals, etc.) to impose their own ideas about the meanings of logistics terms in the "definition section" of these documents.

> In January 1970, the Air Force Institute of Technology published "A Compendium of Authenticated Logistics Terms and Definitions" containing 8,300 logistics definitions and 3,300 abbreviations taken from the definition sections of DOD and military-service source documents. At that time, the compendium's author noted in his foreword:

> . . .A large number of key logistics terms have multiple definitions and/ or meanings within the defense establishment. It is evident that some action must be taken to correct the generation and use of multiple meanings of logistics terms.

Without belaboring the point further, everyone in management, and more especially every software developer, has in their minds exactly what software quality assurance and software quality management are — or ought to be. It is for this very reason that the IEEE Computer Society Technical Committee on Software Engineering has established Project No. 730, entitled "Standard for Software Quality Assurance Plan," to provide for the uniform preparation and conduct of software quality assurance plans [2]. This project is going forward with the active participation, cooperation, and support of the National Bureau of Standards. The IEEE's basic premise is that without standard, clearly stated written definitions of software terminology, we all will continue to flounder in a sargassum of misunderstanding and confusion.

SQA, V&V, CERTIFICATION, AND AUDITING

In addition to all the above activities, the emerging disciplines of software verification, validation, and certification (including the processes of product assurance design reviews, performance auditing, and product testing and inspection) come within the SQM purview. However, as indicated in chapter 15 on software verification and validation (V&V), the V&V processes are mostly engineering-support jobs or functions and are really subordinate to the total SQM effort. Only software certification and Q.A. auditing may be recognizable as

SQA functions — at least from the Q.A. director's viewpoint. For many reasons the individual holding that post may be unable or unwilling to take on the broader task of SQM. This is usually the case in engineering companies having large, highly structured hardware quality or product assurance departments. That means that most of the functions having to do with *real* SQM (as a software professional would view it) "fall on the floor" and the software developers are then left with a feeling of great frustration. It's not because the Q.A. director is malevolent, either; it's just that without top management's commitment, the director has neither the trained personnel nor budget to be the corporate SQM authority.

If it isn't the Q.A. director's job, then whose job is it to provide SQM? The Q.A. people will say it's engineering's job; the engineering lab boss will say it's the PMO's job; and the PMO will say that it isn't his job unless he makes it so. If he does that, then it will apply *only* to his contract and *no one else can use the facility!* So, once again, without top management support in resources (dollars, people, space, etc.), SQM is given short shrift, causing software developments to get into difficulty.

The next logical question, then, is how can this situation be avoided? Is there a better way to organize from a business viewpoint? The solution to this situation is through the formal establishment of a software quality management organization. This new unit should report either to the director of product assurance or, better yet, to the same vice-president that the director of product assurance reports. However, such side issues should be resolved on a company-by-company basis. In any case, the SQM will be a "bridge" organization embracing some PMO, engineering, Q.A., and accounting roles. The nature of its operation is of the PMO variety, but it should be a line organization.

SQA FUNCTIONS, BOTH MANAGEMENT AND TECHNOLOGY

Within a fully functioning software quality organization the following list comprises a minimal (nonchronological ordering) subset of software quality functions:

Review design inputs
Prepare test plans and procedures
Prepare acceptance plans and procedures
Prepare test code generator and create test scenario tapes
Execute test scenarios
Write software problem reports and establish action items

Establish audit trails for problem fixes and follow-up

Manage the software change control boards for all projects

Review and critique Part I (A-level) and Part II (B-level) specifications

Control delivered data base and any changes thereto

Monitor all software development processes and organizations

Control computer hardware configuration for program generation center

Handle PMO interface to software configuration control, document, vaulting and reproduction

Now, that's quite a list and, no doubt, many managerial toes were stepped upon. In one instant, a vast new organizational structure was created with its concomitant pyramid of chiefs and Indians and, since it would be staffed in the main by ex-software people, every bit as arrogant, hard to deal with, and non-businesslike as any present-day software organization. However, the managerial alternative is worse. Without an SQM function the situation exists for continued finger pointing when software crises occur. Within certain companies there are managers who thrive on such crises and use these as opportunities to embarrass other managers they don't like or in order to achieve a higher-level job in the firm. An SQM function will not entirely eliminate this "politicking," but it will certainly make doing it tougher. In the process such an entity will save a great deal of money and avoid much human anguish and time lost from meaningful work.

MODEL SQM ORGANIZATION

SQM must be placed on a formal business foundation. To begin with, a permanent staff to perform these functions will number about six software personnel. This would, of course, build up to a larger number during peak load periods. There would be a department-level manager appointed. This is the SQM team concept. It is best to start small and then grow so that any new entity created, such as the SQM team, can be controlled and directed in its growth. Furthermore, it is not unthinkable to even start on a project basis—bearing in mind that the SQM team should not report to the PMO, but rather through a corporate line or staff organization at the vice-president level. Let us create such an SQM team and have them do all that has been suggested on a pilot basis with one single project. Since the following subfunctions are required on all software jobs, let these tasks be performed by the SQM team:

1. Test plans and procedures creation
2. Test scenario generation
3. Test team leader/interface control
4. Software configuration control
5. Parts I and II specifications review/audit
6. Data base control and acceptance test(s) procedure

The SQM team should also be given sufficient managerial latitude that they be allowed to stay abreast of the happenings taking place outside their immediate firm.

SUMMARY AND CONCLUSIONS

In this chapter it has been shown that the following real-world situation vis-à-vis software quality exists:

1. SQA organizations exist from place to place, are poorly funded (unless attached to a strong PMO), and are given mostly lip service by engineering managers.
2. SQM organizations usually don't exist, and if they do, are pilot or prototype organizations.
3. There is a *need* for SQM and SQA organizations.
4. The lack of management attention to SQM functions impacts software development organizations directly and corporate "bottom lines" indirectly with hand-wringing cost overruns and managerial crises.
5. Getting into SQM doesn't need to be expensive—you can start small if you plan for growth.
6. The most plausible method to initially obtain SQM may be under the SQM team approach.
7. The SQM team, once formed, must be as free as possible from PMO or engineering design pressures.
8. Nothing can really take place in SQM until top management makes a real (as opposed to token) moral and financial commitment to SQM.

Thus, it may be seen that software-related quality activities extend far beyond the traditional hardware quality/product assurance roles and have a wide impact upon any business entity.

References

1. Gluck, Fred. "The Communications Barrier of Nonstandardized Logistics Terminology," *Defense Management Journal,* July 1978, pp. 18-20.
2. Buckley, Fletcher. "Standard for Software Quality Assurance Plan," draft document project No. P730, 5 April 1978, Institute of Electrical and Electronic Engineers, New York.

CHAPTER 4

Management Control Practices for Software Quality

JON A. WHITED

INTRODUCTION

The use of MIL-S-52779, Software Quality Assurance Program Requirements, has generated an increased awareness of software quality assurance (QA) program requirements by both contractor and Government customers. Recently, many Department of Defense projects have tried to implement this specification and found that there has been an equal degree of frustration as well as success in the establishment and implementation of a software quality assurance program. While the purpose of such a program is almost always to assure that software delivered under the contract complies with the requirements of the contract, the implementation of procedures to perform that function have been as varied as the number of contractors and customers involved. MIL-S-52779 does not do what MIL-Q-9858A, Quality Program Requirements does. Since 1963 the quality program requirements established by MIL-Q-9858A have had the same contractual intent to assure compliance with the requirements of the contract as MIL-S-52779. However, MIL-Q-9858A requires the establishment of a quality program or *system* by the contractor that is effective, economical, planned, and developed with cognizance of the contractor's other administrative and technical programs. Those programs are to assure adequate quality throughout all areas of contract performance, for example, design, development, fabrication, assembly, inspection, test and maintenance, etc. Unfortunately, most *software* quality assurance program requirements have been fragmented and are not required to be developed as part of a company quality system. This is not to say that MIL-S-52779 is bad. It is, in fact, good. Some of the applications of this specification have been very successful. This can be illustrated by the number of contracts that the Department of Defense issues with MIL-S-52779 included. In addition, the Navy has just completed MIL-STD-1679 which again requires even more stringent software quality assurance program requirements to be applied on their contracts. But, without a company system to manage software QA program requirements, internal company observations and results of such programs leave project managers feeling that there is a lack of direction or understanding. Observations often include an absence of a software product assurance charter, and therefore varying specific quality task assignments for the projects, a resentment toward quality personnel by project personnel because there is not a clear understanding between development and quality tasks, and a lack of quality assurance independence because the quality personnel become ingrained in the actual project. Again, without a system to support software quality assurance program requirements, there is quite often an absence of training and instruction for new personnel in the quality assurance areas.

What is the answer then to implementing an effective software quality assurance program? All documentation detailing program requirements agree that the quality assurance organization must be separate and independent from the organizations being supported. To be effective in this role, the quality assurance personnel must receive direction, instructions, and task statements from management in a consistent and supportive manner. This requires more than just a program designed to assure that software development complies with quality program requirements under a single contract. To be cost effective and to provide the proper training and management perspective, the software quality assurance program should be an extension of the contractor's existing product or quality assurance program. It should be planned and developed with cognizance of the contractor's other administrative and technical programs as part of a quality *system*. This chapter will stress the policies, procedures, practices, and standards that are useful in establishing a software quality system.

COMPANY POLICIES AND PROCEDURES

To develop a system that is supportive of software quality assurance, management within contractor establishments needs to define policies and procedures pertaining to quality activities within their organization. These policies and procedures should apply to all activities within their organization which affect the quality of delivered products and services. A policy needs to state the primary company interests and goals in relation to software quality assurance in a way that does not parrot the exact paragraphs of MIL-S-52779 (see Figure 1, para. 3.0). It is important to have the company establish quality goals that satisfy the requirements of MIL-S-52779, but at the same time fit their unique environment and type of contract applications. The implementation of requirements varies significantly for the type of software being developed. Different standards can be implemented to satisfy the basic requirements for different software such as operating system software, application software, simulation software, utility software, test or test tool software, compiler software, other support software, or firmware. The policy should state requirements in terms of company goals. For example:

Software quality contractual commitments will be provided in a cost-effective manner.

Work will be done so as to minimize defects, mistakes, and wasted effort.

A quality assurance system will be maintained which satisfies Government requirements such as MIL-S-52779, Software Quality Program Requirements, MIL-S-1679, Weapon System Software Development, etc.

The software quality assurance program will be documented in a system of manuals or other controlled documents which include standards and instructions.

The company will encourage coordination and cooperation with the resident Government contract administration office and its quality assurance representative.

The responsibility of those individuals to implement the company goals and requirements should also be stated in the policy and procedures. This includes the employees, managers and supervisors, division general managers and directors of product assurance. *It is important that these responsibilities be clearly defined to establish the organizational relationship for implementing a software quality assurance program with a systems approach.* The procedures needed to implement the requirements in the policy and procedures must state what activities are required for the satisfaction of the company quality systems (see Figure 1, para. 4.0). These procedures may be in relationship to software quality assurance functions performed in support of

FIGURE 1. *QA policy and procedure example*

POLICY AND PROCEDURE

No.

Date:

SUBJECT: QUALITY OF PRODUCTS AND SERVICES

APPROVED

1.0 PURPOSE

To establish policies, responsibilities and procedures pertaining to quality activities.

2.0 APPLICABILITY

This Policy and Procedure applies to all activities which affect the quality of delivered products and services and the quality of contract work. Both computer software and hardware products are included.

3.0 POLICY

(a) Contractual quality commitments shall be met in a cost-effective manner. Products, documents and services offered to customers for acceptance shall be of high quality, shall be as represented and shall be supported by evidence of conformance to contractual requirements.

(b) Work shall be performed so as to minimize defects, mistakes and wasted effort. Employee training shall be employed when appropriate.

(c) A quality assurance *system* shall be maintained which satisfies the documents listed below. The system shall be structured to have sufficient flexibility so that project quality plans may be tailored to fit individual project requirements.
   (1) Armed Services Procurement Regulation, Section XIV, "Procurement Quality Assurance,"—paragraph 14.102, "Responsibilities of the Contractor"
   (2) MIL-Q-9858A, "Quality Program Requirements"
   (3) NHB 5300.4 (1B), "Quality Program Provisions for Aeronautical and Space System Contractors"
   (4) MIL-C-45662A, "Calibration System Requirements"
   (5) MIL-S-52779, "Software Quality Program Requirements"
   (6) Other Government standards and specifications commonly invoked in contracts accepted.

(d) The quality assurance system shall be documented in manuals and in other formal and controlled documents. Manuals which contain this documentation include:
   Policy Manual
   Quality Assurance Manual
   Reliability Manual

46

Specification Manual
Configuration Management Manual
Drafting Room Manual

(e) Personnel shall cooperate with the resident Government Contract Administration Office and its quality assurance representative in their performance of the functions prescribed in ASPR-XIV and as delegated to them by customer purchasing officers.

4.0 RESPONSIBILITIES

(a) *Employees*

Strive to perform their product-related work in the proper manner and without defects, mistakes or wasted effort.

Report observed or caused defects to their management so that corrective action may be taken.

(b) *Managers and Supervisors*

Emphasize quality of work in exercising their managerial responsibilities.

Evaluate their operations and take corrective action as necessary to meet quality objectives.

(c) *General Manager*

Provides operational direction to the assigned Product Assurance Manager.

(d) *Director of Product Assurance*

Acts as the quality assurance authority and defines the quality assurance system.

Provides for the maintenance of the Quality Assurance Manual, which is the principal manual delineating the quality assurance system.

Reviews and concurs with other Functional Manuals which are part of the quality assurance system documentation.

Evaluates activities affecting product quality and recommends improvements to management.

Manages the Product Assurance Organization.

(e) *Product Assurance*

Performs quality functions including:

Inspection
Quality engineering
Quality records maintenance and analysis
Nonconforming material disposition
Corrective action administration
Calibration
Audits
Operator and special process certification
Supplier and subcontractor quality assurance
Project quality assurance management

5.0 PROCEDURES

(a) Quality assurance activities for individual contracts shall be planned, di-

FIGURE 1. *Continued*

POLICY AND PROCEDURE

No.

Date:

---

rected and conducted in accord with the project management system. Responsibility for quality tasks in the project work breakdown structure (WBS) shall be assigned to the Manager for Product Assurance, or equivalent title, who shall be a member of the Product Assurance Organization. The WBS shall be structured to facilitate management and cost analysis of quality activities.

(b) Proposals which have quality assurance requirements shall receive Product Assurance Manager concurrence prior to submission to the customer.

(c) Project quality plans shall be approved by the Product Assurance Manager. Any contractual or customer requirement which requires a change to the quality assurance system shall be referred to the Director of Product Assurance for authorization.

(d) Product Assurance management may issue stop orders against work being performed in an improper manner. Stop orders shall be in writing and shall state the problem and the action needed before work may be resumed.

(e) Product Assurance personnel shall emphasize the prevention of defects and mistakes and shall assist operating organizations in achieving proper and efficient work performance. The Product Assurance Organization shall promote the exchange of quality related information and standardization of methods and procedures affecting quality.

---

configuration management, testing, corrective action, library controls, computer program design, software documentation, reviews and audits, tools, techniques and methodologies, or subcontractor control, just as a few examples. The policy should also recognize that many quality functions may be performed by people in other organizations besides the quality organization. In fact, a successful software development has the mark of quality that was designed into the software rather than tested in or just monitored until the code worked. Designing quality in is done often by the development organizations implementing quality policies and procedures required for design, development, test, and maintenance of software.

By establishing top-level policies and procedures in the company, the software quality assurance organization receives a charter from which to perform its work. Without that charter it is difficult to accomplish tasks that have not been defined or, even worse, to perform tasks that are not understood or agreed to by upper management. The initial quality planning for software quality assurance should be conducted to identify specific quality objectives of the corporation, and commit management to support the implementing quality organizations.

SOFTWARE QUALITY ASSURANCE FUNCTIONS

The next few sections describe the various functions that should be performed by the software QA organization during the different phases of software development.

Proposal Support

Analysis of requirements affecting quality assurance should be made during proposal preparation by quality assurance personnel. Quality and configuration management inputs as required by the proposal need to be formulated into quality assurance and configuration management plans that are responsive to the request for proposal/ statement of work (RFP/SOW) while at the same time still utilize as much of the company quality system as possible. To do this there needs to be a thorough review of the project plan and then preparation of a quality assurance plan that is responsive to the project plan. If necessary, quality assurance policies and procedures that would be in support of unique contract requirements may be formulated. All quality assurance requirements as defined by either the RFP or by company quality policies and procedures should be related to the contract development life cycle. Special care should be taken to describe what quality requirements apply to subcontractors and vendors and how the software quality assurance program guarantees that software furnished by subcontractors meets contract requirements. The software quality assurance plan should also include those functions and procedures or standards required by the project for the development of software. The QA plan should treat in detail independent quality audits; reviews and audits that are necessary by formal technical contract requirements; what responsibilities are associated with the quality assurance organization in regard to monitoring the software test program; quality assurance activities related to discrepancy reporting, trend analysis, and corrective action; software development tools, techniques, or methodology that will be used to support quality objectives during the software development; and the procedures related to the monitoring of configuration management.

Requirements Definition

The software quality assurance organization should assist in the review of the requirements to help analyze and evaluate the software requirements specification for its contractual and technical acceptability. All problems should be recorded in a formal manner. Requirements should be reviewed and problem descriptions written in the areas of typographical errors, ambiguous requirements, requirements that are not needed, incorrect statements, inconsistency with other requirements, better design possible, more information needed, requirement not testable, etc. In addition, technical documentation and specification should be reviewed to assure the control of functional performance of the interface requirements for software products. All requirements should be traceable to the test program and be addressed in Section 4 of the Part 1 Specification. The quality assurance organization also needs to review this section to assure that it deals with providing the test strategy that the project intends to use to show satisfaction of all the requirements. The types and levels of tests should be defined clearly and be related to the specific requirements to be tested, and any special acceptance criteria should be stated. Examples of special acceptance criteria could be the math models necessary to calculate acceptance values, special limit criteria, volume of stress data, whether real data has to be captured for system acceptance runs, etc.

Design Phase

The quality assurance organization should work with the project to help recommend and maintain project standards affecting design, coding, data base, retest criteria, etc. Standards should be selected and applied during the design phase which promote uniformity, readability, understandability, and other quality characteristics of software products. Additionally, all software development project plans should be reviewed. These may include the configuration management and quality assurance procedures necessary to comply with the quality assurance plans either delivered or being written during the design phase.

Development

There are numerous quality assurance monitoring functions that are performed during the development phase (see Figure 2). Typically, programmer notebook or unit development folder audits are conducted to verify that development personnel have implemented all requirements and complied with project standards. This can involve coding and flowchart requirements tracing as well as the inspection of code and documentation for final standards compliance. The standards compliance can be checked either manually or through the use of automated quality programs such as a code auditor which automatically checks standard compliance with each compilation. Documentation reviews should include specifications and test plans and procedures to show satisfaction of requirements. The development test effort should be monitored to assure that all functional requirements in addition to contract requirements are satisfied, and that development test plans and procedures have been complied with prior to turnover of internal code to an independent test organization. This is a most important step in that it is a milestone that checks progress between the critical design review (CDR) and functional/physical configuration audits (FCA/PCA).

Another very important quality assurance role is that of conducting independent quality assurance audits. They should be conducted to determine compliance with the appropriate company software policies and procedures, software standards and/or contractual requirements (see Figure 3).

While the independent audits are not a continuous function during the software development effort, they are independent and become spot checks for smaller programs that cannot afford a full software quality assurance program. They tend to be highly effective and give good visibility to problems. The principle of auditing is to relate contract requirements to the quality of the product being developed. Independent audits can also verify all quality program requirements, but not require full-time QA support for a project and therefore tend to be very cost effective even for large programs.

A typical audit approach consists of reviewing the contractual requirements and the quality section of the statement of work (see Figure 4). The quality review of related contract items is emphasized. Project documentation which may be in the form of standards and procedures specifications, plans, procedures, reports, etc., is reviewed to verify compliance with contractual and/or company standards. Any noted discrepancy should be formally documented and presented for resolution to the project manager, and a final report prepared. As the discrepancies are eliminated, it is the audit team's responsibility to revisit the project and verify which problems have, in fact, been corrected. Care should be taken to schedule audits early enough in the development program in order to assist the project manager. Coming in with an audit team toward the end of the development cycle does

FIGURE 2. *Sample quality directive*

	NO:
SUBJECT: Quality Assurance Support	DATE:
of Software Projects	REFERENCE:
	APPROVED:

1.0 REFERENCES

MIL-S-52779, "Software Quality Assurance Program Requirements."

2.0 PURPOSE

This directive describes the role of PA in providing quality assurance support to software projects.

3.0 APPLICABILITY

This directive applies to PA quality assurance support of all new software projects developing computer programs for use by someone other than the developer.

4.0 POLICY

To the extent that MIL S-52779 is compatible with the other referenced documents and with a project's contractual requirements, technical complexity, and resources, it shall be the governing specification for PA support, and each of the following topics of MIL-S-52779 shall be considered a standard element of such support:

a. Identification and monitoring of work tasking and authorization procedures in relation to PA tasks (paragraph 3.2.1).

b. Quality assurance of software configuration management (paragraph 3.2.2).

c. Quality assurance of testing (paragraph 3.2.3).

d. Quality assurance of corrective action process (paragraph 3.2.4).

e. Establishment and identification of software development library controls (paragraph 3.2.5).

f. Review and evaluation of computer program design documentation (paragraph 3.2.6).

g. Quality assurance of documentation (paragraph 3.2.7).

h. Quality assurance of reviews and audits (paragraph 3.2.8).

i. Identification and evaluation of quality assurance tools, techniques, and methodologies (paragraph 3.2.9).

The two following activities also shall be considered standard elements of PA QA support, within the limits stated above:

a. Monitoring of quality standards and procedures.

b. Participation in project reviews, audits, and control boards.

5.0 RESPONSIBILITIES

5.1 *Software Project Manager.* Each Software Project Manager shall have the following responsibilities:

52

FIGURE 2. *Continued*

---

    a. Preparing a project software QA Plan in accordance with the contract and with company policies and standards, and obtaining approval of the plan by the PA Manager within one month of project startup.
    b. Maintaining the project software QA Plan.
    c. Identifying and approving jointly with the PA Manager and each Software QA Engineer assigned to a project.
    d. Providing development direction to the Software QA Engineer for each project.

5.2 *PA Manager.* The PA Manager shall have the following responsibilities:
    a. Reviewing and approving each software project's QA Plan.
    b. Approving jointly with the Project Manager the Software QA Engineer for each project.
    c. Reviewing quarterly plans for independent quality audits of SEID software projects, notifying SEID Division and operations management of the audit plans, and reviewing the audits.
    d. Preparing Quality Directives pertaining to software QA.
    e. Maintaining a staff to develop advanced QA techniques.

5.3 *Software PA Department Manager.* The Software PA Department Manager shall have the following responsibilities:
    a. Approving (jointly with the SEID/PA Manager and the Project Manager) the Software QA Engineer for each SEID project.
    b. Providing functional direction on QA matters to each Software QA Engineer assigned to a SEID project.
    c. Reviewing and approving project-specific QA procedures.
    d. Otherwise supporting projects with respect to required product quality requirements.

5.4 *Project Software QA Engineer.* Each project Software QA Engineer shall have the following responsibilities:
    a. Providing independent assurance that the software products being developed meet appropriate standards for quality as defined in the project QA Plans and in the above policy statement (4.0).
    b. Complying with operational direction from the Project Manager.
    c. Complying with functional direction from the Software PA Department Manager.

---

nothing but make the project manager aware that there isn't enough time to fix the discovered problems. When the audits are conducted properly and early enough in the development cycle, they become a very effective way to conduct a low-cost software quality assurance program.

FIGURE 2. *Continued*

Participation in software project quality assurance functions

Quality assurance function number	Quality assurance functions	PA participation			
		Category 1. PA is qualified candidate	Category 2. PA is recommended candidate	Category 3. PA representative shall be included	Category 4. PA is only approved candidate
1.0	Interpret RFP and contract PA requirements 1.1 Review project plan 1.2 Prepare QA plan 1.3 Prepare QA policies and procedures 1.4 Assist in proposal preparation	X			X
2.0	Recommend and maintain project standards 2.1 Coding, data base, retest criteria 2.2 Dictionary/glossary, administrative	X		X	
3.0	Participate in internal and formal reviews 3.1 Systems requirements review (SRR) 3.2 Software system design review (SDR) 3.3 Preliminary design review (PDR) 3.4 Critical design review (CDR)	X		X	
4.0	Oversee and coordinate QA and CM tools program 4.1 Selection and/or design of QA and CM tools 4.2 Tools design review chairman 4.3 Tools maintenance	X	X		
5.0	Perform monitoring functions 5.1 UDF (unit development folder) inspections 5.2 Code/flowchart requirement trace 5.3 Inspect code and documentation for standards	X		X	

5.4 Turnover inspection to test			
5.5 Inspection/test surveillance			
5.6 Validation and acceptance test surveillance			
5.7 Retest decision review			
5.8 Requirements validation check			
5.9 Problem report technical review			
5.10 Subcontractor quality assurance program			
6.0 Conduct independent audit	X		X
6.1 Review project procedures			
6.2 Assess standards procedures adherence			
6.3 Determine contract quality assurance compliance			
7.0 Assess Project quality status	X		X
7.1 DPR/SPR/DR trend analysis			
7.2 Availability/reliability estimation			
7.3 Error prediction			
7.4 Logic path analysis for safety			
8.0 Review and recommend approval		X	X
8.1 Test plans			
8.2 Test procedures			
8.3 Product waivers and deviations			
8.4 Test analyses and reports			
8.5 Test readiness review			
9.0 Participate in test review board		X	X
10.0 Participate in formal acceptance		X	X
10.1 Functional configuration audit (FCA)			
10.2 Physical configuration audit (PCA)			
10.3 Formal qualification review (FQR)			
11.0 Certify the product	X		X
11.1 Witness acceptance and demonstration test			
11.2 Review CDRL items and recommend approval			
11.3 Confirm discrepancy report close-out			

FIGURE 3. *Timing and topics of software QA audits*

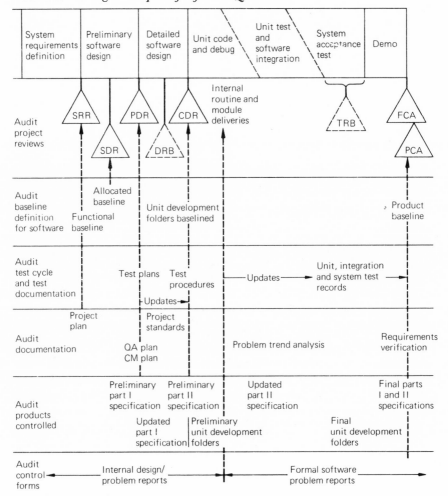

Dedicated software quality assurance personnel also should conduct an assessment of the project quality standards compliance. This can be done by conducting a trend analysis of software problems or discrepancies. Corrective action of deficiencies should be monitored to prevent noncompliant software to contract requirements. This may be performed by analysis of data and problems or of deficiency reports to determine the extent and cause of problems, analysis of trends in performance of work, and review of adequacy of corrective action measures (see Figure 5). Care should be taken when considering what data

4. Management Control Practices for Software Quality

FIGURE 4. *Audit activities*

4%	21%	33%	25%	17%
Organization review	Documentation review	Investigation	Report preparation	Briefing
Project management	Contract	Evaluation	Findings	Preparation
WBS	Software quality provisions	Analysis	Recommendation	Presentation
Customer interface	Specifications	Verification	Project review	
	Plans (test, management, CM, QA)			
	Procedures			

FIGURE 5. *Sample of S/W trend analysis (see reference 8)*

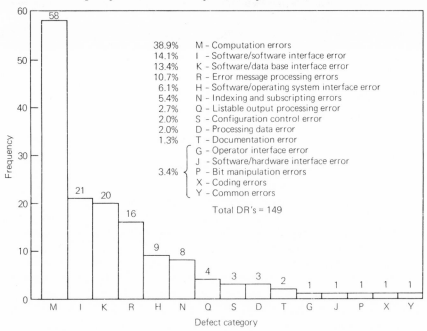

38.9% M – Computation errors
14.1% I – Software/software interface error
13.4% K – Software/data base interface error
10.7% R – Error message processing errors
6.1% H – Software/operating system interface error
5.4% N – Indexing and subscripting errors
2.7% Q – Listable output processing error
2.0% S – Configuration control error
2.0% D – Processing data error
1.3% T – Documentation error
3.4% {
G – Operator interface error
J – Software/hardware interface error
P – Bit manipulation errors
X – Coding errors
Y – Common errors
}

Total DR's = 149

FIGURE 6. *Sample S/W quality instruction*

Date Issued: CONFIGURATION VERIFICATION

1. PURPOSE

This policy statement describes software verification and certification policy for:
(1) Software changes
(2) Validation testing
(3) Discrepancies

2. SCOPE

This Quality Instruction delineates concurrent QA and other organizations' activities as they relate to software configuration verification. This policy applies during validation and demonstration testing phases of software development. The fulfillment of this policy rests as a shared responsibility among all organizations involved in software development.

3. REFERENCES

The documents listed below are either referenced within this Quality Instruction or contain additional background or detailed procedural information regarding the policy established herein:
(1) Software Product Assurance Plan
(2) Configuration Management Procedure: Change Control
(3) Inspection and Test Surveillance
(4) Software Test Program Plan

3.1 *Related Documents*
None

4. POLICY

4.1 *Software Changes*
Software Product Assurance shall verify that approved changes by the CCB to software are incorporated in the computer program and its documentation; and that proper notification of the completed changes are documented.

4.1.1 The following change processing forms shall be used to document changes and shall require a PA sign-off:
(1) Software Problem Report (SPR)
(2) Software Change Order (SCO)

4.1.2 The DPR shall identify changes to baselined code and shall require CCB approval prior to incorporating the changes.

4.1.3 The software development library shall record the actual changes made to the computer program for each program modification. Completed modifications shall be verified by PA by comparing the computer program output to assure that the proper changes were incorporated. Product Assurance shall also verify the configuration for all subsequent tests or retests of the program.

4.2 *Software Configuration Verification During Validation Testing*
Software Product Assurance shall verify that the configuration of the program

under test is the current version and properly relates to other interfacing software, test driver, test plan, test definition, and proper version of test procedures.

4.3 *Discrepancies*

Product Assurance shall maintain a log of those DRs which requires changes to documentation, computer program code, and the data base. PA shall also insure that corrective action is timely, that the DR is not closed until the changes are processed, and that subsequent testing uses the corrected version.

Approved by: _____ _____
           Manager for   Project Manager
     Product Assurance

DATE ISSUED: CONFIGURATION VERIFICATION

Configuration verification responsibilities   *Responsibility*

No.	Requirements	PA	SI&T	CMO	Design and Development
1.	Verify and certify software changes	P*	S	P*	S
2.	Verify closure of discrepancy reports	P	S		S
3.	Verify that configuration of program under test is the current version and properly relates to other interfacing software, test driver, test plan, test definition, and proper version of test procedures.	P*	P*	S	S

*As applicable
P (Prime) — Has overall responsibility for the required action
S (Shared) — Furnishes support, as necessary, for the performance of the required action

needs to be recorded. Data can be expensive, and more than one project has stored data that was never used.

The quality assurance personnel should also participate in internal and formal reviews. These include System Requirements Review (SSR), System Design Review (SDR), Preliminary Design Review (PDR), Critical Design Review (CDR), internal Test Review Boards (TRB), Functional Configuration Audit (FCA), Physical Configuration Audit (PCA), and, when required, a Formal Qualification Review (FQR). The software QA personnel should reference the procedures and standards required for the conduct of formal reviews and audits during the development cycle and the quality assurance measures to be employed to insure that the reviews and audits are conducted in accordance with the contract requirements. This includes early participation and planning to assure the formal reviews go smoothly while the customer is there. This should include compliance to the format of specification requirements, the content required by data items on the contract, and the verification that all requirements have been addressed.

Testing

The quality assurance role in regard to testing software products requires that project test plans and procedures be carefully reviewed. This includes the development of test documentation, which is normally not deliverable to the customer, as well as the preliminary Qualification Test (PQT), Formal Qualification Test (FQT), and Acceptance Test documentation. The review should trace requirements from the specification to the test plans, procedures, and finally to the test reports to show that the requirements have been tested satisfactorily. In addition, all testing associated with those plans and procedures should be monitored for compliance to customer-approved documentation. Other activities that should be monitored carefully are the retest decision review made by the project, problem report technical review, close-out of those problem reports, and participation in test review boards which determine whether the proposed product is ready to be submitted for the acceptance test phase.

Certification

All of the quality assurance support during the test effort is important background for the Functional Configuration Audit (FCA) which will once again require formal review of all testing of the software development, including the test reports that are generated. Final certification of the test results should be provided by the quality assurance organization for review of the requirements traceability against the test reports to show that all design requirements have been satisfied and successfully tested. Immediately following the Functional Configuration Audit, all documentation that is deliverable by the developing organization to the customer should be finally reviewed at the Physical Configuration Audit (PCA) and any remaining test discrepancies can be closed at a Formal Qualification Review (FQR), if required. The FQR is not normally performed during software development, but when it is required, the quality assurance organization should perform the same role as it does during the FCA. During certification of the product, software quality assurance personnel should witness the acceptance demonstration test. All documentation that is deliverable should be reviewed against the CDRL items and Data Item descriptions (DIs) so that the quality organization can certify that the documentation is as required by contract. The final step in the certification process involves confirming that all discrepancy reports have been closed out properly.

SOFTWARE QUALITY ASSURANCE INSTRUCTIONS

As part of the quality system for a company, the quality instructions are the very important implementing devices needed to complete that system. Without the instructions it is difficult for personnel to be consistent in their approach to software quality assurance work. It is also difficult for middle management to provide any training or management support without knowing what type of instructions are to be complied with in support of software projects. One of the more consistently glaring problems in software product assurance is the staffing of jobs by experienced software engineers with any product assurance background. Before assignment to specific projects, quality assurance representatives should receive training. Personnel need a clear understanding of what is expected, and the implementing quality devices for training and project performance should be the quality instructions.

Instructions can be in a variety of forms. They can read somewhat similar to the policy and procedures but be simply stated with more detail (Figure 6), or they may even take the form of checklists (Figure 7) with direction given on how to evaluate a software project effort. As an example, MIL-S-52779 requires contractors to develop and implement a software quality program which includes detecting, reporting, analysis, and correction of software deficiencies and the identification of software quality functions and activities. From a systems standpoint, the policy and procedures would provide the direction for application of these functions. However, the instructions would have to provide the details required by quality assurance personnel to perform evaluation of the basic requirement. The instructions would have to address questions such as, does the quality assurance plan identify all the organizations (including design and development) involved in the software quality assurance efforts? Do software quality assurance personnel have authority, responsibility, and freedom of action to evaluate the software design and production and to initiate and/or recommend changes? Another example could be where MIL-S-52779 requires independent quality assurance audits of the configuration management

61

FIGURE 7. *Sample CM plan audit checklist*

QUALITY ASSURANCE AUDIT CHECKLIST
SOFTWARE CONFIGURATION MANAGEMENT
No. 17

Auditor _____   Area Audited _____

Project Responsible Individual _____   Date of Audit _____

Audit Item	S/W configuration management plan	Reviewed			Acceptable		Findings	Corrective Action
		Yes	No	N/A	Yes	No		
17.1	Plan approved prior to SRR							
17.2	Format complies with contract and/or "SEID Software Product Standards"							
17.3	CM Plan includes:							
	(1) Project baselines (requirements, design, test, product)							
	(2) Baseline definitions in terms of product and review and approval events for each							
	(3) Configuration identification ground rules							
	(4) Configuration control mechanism							
	(5) Problem reporting system							
	(6) Configuration status accounting system							
	(7) Configuration verification approach							
17.4	Project control issuance, retention, change control							

17.5	Establish and operate a product development library						
17.6	PAM approves CM Plan						
	CM review and guidance						
	CM interpretive documentation						
	CADM physical media control as defined in CM Plan						

on a project. The quality instructions should provide the means to perform an analysis of the configuration management plan as well as the steps required to perform an audit of configuration management. Instructions should include such things as audit methodology and forms and the requirements placed on the selection of audit personnel.

PERSONNEL

It is necessary that software quality assurance team members be recognized as being proficient in the area they are reviewing. Therefore, quality assurance personnel should be recognized as specialists by the software development community. Depending on the size of the software development organization, the quality assurance personnel backgrounds should collectively include requirements analysis, software development, specification writing and analysis, testing, software tools development, operational support, former quality assurance and configuration management managers and, if possible, some project management experience. The quality assurance teams should be selected to match the project's needs throughout the entire development cycle. Once the quality personnel have been selected, they should be familiarized with appropriate quality policies, procedures, and instructions so they can approach quality functions in a standardized way in support of their projects. Once this has been accomplished, a quality system has been completed.

By using recognized experts in various software development fields, the personnel performing services to the project as members of an independent organization do not have to sell themselves to show that they are worthy of reviewing and critiquing the project's procedures and products. There are also many jobs from a quality or configuration management standpoint in software that do not require years of experience in software development. Those jobs can be filled by less experienced personnel. But the importance of policies, procedures, and instructions becomes even more obvious. Not all personnel will be as broadly experienced as desired, and it is only through a standardized approach that represents a company quality system that adequate training and management support may be given to those individuals performing the quality functions for the company.

SUMMARY

While the major message for establishing a software quality organization is to have support from top management and to design a company system for software quality assurance as part of an overall company system, there is no need to assume that the system needs to be complex. It can quickly be seen that the amount of paper used to provide the policies, procedures, instructions, and checklists may outweigh the personnel dedicated to the software quality assurance organization. In fact, the simpler the system, the more successful it will probably be. If a company is smaller and less diversified than a large software development organization, that company could probably combine quality policy, procedures, and instructions into one document for each quality function. More complex organizations may benefit from a more structured approach which could develop something like the policies and procedures illustrated. Companies should be extremely careful to keep the system they design as simple as possible. Simple systems are more flexible and tend to be more responsive to the project needs over a longer period of time. The seniority and the expertise of the personnel supporting the software quality assurance organization can provide the ingenuity and common sense needed to implement the simpler company systems and still be responsive to changing customer needs.

Even though the software quality assurance organization may take on the appearance of supporting a customer's requirements more than the project's requirements, it should always be emphasized that software quality assurance is providing an independent service to the project managers. While independence is extremely important, it should never be divorced from the fact that the project managers have a commitment to deliver a product to a customer. It is through the company system that it is clearly understood by all members of the company, not just quality assurance, that the development and quality organizations can work together and benefit from each other.

References

1. McKissick, John, Jr. and Price, Robert A. "Quality Control of Computer Software," *1977 ASQC Technical Conference Transactions*, ASQC, 1977.
2. Fisher, Matt; Jelinski, Zyg; Whited, Jon. "Software Quality Assurance and Reliability As It Relates to Configuration Management," *EIA Data and Configuration Management Workshop*, October 17, 1977, pp. 129-170.
3. McCall, J. A.; Richards, P. K.; Walters, G. F. "Factors in Software Quality," *Interim Technical Report No. 1*, Electronic Systems Division and Rome Air Development Center, October 1976.
4. Neil, George and Gold, Harvey. *Software Acquisition Management Guidebook: Software Quality Assurance*, ESD-TR-77-255, August 1977.

5. *TRW, Airborne Systems Software Acquisition Engineering Guidebook for Quality Assurance,* November 1977.
6. Boehm, B. W.; Brown, J. R.; Lipow, M. "Quantitative Evaluation of Software Quality," *Proceedings of the Second International Conference on Software Engineering,* IEEE, October 1976, pp. 592–605.
7. Ingrassia, F. S. and Thayer, T. A. *The Role of Product Assurance in Improving Software Reliability,* March 1976.
8. Thayer, T. A.; Lipow, M.; Nelson, E. C. *"Software Reliability Study, Final Technical Report,"* Rome Air Development Center, RADC-TR-74-250, October 1974.
9. Computer Software Staff, Product Assurance Directorate, *Software Quality Assurance,* December 1976.
10. Boehm, B. W.; Brown, J. R.; Kaspar, H.; Lipow, M.; MacLeod, G. J.; Merritt, M.J. *Characteristics of Software Quality,* December 1973.
11. MIL-R-83313 (USAF), *Reviews and Audits, Technical, for Communications—Electronic—Meteorological Systems and Related Equipment,* 2 January 1975.
12. Proposed MIL-STD-1679 (Navy), *Tactical Software Development,* 1 August 1977.
13. MIL-Q-9858A, *Quality Program Requirements,* 16 December 1963.
14. MIL-S-52779, *Software Quality Assurance Program Requirements,* 5 April 1974.

CHAPTER 5

Contractual Controls for Software Quality

H. M. LEAVITT, Jr.

INTRODUCTION

The discussion of contractual controls to insure quality software as part of the development of a tactical computerized system will follow the acquisition process and, in fact, concentrate on certain aspects of acquisition strategy. Although Navy terminology and references will be used, the procedures should be applicable to others.

QUALITY SOFTWARE

Tactical systems have known, established requirements which must be well understood at the start of the acquisition process. These systems must be operable and maintainable by some combination of trained officers and enlisted personnel. They must also interface with other military systems. These other systems may be analog, digital, or human. A given new system will usually have to receive or send specific information to different systems depending upon the class of platform in which it is installed.

Tactical systems will be in service for a considerable period of time.

During their service life, their interfaces will change and their functional performance will be modified to meet changing threats. They must be as immune to damage and failure as possible; that is, they must degrade gracefully, have some redundancy, and be quickly repairable. Therefore, the acquisition manager seeks a system which can grow to meet new threats, interfaces with all required systems, has low failure and high survivability, and which may be installed in modified configurations which are subsets of a higher system.

The software package which allows this is a quality software product.

ACQUISITION STRATEGY

The plan for development and procurement of a tactical computerized system must be carefully developed in detail prior to any contractual action. Once started, most contractual actions are irreversible. The broad phases of acquisition strategy are shown in outline form in Figure 1. Actually, each phase of the program should be recognized as a series of iterative "subphases" (Figure 2) during which requirements and other governing decisions can be re-examined and, if necessary, changed.

For purposes of discussing acquisition strategy, it will be assumed that a project manager exists and some general requirement has been

FIGURE 1. *Acquisition strategy*

Milestones	0 − − − − − I − − − − − − − − II − − − − − − − III
SOI (statement of intent) Brief to Industry	− − −
RFP (request for proposal) and Evaluation	− − − − − −
Contract Definition	− − − − −
Development Contracts	− − − − −
Production Contracts	− − −

FIGURE 2. *Program plan phases*

Milestone	0	Program Initiation
	1	Demonstration and Validation
	2	Full-Scale Engineering Development
	3	Production and Deployment

stated by proper authority. A competitive development will also be assumed, and only the software aspect of the strategy will be discussed.

Help for the Program Manager

Much help is available to the program manager before he starts and during the execution of a program. This help is in the form of:

Regulations
Instructions
Mil-standards
Standardized computer hardware
Government laboratories
Government industrial activities
Experience of other program managers

INITIAL STEP—APPROVED PROGRAM

The project manager will become responsible for a number of contracts during his tenure. These are not all contracts with industry, but they are all important. Some of these "contracts" are really charters and approved plans within his organization.

The first contract for which he will be responsible concerns requirements. Many projects are doomed because of problems during this first step. This internal contract develops in accordance with DOD Instruction 5000.1, "Acquisition of Major Defense Systems," and is an iterative process as shown in Figures 1 and 2. The final result of this process is an approved program plan, a Decision Coordinating Plan (DCP), which contains requirements, schedules, resources, and thresholds for all three. This document is truly an incremental approval to proceed, since it requires reviews by higher authority at designated milestones before proceeding to the next milestone.

The project manager must realize that all future actions and reviews will use the DCP as the source document. Therefore, he must insist that any exceptions that he requires are included. Specific examples are: Which high-order language should be used? Which computer will be used? Is any concurrency required? Is the establishment of a software maintenance facility authorized? The details of each program should be carefully reviewed to include direction concerning any controversial or specific issues which require exceptions from existing rules or regulations.

The second in-house contract for which he is responsible is the test and evaluation master plan (TEMP). This is an agreement on what, how, and when the product will be tested. The TEMP defines all required resources for conducting the test program. The TEMP must be based on and completely correspond with the approved program plan requirements.

Requirements

The formal requirements document will usually contain certain requirements which cannot be met either because of technology or cost limitations and they naturally should not be set forth as requirements in the approved program. Of more concern, however, is the specific wording of requirements which are to be met. The project manager should not accept any requirements unless they are clear and, most important, they must be testable. Such statements as "must be rapidly available," "provide necessary information to," etc., have to be defined in detail.

Because of the very nature of processing systems, the project manager should consider one or more scenarios and/or event-time line documents as part of his requirements package. This will be invaluable in defining performance specifications to contractors and in writing test plans which demonstrate the system capability. The interpretation of the simultaneity of the system's capability can be a disaster to a system in development. The use of scenarios and event time-line documents cannot be overly stressed.

At this time the project manager should be able to establish a one-to-one track for each element of his requirements from the approved plan, DCP, to test and evaluation master plan, TEMP, to the statement of work and/or specifications of the contract he intends to sign with industry (see Figure 3).

Project Manager's Staff

By this time it is obvious that a one-man show has been exceeded and in any case the DCP requires management to be addressed. The

FIGURE 3.

DCP Requirements =   Requirements   = TEMP Requirements
                              =
                        Contracts to Industry

choice of vertical versus function organization is beyond the scope of this discussion.

Prior to formal program approval the project manager needs the following help. A *test and evaluation manager* is required to insure that the DCP is written in a manner such that compliance with the requirements can be demonstrated by reasonable testing. Also, the costs of testing including the installation and support of the test system are properly chargeable to R&D funds and must be included in the DCP. Direct liaison by the T&E manager with other T&E managers of computerized systems will insure a good start.

A *business and financial manager* with knowledge and access to experienced people in software development costs is required at the start. A detailed knowledge of appropriations and which to use for each required effort is mandatory while the plan is being conceived. He should also initiate a life cycle cost study.

These two functions can be considered as the project manager's conscience. As the program progresses, they will actually be reviewed, audited, and directed by higher authority. Know this, expect it, and prepare for it.

In addition to these two key people, he requires an *engineering development manager*, obviously knowledgeable in software and computers.

A *logistics manager* knowledgeable in software support is also required at the beginning. The project manager must understand that it takes as long to establish a software support capability as it does to develop the software. The two efforts should also be mutually supportive, that is, the software support group should review software documentation during development and they can provide direct support to the developer. More on this later.

With this minimum assistance the project manager should be able to iteratively balance requirements, schedules, and resources to produce an approved program plan.

Development

Prior to seeking contractors for development of the computerized tactical system, the project manager has an approved program plan which clearly states requirements, resources, schedules, and thresholds. He now has a contract with the operational requirement and budget authority.

At this time he relies on a key document among many important ones. This is SECNAVINST 3560.1, *Tactical Digital Systems Documentation Standards.* The project manager and his team now prepare to meet industry. Knowing and understanding SECNAVINST 3560.1, they realize its value and the effort they must display in supporting its implementation.

Following the approved plan, they prepare for the following steps with the contractors:

1. Statement of intent brief
2. Request for proposal
3. Evaluation of proposals
4. Selection and award for contract definition contracts
5. Evaluation of contract definition proposals
6. Selection and award Phase 1 for development contractors
7. Evaluation of Phase 1 development efforts
8. Selection and award for full-scale development contractors

TACTICAL DIGITAL SYSTEMS DOCUMENTATION STANDARDS

This is the title of SECNAVINST 3560.1, and the documents detailed therein are shown in Figure 4. Their use during the steps to contract outlined above will be discussed.

Figure 5 shows the documents divided into the three categories of authorize, approve, and accept. The authorizing documents are in reality part of the approved plan, DCP, in that they must represent goals and requirements of the project. They may be prepared by a contractor and formally approved by the Government to become authorizing documents or they could be prepared by the project managers. The approved documents are those which are reviewed and received by the Government when found satisfactory. They are deliverables of the contract, and when signed for by the Government they become direction documents to the contractor for effort which follows. The acceptance documents are those documents which are reports or descriptions of efforts completed. They do not normally control work to be done; they describe work which has been done.

Statement of intent brief—The project manager, through his contracting officer, announces via the Commerce Business Daily and letters, if desired, that the Government intends to have a briefing for contractors interested in bidding on the development of a system which is generally described.

During this brief the project manager describes the requirements of the system, any design to price goals, the desired schedule, the intended acquisition strategy and Government-directed matters such as

FIGURE 4.

Part	Group/document title
I	System Development Tactical operational requirement
II	Software System Specification System operational specification System operational design Function operational specification Interface design specification Program Specification Program performance specification Function operational design Program design specification Program Description Program description document Data base design Program package
III	Test Plan/Specification Test plan Test specification Test Procedures/Reports Test procedures Test reports
IV	Program Manuals Operator's manual Program design manual User Manuals Command and staff manual System operator's manual

use of AN/UYK-20 is directed, use of CMS-2M high-order language is directed, required reports, etc.

At this time the authorizing documents (Figure 6) should be presented or their preparation should be discussed.

All attendees should be recorded and given both written and verbal invitation to request in writing a request for proposal.

Request for proposal—The RFP should be delivered by mail to the requestors and followed in two or three weeks by a RFP brief. The announcement of the RFP brief should request that all questions be submitted in writing some suitable time prior to the brief. The brief

FIGURE 5.

Part	Group/document title	Action		
		Authorize	Approve	Accept
I	System Development			
	Tactical operational requirement	X	X	
II	Software System Specification			
	System operational specification	X	X	
	System operational design		X	
	Function operational specification	X		
	Interface design specification		X	
	Program Specification			
	Program performance specification		X	
	Function operational design		X	
	Program design specification			X
	Program Description			
	Program description document			X
	Data base design			X
	Program package			X
III	Test Plan/Specification			
	Test plan		X	
	Test specification		X	
	Test Procedures/Reports			
	Test procedures			X
	Test reports			X
IV	Program Manuals			
	Operator's manual		X	
	Program design manual			X
	User Manuals			
	Command and staff manual	X		
	System operator's manual	X	X	

should cover in detail the high-level requirements and all Government direction, as well as Government-furnished material and information. Specifically, the contractors should be provided with a statement of the tactical operational requirement, the system operational specification, the functional operational specification, and scenarios in which system requirements are to be demonstrated. The objective of this first RFP is to receive proposals on how the contractor intends to approach and solve the problem stated. The RFP must clearly state the evaluation criteria.

FIGURE 6.

Part	Group/document title	
I	System Development Tactical operational requirement	These documents must track with the DCP and the TEMP
II	Software System Specification System operational specification System operational design Function operational specification	

Evaluation of proposals primarily concerns the contractor's demonstrated understanding of the requirements and his proposed approach to meeting those requirements.

Selection and award for contract definition contracts—After completing the evaluation process, competitive contractors are given a contract to write a detailed development contract to meet the system requirements and observe all Government direction. This is the key contract, since response and subsequent evaluation of this effort will most likely determine the final contractors or contractor and the end product.

It is at this point that the project manager should direct that the response include a two-phased effort. The first phase should be a proposal to develop sufficient data to demonstrate that phase 2 of the development would meet the stated requirements. While each project would require a tailored approach to the deliverables of phase 1, they fall into two categories: software documentation, and hardware specifications including a detailed system architecture.

Referring to SECNAVINST 3560.1, phase 1 should include as a minimum:

1. The system operational specification, an overall system performance specification
2. Performance specifications of all hardware units
3. The computer program performance specification
4. Description of all interfaces
5. Documentation to confirm that hardware will meet size and environmental requirements.

The inclusion of additional documentation in phase 1 or a phase 2 for additional documentation followed by system development must be very carefully considered by the project manager. Probably the most important additional documentation are the program design budget of the system operational design and the specific operator actions of the functional operational specification.

Evaluation of contract definition proposals—This effort provides an additional measure of insight into the contractor's intention and capability to produce a quality software product. The project manager will need the expanded software support part of his logistics manager for this evaluation.

The selection and award for phase 1, evaluation of that effort, award of subsequent phases and evaluations until full-scale development is awarded will require the project manager to have an ever-increasing amount of assistance in all areas concerned with the documentation of software.

The development contract—Assuming the project manager has awarded the initial development contract, he is now faced with contractual obligations to the contractor. He must be prepared to evaluate, approve, and control a series of contractor-generated documents *concerning software.* These documents become detailed statements of performance requirements of the contract. He must be able to review them for compliance with the DCP, question and define areas of vagueness, omission, error and confusion until the document satisfies its intent. The documents he must approve and control and to which the contractor must perform in accordance with SECNAVINST 3560.1 are listed in Figure 5.

Also as part of the development contract, a logistic support analysis will be required. This too has software implications in that it is the plan for maintenance and support of the system when it is operational.

All of the above items will be addressed in the contract as to scope, due date, Government response time, and format. They will be covered by data item description documents, listed in the contract data requirements list, provided for by effort in the statement of work and they will be in consonance with specifications. All these are part of the contract for which the project manager is responsible.

DEVELOPMENT CONTRACT CONTROL

At any time during the development contract, the program manager should review the software documentation from two main points of view. First, did he contract for the right system, and, second, is the contractor designing the system in accordance with the contract?

The first step in checking on a contract involving the design and delivery of computer software is to review the documents shown in Figure 7 to see if they reflect the requirements of the approved plan, DCP.

FIGURE 7.

Part	Group/document	
I	System Development Tactical operational requirement	
II	Software System Specification System operational specification System operational design Function operational specification Interface design specification	
	Program Specification Program performance specification Function operational design Program design specification	DANGER If these documents do not track DCP and TEMP, you are developing the wrong system
III	Test Plan/Specification Test plan Test specification	

The next step is to check the contractor-generated documents which describe the details of his software design against the requirements type documents. Figure 8 shows this action.

These two checks can quickly identify the existence of problems during development. The first check, "Did I tell the contractor to design the right product?" is most important early in the development. The second check, "Is the contractor designing what he contracted?" becomes increasingly important as the development progresses and the documentation is submitted for approval or acceptance.

Project Manager's Obligations

Before the developmental contract with industry is completed, the project manager finds himself party to a series of contracts. They are:

1. The DCP which states the requirements, schedule, and resources as well as exceptions and limitations of the project.
2. The procurement plan which approves and limits the business execution of the project.
3. The test and evaluation master plan which outlines how he will demonstrate that the project has complied with the DCP.
4. The integrated logistic support plan which outlines the projects, planning for support to the user.

FIGURE 8.

Part	Group/document title
I	System Development Tactical operational requirement
II	Software System Specification System operational specification System operational design Function operational specification Interface design specification Program Specification Program performance specification Function operation design Program design specification Program Description Program description document Data base design Program package
III	Test Plan/Specification Test plan Test specification Test Procedures/Reports Test procedures Test reports
IV	Program Manuals Operator's manual Program design manual User Manuals Command and staff manual System operator's manual

DANGER. If these documents do not track those circled, the contractor is not performing

5. The training plan which details the acquisition of a training course, the training of instructors, and a schedule to support training of personnel required for system installation.

Simply put, he is party to agreements which provide for a clearly defined requirement to be developed and installed on a given schedule for a known cost that will be properly supported during its service life by trained personnel.

Who is the project manager?— At this point it is important to review the commitments of the project manager and define his capabilities. Obviously, he is a team and a member of other teams.

A single point of contact at the requirements and budget authority level is the project coordinator. In the iterative process of developing requirements, schedules, and resources, he focuses on all user and program beneficiaries inputs as alternatives are developed by the project manager. He is the focal point and director of the DCP approval cycle and all other user-oriented issues.

The project manager's team must be able to support the previously discussed contracts. These people must have an understanding of at least two disciplines: they must be knowledgeable in the field of the project such as surface to air missiles or torpedoes or fire control, and they must be knowledgeable in digital systems.

To accomplish this end, these people need expertise in the chosen computer, the chosen high-order language, and microcomputers. They have to understand the implications of these subjects with respect to development including development tools, testing, and service life support which includes training.

Regardless of whether the project manager operates in a vertical or functional manner, much of this expertise will require significant funds either for in-house facility support or contractor support.

The project manager's team for software should include a number of elements as either staff function or supporting activities.

Test director—A test director should be assigned to the project manager's staff whose main concerns are the test-related documents (i.e., plans, procedures, reports, and specifications). He will review and comment on the program performance specifications, functional operational design documents, and maintain all WBS reports on schedules and costs. He will also review all other system-related documentation for information.

The primary duties of the test director are to insure that the PPS and FOD reflect the system specification and that tests are designed to adequately verify this. Additionally, he must interface with independent testing agencies for test plans, schedules, and budgets for all test efforts.

Software development manager—A software development manager should be assigned to the project manager's staff whose main concerns are all documentation developed which relate to software and system performance. His primary duties are to make final recommendations to the project manager on all approval or acceptance actions for software documentation. He must also insure that all deliverables are reviewed for scope and completeness, and he must insure the capability for testing of incremental software deliveries.

Software interface manager—This manager, also assigned to the project manager's staff, is concerned with software system specifications and program specifications. His primary duties are to insure that development satisfies all required interfaces and that user data and data handling systems are compatible with the developing system.

Fleet user team — One of the most valuable sources of operational expertise which can be made available to the program manager is a team of experienced users from the fleet. A fleet user team dedicated to the development program with frequent users to the contractor facility can provide realistic and timely assessment of the operational impact of any system-related issues. The main concerns of the fleet user team include the tactical operational requirements, user manuals, test procedures/reports, and function operation design. In addition, the team should review and comment on all other system documentation. Their primary duties are to advise the project manager on questions concerning high-level requirements, to provide resolution of man-machine interface issues, and to assist in development training plans.

In-service software support center — The software support center must be initially established early in the definition phase of the development program to provide for learning and growth in capability to ultimately provide full system support. The main documentation concerns of the support center include program design specifications, program description documents, data base design documents, program packages, program operator manuals, and program design manuals. The support centers should also review and comment on test plans/specifications and user manuals and review all other documents for information. The primary duties of the support center are to provide complete support to the system user, to provide audits during development as required, and to perform the configuration control function beginning with the establishment of a software baseline.

The training authority, in coordination with the program manager, must be familiar with the tactical operational requirements and insure that the user manuals are fully supportive of these requirements. This activity must be familiar with all relevant system documentation. Their primary duties are to provide information on the system to the training command and to budget for training requirements.

The *system modeling lab* may be very productively used by the project manager. The main documentation concerns include the software system specifications, program specifications, test plans and specifications. The primary duty of the modeling lab is to provide the project manager and team members with modeling results as requested and to identify risk areas, review contractor proposals, and identify areas for concern in testing.

SUMMARY

Effective contractual control of a software acquisition program requires:

1. That clear, measurable, testable requirements be established before contract
2. That a project management team be in place before contract
3. That continuous, clear communications exist between the project office and the contractor throughout the contract
4. No changes

CHAPTER 6

Organizational Planning for Software Quality

BARNEY M. KNIGHT

INTRODUCTION

This chapter discusses the software quality assurance organization. An understanding of the organization is presented through an analysis of organizational objectives and attributes.

"Why do you need a software quality organization?" "What are you going to do for me?" "What are you going to do?" "What will it cost?" "How do I know we are not wasting money, time?" "Oh, just what I need, another person looking over my shoulder!" These are questions and comments most often heard when one proposes a software quality assurance organization (SQA). Some answers are appropriate.

Why Do We Need a Software Quality Organization?

Quite simply because the way we have been doing business has not worked. Quality assurance organizations have long been accepted in the hardware world as an extension of management necessary to deliver good product. What has worked well for the hardware system will work, perhaps even better, for the software product.

As software development activities move out of the artistic realm into a more disciplined environment with proven processes, the more necessary it is to have assurance of process fidelity. Faithful compliance with and correct use of development standards, plans, tools, procedures, etc., will take us a long way toward achieving product quality objectives. A quality assurance (QA) organization or at least a QA process is an essential and effective means of assuring process fidelity.

It is improper to assume that a QA organization is required in every instance or for every development effort. Certainly, the decision to form a separate organization with distinct and dedicated resources must be a function of the size, importance, and duration of the development project. A QA organization seems clearly indicated in a facility with a significant software business base and where significant numbers of programmers are employed beyond the development of a single program. A QA organization seems clearly not indicated in the environment where small, stand-alone or occasional programs are generated to satisfy a short-term requirement. It should be evident that quality objectives in a small organization can be attained without a separately chartered organization.

What Are You Going to Do for Me?

It should be understood that quality is everybody's business and that the achievement of higher quality software will be attained by the people who specify the requirements, do the design, write and test the code. However, as an organization, the quality assurance function can materially aid that process by adopting a set of organizational objectives which are clearly consistent with and understood by the overall business organization and its objectives. If product quality is fixed at some minimum acceptable level as a business objective, then the other three basic business objectives (cost, schedule, and performance) are certainly affected by the ability to achieve the desired quality level. The QA organization should be chartered to ensure the attainment of the desired quality level within program cost and schedule constraints.

QUALITY ORGANIZATIONAL OBJECTIVES

Understanding quality organizational objectives is so important in answering the question "What is the organization going to do for me?" and for establishing a software QA organization, we devote this section to a discussion of basic objectives.

A Net Measurable Improvement in Software Quality

Most everyone has his own concept of what "quality" is. The new quality assurance manager is likely to get "wrapped around the axle" very quickly unless he establishes and gets agreement with organizational peers and upper management as to what the quality measures are. Everyone in the existing organization has his own unique set of problems and will tend to look to the quality organization either as the solution or for the solution.

The key word in this objective is "measurable." The first thing the manager must do is evaluate carefully the development process and organization; the evaluation results in a flowchart which shows in detail the development steps, product flow, and organizational entities. With this analysis in hand, he may approach the various organizational entities and propose and discuss, perhaps compromise but at least agree on, entry and exit quality criteria for each development step and how they are to be measured.

This procedure is imperative because there are as many valid variations in software development processes as there are in programming languages, and it is essential to operate from a common base. Furthermore, the quality manager cannot wait until the product is ready for delivery to measure its quality because for software this is impossible without knowing something of its development history. The quality manager who stops product delivery on the day due without having developed a position long before will have no friends. After all, the objective is not to stop product delivery but to ensure it.

Definition of Useful Quality Measures

There have been a number of talks and papers written on quality measures or metrics, and this chapter is not intended to reiterate those topics. However, a comment on this most vital area is appropriate. Most rational managers will look for a single indicator as an index of performance. Those who own a stock portfolio, for instance, may look to the Dow Jones averages every day for an indication of the performance of his holdings — that is, if the Dow Jones industrials happen to be indicative of the portfolio. If you own a single stock, you most likely will track the price of the stock or its dividend record depending upon your investment objective. Our nature and need in the software quality stock market is quite the same: To establish a single measure (or as few as possible) that is clearly indicative not only of the software quality performance today but of what it will be . . . at and beyond delivery, indeed, throughout its projected useful life.

FIGURE 1. *Reliability growth in development*

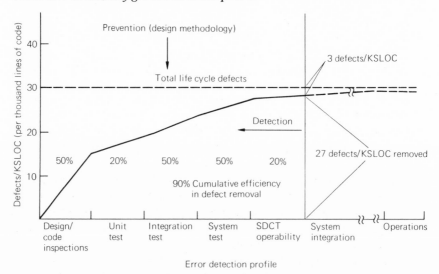

Error detection profile

A most useful quality measure to serve this need is defect detection rate. Figure 1 gives an example of how the defect detection profile can be an extremely effective quality index for management. This measure seems appropriate because finding and fixing errors represents about one half to total life cycle cost of a program [1]. In a National Security Industrial Association, Quality/Reliability Assurance Committee (NSIA, QRAC) meeting in 1977, it was reported that the Department of Defense spends about three billion dollars a year on the procurement of specialized software [2]. This figure did not include general-purpose data processing software and may have been a conservative estimate. If one-half of this cost is error related, then it is proposed that the DOD has a 1.5 billion dollar a year software quality problem.

The point is that software error prevention technology is not perfect. There is an inherent error rate associated with every development process. This inherent error rate is a function of many things in the programming environment. Most notable of these are the size and complexity of today's systems and the human inability to deal with the increasingly abstract structures [3]. There is much being done today to understand and deal with these error-producing mechanisms. But, we cannot wait until we can write perfect code before we deliver high-quality software. It can be dealt with immediately by establishing the current defect density (errors per thousand lines of code generated) for a given program, program type, or development process. Then aggressively apply detection steps until the latent error density/severity is at an acceptable level.

Definition of Acceptable Quality Levels

Acceptable quality levels (AQL) is a concept used quite often in managing production of hardware systems. When an item is produced in sufficient quantity, a sampling technique can be used to ascertain the percent defect rate of the item. The AQL then is a number which will support the production goals and cost target of the part or the higher assembly into which the part is assembled. For example, if a production goal for an assembly is 100 per month and a part for that assembly is purchased or made at a rate of 100 per month, the AQL required is obviously 100 percent, unless the defective parts can be reworked at a 100 percent rate within the production schedule. The cost of the part and hence the assembly will be achieved only if the percent defects have been anticipated correctly and the rework costs planned in. AQL is obviously a very important management tool in the production of hardware systems.

A similar concept can and should be established for software systems. Proposal managers price software based on two prime factors: size and programmer productivity. Both program size and programmer productivity are derived with considerable Kentucky windage. The proposal manager will attempt to bid the lowest productivity rate he thinks will win and browbeat the programming manager to reduce the size estimate until he has a cost target which fits his proposal goal. The quality organization, then, has a golden opportunity to assist the program manager in removing some of the Kentucky windage in the estimates by collecting data and establishing the actual error rate of each development step of current programs (and past programs where data is available). This data can then be used to more accurately determine real "net" productivity from which cost and schedule can be developed. After the proposal is won, the quality organization can then track the development against the derived AQL for each step and provide additional insight to management much earlier and with more accuracy as to probability of success.

Interpretation/Implementation of Contractual Quality Assurance Requirements

In the not too distant past, there were no quality assurance requirements placed on the software in a contract. Occasionally, one could find some maverick Defense Contract Administration Service

(DCAS) organization trying to impose MIL-Q-9858A on the software organization. But that was generally ineffective because neither DCAS nor industry really believed MIL-Q-9858A was a viable specification for the software product. Indeed, the existing organizations did not know how to apply the specification to the product. Attempts to blindly apply a specification written twenty years ago to today's software systems are, in fact, counterproductive.

There has been a flurry of activity in the past couple of years on the part of Government and industry to correct this situation. We have seen attempts to rewrite MIL-Q-9858A. We have seen proposed several new specifications, MIL-S-52779 and MIL-STD-1679, to cite a few. The Government has funded many studies which advocated sweeping reforms in the software acquisition process [4]. The company or organization that ignores these trends and fails to recognize the problem will find itself going the way of the buggy whip manufacturer.

Under these conditions, quality assurance for software cannot be a part-time assignment or a one-shot deal. Things are changing too fast. Dedicated and professional attention is required to keep up. Keep up, indeed — the idea is to get ahead. The quality organization then must grow some software professionals, or the software organization must grow some quality professionals — and quickly!

A Quality Assurance Discipline that Survives the Development Organization

Quite often, a project organization is formed to address new programming requirements. Hence, when that particular effort is complete, the resources are disbanded and applied to other existing or ongoing projects. Many companies today are going away from the project organizations to a functional organization or to a project/functional matrix. Certainly, this seems most applicable where in a given business area, division operating unit or company, there are several "projects" ongoing, phasing in and out at different times and requiring the same generic skills. The savings in management overhead, redundancy in procedures, tools, and so forth are quite apparent by putting all the necessary resources in a functional organization which then interfaces with as many project managers as there are projects. Figure 2 shows how software quality assurance might fit into such a scheme.

There are advantages, of course, to having QA resources reporting directly to the project manager or to the software development manager. However, where business reputation and potential for new business depends on quality performance, product quality usually becomes a higher level business objective and hence more closely monitored by

FIGURE 2. *Software quality in the project/function matrix*

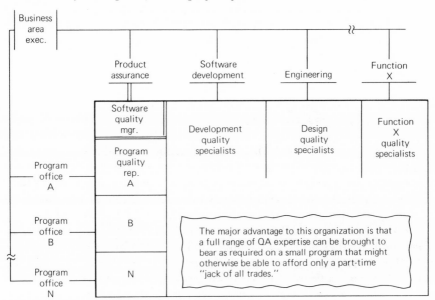

the business executive responsible for the overall project functional matrix. The reporting relationship of the quality manager surely has significant effect on his ability to be objective and independent.

A functional QA organization also is more apt to address the long-term business needs because the mission extends beyond the current programs. In this regard, the software QA manager is well advised to develop a new business arm and maintain close ties with the marketing area. It is often advisable to provide a member to the proposal teams such that quality requirements and statement of work language can be tailored to the best needs of the customer and the program.

Provide Management an Independent Assessment of Software Product Quality

In spite of the new disciplines, procedures, tools, and techniques, the software product, up until its final functional performance demonstration, remains somewhat an intangible or abstract item. Executives who can get a warm feeling by going to the manufacturing floor or engineering lab and viewing the hardware have no similar opportunity for attaining such firsthand insight for the software. This problem sometimes slips down into the ranks of the software development management itself. An independent organization chartered to operate in a fashion to provide that missing insight is an invaluable aid to the whole management team in terms of assessing progress, problems, and risks. When it comes to software visibility, people have only one eye and hence no depth perception. The quality manager working with the development manager can provide a much better picture with two eyes between them.

Provide a Net Reduction on the Indirect Work Load of the Development Organization

One of the most important tasks facing the quality-oriented development organization is keeping track of its problems. Left to the programmers, problem tracking will be done in a spurious fashion. The individual programmers may feel quite capable of keeping track of their own problems, and management-imposed problem reporting/ tracking systems are a burden which does not contribute to their success and, furthermore, may even be an invasion of privacy.

The QA organization can be a positive factor in solving this problem. Setting up simple but accurate procedures, the QA organization can remove a great deal of the burden from the individual programmer. The tracking system operated by the QA organization can tell both management and programmer needed information during the development process as well as forming the data base required for prediction and future improvements to the programming process. The quality data system is just one example of a management tool that can be turned from a burden to a boast. Every quality procedure, indeed every management procedure, should be evaluated in the same fashion. The idea is to free the programmers from as many of the non-direct programming tasks as possible.

ORGANIZATIONAL ATTRIBUTES

One way to understand an organization is through its purpose or its stated objectives. But, to be very clear, the charter must also describe the organization's style, its attitude and approach to the stated objectives. These attributes are what gives the organization its personality. Indeed, before any objectives are achieved, the organization will be judged in terms of its visible attributes.

There are at least three attributes which endow the infant software quality organization with the ability to survive the early growth period and mature into a viable, contributing part of the overall organization.

These are vital signs through which management can and will monitor the health of the organization and gain confidence in its ability to achieve. The software quality organization must fit the business organization, have technical credibility, and be cost justified.

Fit the Business Organization

Even at the risk of sounding trite, this is perhaps the most important attribute the quality organization can have. We have touted "independence" or the ability to provide an independent assessment of quality as a key factor. However, to function most effectively, the business organization must operate as a whole with clearly defined interfaces and responsibilities. The quality organization is therefore a part of the overall organization and must develop its interfaces with every other functional entity in a manner which ensures that all elements are covered and redundancies are minimized.

The lifeblood of the quality organization is data. The source of this data is the interface with the other functional areas and the development process. One way to approach this is to develop a diagram similar to the one shown in Figure 3. This diagram should contain every functional area involved in the program or project with the program manager at the center of the universe and showing clearly and briefly the mission of each satellite organization. This chart will allow the quality manager to evaluate, from a quality assurance point of view, whether all necessary development steps or activities are covered in the overall organization.

Next, it is necessary to develop a life cycle diagram for the software product or products showing clearly the functional responsibilities throughout the cycle. Again, the software quality assurance (SQA) manager should evaluate this from a quality point of view. It is important that this diagram be reviewed as accurate by each organization to prevent an analysis of what *is thought* to be the plan rather than what *is* the plan. The evaluation by the SQA manager should emphasize the phasing of the various functions. No program manager worth his salt will carry resources on his program until they are absolutely required and then no longer. Therefore, the program manager will be pushing to minimize cost by tight phasing in and out of functional resources, and it is up to the SQA manager to blow the whistle when, for example, the software control function or subfunction comes in too late in the program to achieve quality objectives.

Thirdly, it is recommended that the universe be reconstructed with software quality assurance at the center (Figure 4). Each interface can then be characterized as two-way communications channels between

FIGURE 3. *Software program management functional interfaces*

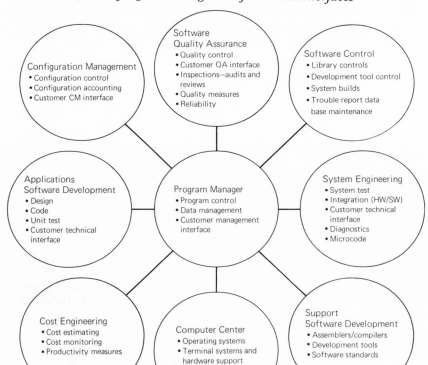

quality assurance and every other functional element. Success of the QA organization will depend greatly upon the interfaces being two-way channels. Feedback, discussion of and healthy contention over analysis of quality data, is expected by the affected areas. Without this feedback process, corrective actions will not, indeed cannot, be taken by the development groups. This feedback should be designed to address every level of the organization and be timely to the need. For example, the programmer whose code has just undergone initial inspection should leave the session with his defect list in hand. The programmer's manager should receive weekly summaries of all inspections conducted in his area together with a quality analysis of significant trends developing which may require management attention. Higher levels of management should expect and receive reports tailored to their level of concern at regular intervals—monthly, quarterly, or at predefined points in the software life cycle as appropriate.

FIGURE 4. *Project software quality assurance functional interfaces (This figure depicts an example of typical QA/interface data exchange from a NASA Space Shuttle program.)*

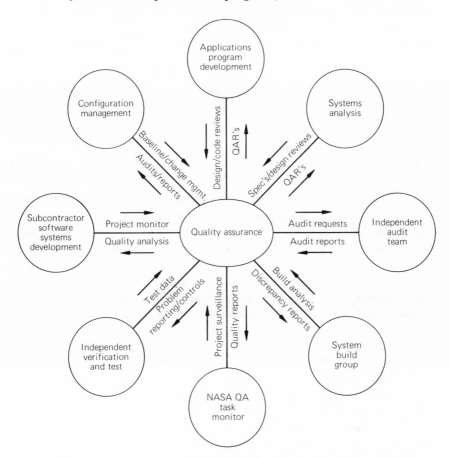

The customer or user of the software is an important interface for the SQA organization. As much care and planning should go into developing that interface as is given to the internal organization. If the customer happens to be the U.S. Government, there may well be contract data requirements imposed which the quality organization is obliged to provide. It is suggested, however, that a lot of credibility can be bought from the enlightened customer by going beyond the contract requirements and sharing openly and honestly the quality data during the development cycle. The rational manager will of course carefully coordinate all customer communications with the program manager. There are several good reasons for this: to safeguard proprietary information, inadvertent changes in contract scope, and assurance of internal coordination on issues, just to cite a few.

The quality manager should pay particular attention to how problems are handled across the various interfaces. Many times problems are discovered as a result of a quality audit, inspection, or analysis of data to show a trend. It should be obvious that a problem is best brought first to the lowest level necessary to get resolution. The rule might be stated: Take a problem (and preferably a solution) to the lowest level you can but to the highest level you must. In order to do this, the organization must have technical credibility to establish and back a position, which is the second organizational attribute for discussion.

Have Technical Credibility

It's been said that QA lives on data. However, there is a significant amount of technical judgment and expertise required to collect the right data and perform a meaningful analysis. Nothing is more ineffective or inconsistent with organizational objectives than a group of bean counters perfunctorily pumping out reams of inconsequential data. The truly effective software QA engineer has the respect of his peers and all levels of management with whom he must interface. This respect is born out of technical competence on the part of the individual. The organization, to have technical credibility, must be staffed with technically competent personnel. The problem is that there is not a readily available pool of the right talent to draw upon. The ideal individual is one having both a quality and a programming background, but they are scarce. The QA manager, then, is faced with two problems: bringing programmers into the quality organization and teaching quality engineers the programming process. Both actions present a challenge to the QA manager.

Programmers must be convinced that an assignment in a quality organization is a viable way to maintain and grow in competence as a programming professional. They must be convinced that bringing discipline to the programming process is essential to meeting the growing demands placed on today's business environments. They must be shown that their experience and innovative ability is essential to the realization of the discipline. It cannot happen through decree alone. This would surely result in a perfunctory organization having no impact on the development process and no assurance that delivered products are quality products.

Traditional quality engineers (QEs), on the other hand, are apt to spend too much time drawing inappropriate hardware analogies (in-

FIGURE 5. *SQA roles*

Positive	Negative
Advocate	Adversary
Partnership	Confrontation
Collaborator	Wrecker
Contributor	Parasite
Inspector, Reviewer	Rubber stamper
Counselor	Informer
Standard enforcer	Nit-picker
Objective auditor	Whimsical critic
Watchdog	Scarecrow
Data collector	Spy
Data analyst	Fortune teller

ertia). They must be convinced to resist the temptation to oversimplify the programming process and to make it fit current hardware quality techniques. QEs can be taught programming concepts and methods, but they lack the essential ingredient of experience required to have an impact on the programming process. The immediate necessity for implementing the software quality discipline does not allow the time required to approach the problem solely through the retraining of quality engineers.

There are other personal characteristics which are required of the key personnel (those who have prime responsibility for a program). They must have good communication skills and be of strong logical persuasion. The success of the organization will depend on the individual's ability to sell his ideas for improvement. If the SQA organization is to be a positive organization, the QA programmer must be a positive individual. Figure 5 contains a list of the positive versus negative roles the QA programmer/engineer should use to approach the job.

Having technical credibility is one way to ensure that the QA organization is a cost-effective organization, which is the third attribute the software QA organization must be concerned with.

Be Cost Justified

The charter of a software quality organization to manage, monitor, and control the implementation of a software quality program will add apparent cost to the development cycle. At least the initial implementation will add apparent cost. This "added cost" is a source of concern to everyone associated with the program, particularly the program manager and the customer. The term "apparent cost" is used

95

because just as an improper reading of true power is obtained if the voltage and current are out of phase, an improper reading of true cost is obtained if application of resource and benefit are out of phase. The true benefit of the quality program/quality organization is not realized until after the development cycle is complete and the operational phase begins. It was mentioned earlier that as much as half the life cycle cost of software systems is related to finding and fixing errors or defects. A great deal of this expense has been incurred after delivery. Therefore, if the quality organization achieves its stated objective of reducing defects, the potential for saving money on a life cycle basis greatly outweighs the potential "added cost" of the quality program during development. This intuitive argument will not be belabored since there are many good references on the subject which deal with the topic in quantitative and exhaustive fashion.*

A more pressing concern to the software quality manager is how cost efficient are the QA operations during the development cycle. The QA organization, just as all elements of the development process, will and should be subject to detailed and continuing scrutiny regarding the cost of doing business. There are several valid ways to measure the cost of quality assurance for software. Care should be taken not to pick too gross a measure. An example of a gross measure is as follows:

$$\frac{\text{Cost of defect detection and rework}}{\text{Program size (K lines of code)}} = \text{Dollars per K lines of code}$$

This measure is useful to management for preparing proposals and evaluating in a relative fashion the efficiency of one program against another. It is of limited use in the day-to-day evaluation of QA performance. It is more meaningful to the QA manager to break down the software QA program costs into its basic elements and then track QA cost versus development cost. Table 1 will aid in that process.

Error prevention technology in terms of improved programming techniques is the other large investment area. Although these efforts have tremendous potential impact on the ultimate quality levels of the program products, the costs, in general, go far beyond the quality organization. (A discussion of this interesting area is in chapter 13.)

The question on everyone's mind is, of course: If you must gather more data before you can tell what the true or real cost of quality assurance is, can you tell me now what the apparent costs are to implement a software quality program? The answer is a qualified yes. A qualified yes to the extent that some generalizations are required

*Particularly recommended is reference 1.

TABLE 1. Sample SQA Cost Elements

	Accomplish	Participate	Monitor	Audit	% of SQA Budget
1. Quality Planning and Organization	X				8.9
Quality plans	X				0.7
QA tools, procedures	X				5.4
QA training	X				0.3
QA cost proposal and tracking	X				2.5
2. Standards, Design and Implementation Reviews		X	X		3.5
3. Software Configuration Assurance				X	12.4
Library controls	X		X		3.2
System build inspections					6.1
Change control board		X			3.1
4. Documentation Inspection	X				4.5
5. Test Verification and Controls					14.7
Test readiness reviews	X	X			2.4
Test-bed validation					0.7
Test execution			X		10.1
Test data and records				X	1.5
6. Nonconformance Control (Process/Product)	X		X		10.1
Corrective action					5.1
Data base maintenance	X				2.7
Reporting	X				2.3
7. Quality Records Control	X				3.1
8. Subcontract QA			X	X	3.5
9. Quality Data Analysis	X				3.3
10. Administrative Activity	X				2.2
11. Meetings and Coordination		X			16.6
12. Presentations and Writing	X				12.0
13. Other (reading, proposals, misc.)	X				5.2
					100.0

Note: These are actual data taken from an SQA organization of approximately 14 people over a 2-year period.

FIGURE 6. *Approximate range of SQA cost (Based on a functional QA approach with activities as described in Table 1)*

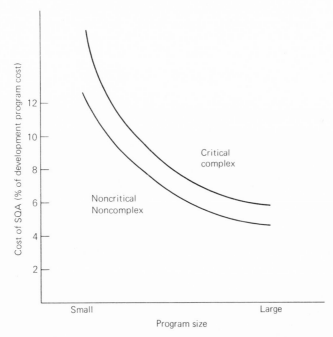

without knowing some specific information about the development process and program to which it will apply. The cost can be broken down into two basic elements: (1) nonrecurring or start-up costs and (2) recurring costs.

Nonrecurring costs include generation of initial program plan, development of tools, procedures, and training unique to the program. Recurring costs may be considered to include all other activities covered in the QA plan such as reviews, inspections, and audits for each program product unit and every development process step; operation of quality data system, analysis procedures, generation of reports, and participation in meetings.

Figure 6 is a chart showing a range of reasonable costs for an SQA program in terms of a percentage of the program development cost (excluding QA).

Funding the quality organization can be done in either of two basic ways: (1) directly funding as part of the software product cost or (2) indirect or overhead funding as part of the expense of doing business. Experience shows that the quality organization can budget tasks directly in an efficient manner, thereby keeping the overhead cost at a minimum. Indirect funding tends to cause a level-of-effort mentality and is therefore not desirable, especially since things are changing rapidly. The concepts, tools, and techniques for both software development and software quality are rising to new states. The SQA manager and the whole organization must be forward looking and flexible in order to best serve the organizational objectives.

SUMMARY

A great deal of emphasis is currently being placed on development of software quality management as a separate, distinct, and required discipline within the software management sphere. As the efforts of the individuals who are working to fill this gap come to fruition, new, more effective tools, techniques, and methodologies will develop. It is imperative that software quality management organize to anticipate, stay in sync with, and, in fact, act as a catalyst to the changing development process.

As programming requirements continue to force order of magnitude changes in program size and complexity, quality management will be expected to respond with equal reductions in error rates. The QA manager is well advised to plan for allocating a significant portion of his resources to meeting the continuing challenge of change.

References

1. Alberts, David S. "The Economics of Software Quality Assurance," *MTR-5257*, MITRE Corporation, December 1975.
2. DeRoze, Barry C. "Software Management within the Department of Defense," *Proceedings of the NSIA Conference on Software Quality and Reliability*, March 30, 1977.
3. Knight, B. M. "On Software Quality and Productivity," *Technical Directions*, vol. 4, no. 2, IBM, FSD, July 1978.
4. TMC Project 115-9, "DOD Weapon Systems Software Management Study," (MSCB 75.4), *AIA, TMC 75-32*, June 2, 1975.

CHAPTER 7

Department of Defense Software Quality Requirements

DENNIS L. WOOD

INTRODUCTION

The program manager for the acquisition of a U.S. Department of Defense (DOD) system is responsible for the quality of the system. The quality of the system is the composite of all its attributes or characteristics, including performance. Computer resources, in particular computer programs, or software, are usually major elements of defense systems. Thus, the quality of the defense system, especially its performance, is highly dependent on the quality of the software element. The consequence of this dependency is that the program manager must give special attention to software quality, in order to fulfill his responsibility for the overall quality of the defense system as an integrated system of hardware, software, personnel, facilities, and data. The essence of software quality requirements, management, and acceptance is summarized as: (1) contractual specification of both computer program requirements and requirements for a quality program for managing software quality; (2) Government and contractor monitoring and assessment of implementation of the contractor's quality program, including its effectiveness; and (3) Government acceptance of the software upon demonstration of contractor compliance with contract quality requirements, particularly for computer program performance.

The management of software quality for a system acquisition or modification effort is the responsibility of various organizational elements and levels within the military/contractor complex. It can be viewed as that which is necessary to assure that contract requirements regarding software are met.

There is another type of system involved in the acquisition process, different from the defense system itself, which can be referred to as a defense acquisition management system. This is the system of interrelated and mandatory DOD and DOD component (e.g., Army, Navy, Air Force) directives, regulations, and instructions which establish policy and procedures for managing defense system acquisitions. This system governs and assists the program manager and interfacing Government organizations in managing the acquisition of the defense system itself. Figure 1 identifies key quality management-related publications selected from the defense acquisition management system, and shows their interrelationships.

A few of the key elements of this management system, at the DOD level, are the Defense Acquisition Regulation (formerly the Armed Services Procurement Regulation) and DOD Directives 5000.1, 5000.2, 5000.3, 5000.29, 5010.19, and 4155.1.

The policies and procedures in these particular publications address contracting; major system acquisition; the major system acquisition process; test and evaluation; computer resources; configuration management; and quality. These and other directives regulations, instructions, and standards address a range of acquisition management disciplines. Some address software exclusively (e.g.,

FIGURE 1. *DOD software quality requirements framework*

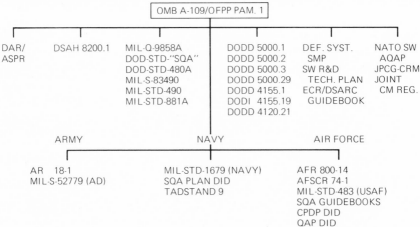

DODD 5000.29); some explicitly acknowledge software as also being within their scope, to an extent, by using the word "software" (e.g., DODDs 5000.1 and 5000.2); and others provide additional explanation for software (e.g., DODD 5000.3). Many are generally applicable to sytems and hardware or software items, but some of these contain sections which have no formally defined counterpart for software (e.g., 6.1, "Materials and Materials Control" in MIL-Q-9858A), and yet do not state applicability or nonapplicability of the questionable sections.

DODD 4155.1 is devoted exclusively to quality assurance. Various aspects of quality assurance are either addressed or underlying in some of the acquisition management system publications. With the issue of the in-progress DOD-STD for software quality assurance, there will be a DOD-level standard dealing exclusively with software quality.

Acquisition Management System and Software Quality

Within the framework of the overall acquisition management system, selected elements of the current and evolving software quality at the DOD/NATO level are:

The in-process NATO software quality assurance publication

The forthcoming DOD standard for software quality assurance

The Navy's draft data item description for a software quality assurance plan, which will be available for use by all DOD components.

The Defense Logistics Agency handbook section for software procurement quality assurance

Complementing this approach to improve software quality management, and thus improve software quality itself, is the software technology base. This is an element of the Defense System Software FY 79-83 Research and Development Technology Plan.

The objectives of this chapter are to:

1. Identify for the reader the principal DOD publications which deal directly and indirectly with quality for systems and software.
2. Identify current DOD efforts to improve software quality management.
3. Provide a perspective for managing software acquisition and quality within the broader context of managing defense system acquisition and quality.
4. Establish a basis from which the reader can track on-going efforts related to DOD software quality management.

MAJOR SYSTEM ACQUISITION

The two most important federal documents that impact acquisition of quality systems and quality software are the OMB Circular A-109 and the OFPP Pamphlet No. 1.

Office of Management and Budget Circular A-109

OMB Circular A-109, "Major System Acquisitions," 5 April 1976, establishes policy for executive branch agencies of the U.S. Government for acquiring major systems (see Figure 1). Some of the stated management objectives of A-109 which are related to quality management are that an agency acquiring a major system should:

Ensure that the system demonstrates a level of performance and reliability that justifies the national resources necessary for its acquisition and ownership.

Ensure adequate system test and evaluation, and conduct test and evaluation independent, where practicable, of developer and user.

Typically include demonstration, test, and evaluation criteria, as well as warranties, in the acquisition strategy.

Quality management comes through clearly in A-109's policy. The circular requires that program managers monitor tests and contractor progress in fulfilling system performance, cost, and schedule commitments, and that significant variances receive attention for corrective action. Software is recognized explicitly in A-109 as an element of major systems. Quality assurance is a fundamental concept on which A-109 relies, as evidenced in specific management objectives of the circular.

Office of Federal Procurement Policy Pamphlet No. 1

OFPP Pamphlet No. 1, "Major System Acquisitions, A Discussion of the Application of OMB Circular No. A-109," August 1976, interprets and expands on A-109 policy. Like A-109, the pamphlet also explicitly recognizes software as typically an element of a major system. It goes beyond A-109 by singling out automated data processing (ADP) systems as examples of major systems for which an agency might establish a different criterion or threshold for classifying the system as major. Quality management aspects are implicit in the policy regarding Government laboratories maintaining technology bases for agencies. Government laboratory support may involve evaluation of contractor technical progress throughout the sequential steps of the system acquisition process, as well as involve independent test of alternative candidate systems.

A-109 and OFPP Pamphlet No. 1 do not explicitly identify quality management policy, as such, for major system acquisitions. However, they do contain certain policy statements which imply quality management as one of the acquisition management disciplines necessary to implement policy.

DEFENSE SYSTEM ACQUISITION AND QUALITY ASSURANCE POLICY

This section discusses a few of the more significant DOD directives and related publications which address, directly or indirectly, quality of software (see Figure 1).

Defense Acquisition Regulation for Contracting

The Defense Acquisition Regulation (DAR), formerly referred to as the Armed Services Procurement Regulation (ASPR), contains quality assurance policy and procedures for specifying, assuring, determining, and accepting that contracted supplies and services comply with contract requirements for quality.

A proposed addition to DAR Section IV, Part eleven, dealing with ADPE, was transmitted to various industry associations for comments on 26 May 1978. It includes policy and procedures regarding computer software, but was not available in time to be reviewed for impact, specifically on software quality management. In the meantime, the 1976 issue of ASPR will continue to be in effect until replaced by the first Defense Acquisition Regulation published under its new title, expected in 1979.

The DAR contains a quality program clause for insertion in the contract. This requires that the contractor establish and implement a quality program per a specified MIL-SPEC, e.g., MIL-Q-9858A or MIL-S-52779 (AD). The DAR states the procurement quality assurance responsibilities of the contractor and of the Government. It assigns both responsibility for, and performance of, procurement quality assurance to the contract administration office.

DODD 5000.29

DODD 5000.29, "Management of Computer Resources in Major Defense Systems," 26 April 1976, establishes DOD policy for management of computer resources over the total defense system life cycle.

This directive includes policy specific to certain aspects of software quality, i.e., software reliability and correctness, and determination of overall system quality (considering integrated computer resources as part of the total defense system). DODD 5000.29 requires that DODDs 5000.1, 5000.2, and 5000.3 be modified to assimilate policy and principles for computer resources, and that DOD components develop and implement a disciplined approach to software management, supported by guidance documents for program managers. To varying degrees, these requirements are being implemented with respect to the software quality aspect. For example, DODD 5000.3 has been revised to explicitly accommodate software. However, DODDs 5000.1 and 5000.2 only briefly mention the word software (in one and three places, respectively).

DODD 5000.3

DODD 5000.3, "Test and Evaluation," 11 April 1978, provides policy for test and evaluation of defense systems over their life cycle, and applies to software as well as hardware components. This is a recent revision and includes a section which amplifies key policy aspects as they apply specifically to software. As expected from the title, DODD 5000.3 is oriented primarily toward *demonstrating* quality, in particular the performance aspect, for the evolving and resulting system. For test and evaluation involving software, the new DODD 5000.3 requires that:

1. Quantitative and demonstrable performance objectives shall be established for each software phase.
2. The decision to proceed to the next phase shall be based on quantitative demonstration of adequate software performance, using test and evaluation.
3. Prior to release for operational use, software shall undergo operational testing under realistic conditions sufficient to provide a valid estimate of system effectiveness and suitability in the operational environment.
4. Operational test and evaluation agencies shall participate in early stages of software planning and development to insure adequate consideration of the operational environment and operational objectives.

DODD 4155.1

DODD 4155.1, "Quality Assurance," 9 February 1972, establishes Department of Defense policy for quality assurance. It requires that materiel conform to specified requirements (this would include computer program conformance to its Type B5 specification); quality audits be conducted; contractors be responsible for controlling product quality and offering for acceptance only materiel that complies with contract requirements; and DOD components assure that contracts specify, and contractors comply with, appropriate quality requirements. DODD 4155.1 is under revision, with publication anticipated for 1979. The draft circulated to industry for comment included explicit recognition of software. It also emphasized that the program manager is responsible for the system's quality, and that quality reviews are required prior to Defense System Acquisition Review Council (DSARC) meetings.

DODD 4120.21

DODD 4120.21, "Specifications and Standards Application," 9 April 1977, established DOD policy and procedures for applying and tailoring specifications and standards to achieve cost-effective acquisition and life cycle ownership of defense items. In support to the implementation of tailoring, DODD 4120.21 recommends that the training curricula of service schools be revised to include, among other subjects, quality assurance and reliability. Presumably, this training would include software quality assurance.

DODI 4155.19

DODI 4155.19, "NATO Quality Assurance," 6 June 1978, addresses Department of Defense quality assurance with respect to NATO countries. The directive was published too recently to be available for review to determine if software is included within its scope.

Defense System Software Management Plan

In 1976, the DOD Software Management Steering Committee (Management Steering Committee for Embedded Computer Resources [MSC—ECR], which was later formally established by DODD 5000.29, formulated a comprehensive management plan for DOD computer resources. The plan comprises policy, practice, procedure, and technology initiatives to provide solutions to key problems in defense system software acquisition management, coordination, and control. It was published as the "Defense System Software Management Plan," 19 March 1976. Software quality assurance and control and software quality specification are two key issues addressed by the plan. The current software quality management efforts at the DOD, Joint Logistics Commanders (JLC), and Army, Navy, and Air Force levels are all an integral part of the response to that plan.

Software Research and Development Technology Plan

Software quality assurance is one of the many issues specifically addressed by the "Defense System Software FY 79-83 Research and Development Technology Plan." This plan is an element of the Defense System Software Management Program. The Office of the Under Secretary of Defense (OUSD) for Research and Engineering is responsible for overseeing implementation of the plan within the military departments and defense agencies. The MSC-ECR, established under DODD 5000.29, is assisting OUSD in this role.

An R&D technology panel, reporting to the MSC-ECR, has been established to assist the Director of Defense Research and Engineering (DDR&E) in execution of the plan. The plan has been approved by the R&D Technology Panel on Software Technology. Technology to improve software quality and reliability, and to advance the state of the art in these two areas, is a major objective of the software R&D technology plan. The military departments, through representation on the R&D Technology Panel of the MSC-ECR, have formulated technology objectives regarding the DOD software technology base. Several of the objectives adopted by the MSC-ECR deal specifically with various aspects of software quality:

1. Development of qualitative and quantitative measures of software quality
2. Establishment of a uniform software error collection and analysis methodology
3. Development of methods and tools for testing to determine adherence to computer program requirements within stated tolerance
4. Quantification of reliability
5. Development of tools and techniques for proving computer programs and specifications are consistent

DSARC Guidebook

"Embedded Computer Resources and the DSARC Process—A Guidebook," 1977, contains various questions of the types which might be asked prior to Defense System Acquisition Review Council (DSARC) meetings, i.e., DSARC I, II and III.

One of the DSARC II questions addresses a key aspect of software quality assurance, i.e., "How will the overall system quality be determined?" The preferred response, of three typically offered, is that, "The system will be measured against the original operational requirements in field tests." Several types of questions which might be asked at DSARC II in the areas of testing, reliability, and maintainability are given, with a range of responses. Among the DSARC III questions, a significant percentage are devoted to topics such as integration and testing results, discrepancy profiles, change activity due to errors, and accuracy of coding to listings.

In searching for quality assurance-related questions throughout the guidebook, it is noticed that there is no question similar to, "Is a software quality assurance plan required of the contractor?"

TRI-SERVICE AND NATO SOFTWARE QUALITY MANAGEMENT

In addition to the various federal and DOD level documents influencing software quality, there are numerous activities sponsored by the services that are intended to directly promote quality for software.

Joint Policy Coordinating Group

The "Charter for the Joint DARCOM/NMC/AFLC/AFSC Commander's Joint Policy Coordinating Group on Computer Resource Management," 6 December 1977, establishes the basis for coordinating policy, procedures, guidelines, and standards related to defense system computer resource management, for the Joint Logistics Commanders (JLC). It is anticipated that various subgroups will be established within the JPCG-CRM to deal with specific subject areas, for example, software quality assurance. A software subgroup, initially established under the *Joint Technical Coordinating Group—Reliability, Availability, Maintainability* (JTCG-RAM), is now under the JPCG-CRM.

There are various new and under-revision DOD directives, instructions, and standards which bear on computer resource management, such as the forthcoming DOD-STD for software quality assurance, and the in-process revision of DODD 5010.19 for configuration management. The JPCG-CRM can be expected to be centrally involved in assuring the consistency of software quality-related aspects with these requirements.

NATO Software Quality Assurance

An effort is under way to help NATO (North Atlantic Treaty Organization) develop an Allied Quality Assurance Publication (AQAP) specifically for software. To accomplish this, a working group for software quality assurance has been established under the auspices of the NATO Advisory Committee (AC)/250 Group. The U.S. has been designated to chair the working group, and the Army has the primary responsibility for developing the publication. Publication is estimated to be near the end of 1979. Current effort includes collecting copies of quality assurance documents from all of the NATO countries.

Reliability Standardization Program Plan

Software reliability is addressed by the DOD "Reliability Standardization Document Program Plan," 10 March 1977. The plan was developed and coordinated through the Defense Materiel Specification and Standards Office (DMSSO)/Joint Logistics Commanders (JLC) Documentation Task Group.

The plan includes a task to formalize and approve a standard set of software definitions which will support development and monitoring of software reliability programs. A revision to MIL-STD-721, "Definitions of Effectiveness Terms for Reliability, Maintainability, Human Factors and Safety," is expected to be published in 1979 and to include definitions relating to software.

Joint DOD Configuration Management

The "Joint DOD Services/Agency Regulation Configuration Management," 1 July 1974, requires that compliance with specifications and other contract requirements be verified by means of functional and physical configuration audits (FCAs and PCAs). Such verification of compliance with contract requirements is an element of the Government procurement quality assurance function, and is a prerequisite to granting acceptance. The regulation specifically encompasses computer programs.

DOD STANDARDS OF QUALITY REQUIREMENTS AND MANAGEMENT

The following publications are DOD standards to be used specifically in contracts for the acquisition of quality software (see Figure 1).

MIL-S-83490/MIL-STD-490

MIL-S-83490, "Specifications, Types and Forms," 30 October 1968, is mandatory for use by DOD components. It requires that a Type B development specification for an item (for example, the Type B5 computer program development specification) specify all functional characteristics required of the item, as well as specify all tests required to demonstrate achievement of those characteristics. These two factors, specified functional characteristics and tests to demonstrate them, are the essence of the computer program quality requirements issue.

MIL-STD-490, "Specification Practices," 30 October 1968, contains a standard for preparing Type B5 computer program development specifications. There are various data item descriptions (DIDs) which contain similar standards for preparing a Type B5 specification. When a properly prepared Type B5 computer program development specification is cited in the development contract, it becomes a legally binding document, requiring the contractor to develop and deliver a computer program which performs according to the requirements in the B5 specification. The objective of the contractor's software quality assurance function is to assure that this happens. The objective of the Government's procurement quality assurance function is to verify that it actually happened, before granting acceptance to the contractor as having complied with this requirement of the contract. The function of the Government quality assurance representative is to monitor and evaluate, on-going as necessary, to assure that computer program development is proceeding according to the contractor's software management plans, primarily with his software quality assurance plan.

MIL-Q-9858A

MIL-Q-9858A, "Quality Program Requirements," 16 December 1963, does not use the term "computer program" or "software." However, its stated applicability for "all supplies (including equipments, sub-systems and systems) or services . . . " implies that computer programs be included (as supplies) within the contractor's quality program. For much of MIL-Q-9858A, the requirements can be easily understood when interpreted for either computer program or hardware items. For example, "the authority and responsibility of those in charge of the design, production, testing, and inspection of quality shall be clearly stated."

Other parts of the specification contain requirements for hardware-oriented areas for which DOD has not yet provided equivalent interpretation for computer programs or software — for example, fabrication, manufacturing, machining, and production tooling. Yet, the specification does not say these areas do not apply to software. Thus the Government and contractor users of not only MIL-Q-9858A, but of similar documents with terms not defined for software, are faced with a dilemma, due to the absence of guidance as to how these terms apply, or that they do not apply.

DOD Software Quality Assurance Standard

The Army has been asked by the Staff Director of Quality Assurance in the Office of Under Secretary of Defense (Research and Engineering) to develop and coordinate a DOD document specifically for software quality assurance. The document is planned to be published as a DOD-STD in 1979. MIL-S-52779 (AD), "Software Quality Assurance Program Requirements," issued by the Army in 1974, is being used as a basic starting point. There have been numerous reviews of MIL-S-52779 (AD) by various Government organizations and industry associations. The comments generated by these reviews can be expected to serve as constructive inputs toward development of the DOD software quality assurance standard.

DOD-STD-480A

The recently issued DOD-STD-480A, "Configuration Control— Engineering Changes, Deviations and Waivers," 12 April 1978, incorporates specific instructions for preparing software engineering change proposals (ECPS). Some of these instructions are related to quality assurance. Page 2 of the ECP Form (DD Form 1692-1) calls for identifying the requirements for repetition of testing and live environment testing due to proposed changes in a computer program development specification. DOD-STD-480A also states that engineering changes should be evaluated by testing, and that the results of testing completed at the time the ECP is prepared should be included, since they may be a factor in the approval decision.

MIL-STD-881A

MIL-STD-881A, "Work Breakdown Structures for Defense Materiel Items," 25 April 1975, governs preparation and use of work breakdown structures (WBSs), and is mandatory for use by both DOD components and contractors. Computer programs are identified as a separate element at Level 3 within the WBS for electronics systems. The quality assurance program is included within the system engineering element (Level 3), which is within the system program management

112

element (Level 2). Development test and evaluation (DT&E) and operational test and evaluation (OT&E) are each included separately in the WBS at Level 3, under systems test and evaluation, which is at Level 2. Test and evaluation involving software would be included within these WBS elements.

CONTRACTUAL FACTORS

Representative contractual implementation of DOD software quality requirements can be highlighted as follows:

1. An ASPR clause is cited which requires that the contractor establish and implement a quality program.
2. A task statement requiring the preparation of a quality assurance plan is incorporated in the statement of work (SOW).
3. The particular data item description (DID) governing format and content in preparing the QA plan is cited on the contract data requirements list (CDRL).
4. The delivery of all software-related data items required by the Government is called for in the CDRL. DIDs for their preparation also are cited in the CDRL.
5. The requirement for a work breakdown structure (WBS), per MIL-STD-881A, is incorporated in the contract.
6. Development, test, evaluation, and documentation of each computer program configuration item (CPCI) are reflected in the WBS, as is the associated software quality assurance effort.
7. If the contract is for the demonstration and validation phase, a task to prepare a Type B5 computer program development specification for each identified CPCI is incorporated in the SOW.
8. A task to develop, test, and integrate a computer program which will meet the requirements of a cited Type B5 computer program development specification, is incorporated in the full-scale engineering development (FSED) phase SOW.
9. A task to prepare a Type C5 computer program product specification for each computer program configuration item (CPCI) is incorporated in the FSED phase SOW.
10. The delivery of the CPCIs is called for in the contract.
11. Functional and physical configuration audits of the CPCI are called for in the contract.

These and related factors in the contract provide the contractual basis for Government and contractor management of software quality.

Computer Program Acceptance

The DD Form 250, "Materiel Inspection and Receiving Report," is used for granting acceptance of specifications and configuration items. Block 21, Procurement Quality Assurance, is used by the Government representative authorized to grant acceptance to indicate that the Government procurement quality assurance (PQA) function has been accomplished and that the item conforms to contract requirements. For software, this means that once PQA has been successfully completed, and the DD 250s for each of the computer programs and computer program product specifications have been signed, with no contingencies noted for deficiencies, the contractor has been given legal evidence of having complied with these requirements of his contract. Recourse by the Government due to latent defects (e.g., coding or design errors) surfacing later are resolved via warranties, assuming warranties were in the contract.

Monitoring Contractor Quality

Defense Supply Agency Handbook 8200.1, "Defense In-Plant Quality Assurance Program," August 1976, is a compendium of selected publications frequently used by Government quality assurance personnel. DSAH 8200.1 contains one section specific to software, i.e., "Procurement Quality Assurance for Computer Software." It represents Defense Supply Agency, Army, Navy and Air Force guidance to the Government Quality Assurance Representative (QAR) for procurement quality assurance (PGA) actions for software.

The Government QAR's PQA actions for computer software (CS), "in addition to witnessing and monitoring tests, will usually be limited to the reviewing, monitoring and evaluation of the contractor's CS planning documents, management practices, and related procedures for control of the CS development effort. By assuring conformance with the plans, that documented procedures exist and are being adhered to, and by assuring quality management over contractors' CS development effort, the quality of the CS product is influenced. Testing is an equally important part of the CS development effort although it does not directly influence the as-built quality of the CS product. Testing identifies the design and coding errors that would degrade quality if permitted to go undetected without corrections."

ARMY SOFTWARE QUALITY

The Department of the Army's software policies have not completely solidified. The documents discussed below represent the current status of the Army's software quality management efforts.

AR 18-1/AR 70-XX

The Department of Army Automation is revising Army Regulation AR 18-1, "Army Information Management," to provide policy for the management of automation of Army defense systems, management information systems, and scientific and engineering systems.

Procedures and guidelines for implementing the new policy will be provided in the in-process "18-100 series" of Army Technical Bulletins (TBs). In this series, TB 18-123 is addressed to quality assurance, and will reflect software quality assurance as an element of total system quality assurance. Software quality will be managed not only during the development phase, but during the post-development phase as well. TB 18-123 probably will be issued during 1979. It is anticipated that the work on AR 70-XX, "Management of Computer Resources in Army Defense Systems," will be terminated and its basic principles reflected in the integrated effort to revise AR 18-1 and develop the TB 18-100 series.

DARCOM Circular 702-4

The U.S. Army Materiel Development and Readiness Command (DARCOM) recently issued a circular, DARCOM-C 702-4, "Army Defense Systems Software Control During the Production and Deployment Phase," 28 March 1978, which bears directly on Army-wide software quality requirements. The circular is one of the few Government publications devoted exclusively to software management for the production and deployment phase. The circular is significant in three aspects, in terms of the software quality management issue:

1. It requires that the software support facility maintain a software malfunction reporting system for assessing software performance and determining necessary modifications.
2. It requires that all software changes be subjected to three types of test, as appropriate—certification, verification, and acceptance.
3. Appendix B, "Outline for Computer Resource Management Plan (CRMP)," identifies specific software quality management requirements to be addressed in the CRMP.

MIL-S-52779

MIL-S-52779(AD), "Software Quality Assurance Program Requirements," 4 April 1977, was prepared as an Army MIL-SPEC, but it has been cited to advantage in numerous Army, Navy, and Air Force

contracts. It is approved, but not mandatory, for use by all departments and agencies of the Department of Defense. The specification is
the equivalent of MIL-Q-9858A, in that it requires that the contractor
develop and implement a Quality Assurance Program (QAP), but
specifically for software. It defines software as computer programs and
related documentation. The QAP is to assure that delivered software
meets contractual requirements. To accomplish this, the QAP must
provide for detection, reporting, analysis and correction of software
deficiencies. Required scope of the QAP covers quality aspects related
to work tasking and authorization procedures, configuration management, testing, corrective action, library controls, computer program
design, software documentation, reviews and audits, tools, techniques
and methodologies, and subcontracted software. The specification recommends that bidders'/contractors' methods and procedures prepared in response to the requirements of MIL-S-52779(AD) be acquired via a software QAP plan.

The effect of MIL-S-52779(AD) on defense software contractors has
ranged from reluctant acceptance or perfunctory compliance, to
grateful appreciation for the specific guidance, which had been lacking in MIL-Q-9858A. The effect on acquisition agencies has been to
fill a virtual vacuum by providing something specific to software quality which can be cited in the contract. It also has reinforced the need to
justify with hard data its impact on overall cost. The favorable effect
on the net quality of acquired software is generally unquestioned.

NAVY SOFTWARE QUALITY

U.S. Navy activities for software quality are partially reflected in the
following documents.

MIL-STD-1679

MIL-STD-1679(Navy), "Weapon System Software Development,"
has been prepared by the Navy for issue as a Navy-wide standard. The
draft standard was distributed to various industry associations for comment, e.g., to the Electronic Industries Association (EIA) and the
National Security Industrial Association (NSIA). A 22 May 1978 draft
replaced the earlier, 1 August 1977, draft. Official issue occurred in
late 1978.

The draft includes a separate section for software quality assurance.
Requirements are identified for the quality assurance organization,
authority, reporting, participation in design reviews, conduct of inde-

116

pendent quality audits, witnessing of tests, record keeping, discrepancy resolution, program design audit and verification, program production standards, and code walk-through. A data item description (DID) for a software quality assurance plan, "Plan, Software Quality Assurance," DI-R-XXX, is among the seventeen DIDs currently associated with the standard. The DID is intended to be cited in the contract, in order to acquire from the contractor a quality assurance plan specific to software. The contractor's implementation of, and on-going compliance with, the plan is subject to monitoring and evaluation by the Government quality assurance representative.

TADSTAND 9

The Navy has promulgated "Tactical Digital System Standard, Software Quality Assurance Testing Criteria," designated as TADSTAND 9. It focuses on testing (rather than in-process control and review) aspects of quality assurance, but recognizes that testing is only one aspect of achieving reliable software. The key requirements addressed are software endurance runs, third-party (other than acquisition manager or developer) conduct of endurance runs which are part of acceptance, allowable software errors, and allowable patches. Endurance runs include stress loading, degraded modes, and on-line maintenance support programs.

NAVSEAINST 4855

A draft NAVSEAINST 4855, "Computer Software Product Quality Program of the Naval Sea Systems Command," has been prepared which establishes policy and requirements for the Naval Sea Systems Command. The policy and requirements are in response to both higher-level Naval Materiel Command quality assurance requirements and DODD 5000.29. The draft also includes an enclosure on software quality practices.

AIR FORCE SOFTWARE QUALITY

The U.S. Air Force approach to software development and software quality is discussed in the following documents.

AFR 800-14

Air Force Regulation AFR 800-14, Volume II, "Acquisition and Support Procedures for Computer Resources in Systems," 26 September 1975, consolidates procedures for implementing Air Force and DOD policies as they apply to acquisition and support of Air Force computer resources. This implementation includes the DOD-level policies and requirements of ASPR; MIL-S-83490; and MIL-STDs 480, 490 and 881A. It contains procedures addressing a broad range of computer resource management disciplines. Procedures for software quality management, as such, are in essence limited to deficiency reporting during the deployment phase. The regulation does, however, call for the computer program development plan to include quality assurance.

AFR 800-14 contains a significant impediment to full realization of the DOD effort for improved software quality management. The problem is in the AFR 800-14, Volume II, requirement (pg. 2-2, Item 2-5a and pg. 4-4, Item 4-9b[7] that the computer program development specification contain preliminary design. This was the first regulation for computer resource management, and although an Air Force regulation, it has been a valuable source of information for all the military services. However, placing preliminary design in a requirements specification can have an adverse impact on computer program quality, e.g., when the preliminary design is incompatible with a performance requirement. There is also additional cost, which results from the fact that, because preliminary design is now in the baselined development specification, changes to it require an engineering change proposal (ECP) and, usually, additional funding.

Contract Management Division Regulations

Policy and procedures for the Air Force Contract Management Division (AFCMD) procurement quality assurance function are provided by AFCMDR 74-1, "Procurement Quality Assurance Program," 3 January 1977. Software is not separately identified in this regulation. Both the recent AFCMD Regulation 800-1, "Contract Management Engineering," 6 April 1978, and the recent AFCMD Pamphlet 800-2, "Contract Management Engineering guide," 20 April, address computer resource management and include aspects of software quality assurance.

AFSCR 74-1

A new Air Force Systems Command (AFSC) regulation, AFSCR 74-1, "Quality Assurance Program," is being prepared and will replace the existing 74-6 publication. The new regulation gives explicit recognition to software quality assurance as a separate, identifiable element of the total quality assurance effort. The regulation probably will be available before the spring of 1979.

MIL-STD-483

The Air Force transmitted a proposed amendment to MIL-STD-483 (USAF), "Configuration Management Practices for Systems, Equipment, Munitions, and Computer Programs," 31 December 1970, to several industry associations on 19 June 1978 for comment. The proposed amendments are to replace Appendix VI, *Computer Program Configuration Item Specification*, and to add a new appendix for configuration item selection. The proposed amendments had not been received at the time of this writing. Thus, it is not known if the proposed changes to the computer program Part I and Part II specification standards contained in Appendix VI will impact Section 4, Quality Assurance. Because MIL-STD-483 is widely cited in Army, Navy, and Air Force contracts, any change in the quality assurance section would have an impact across a wide range of DOD software acquisitions.

Software Quality Assurance Guidebooks

As part of its effort to assist its program managers in the overall acquisition management of software, the Air Force has recently issued two guidebooks for software quality assurance. One is for command, control, and communications systems, "Software Acquisition Management Guidebook: Software Quality Assurance," August 1977. The other is for airborne systems, "Airborne Systems Software Acquisition Engineering Guidebook for Quality Assurance," November 1977. These two guidebooks are part of a series which in toto address the major disciplines for software acquisition management. They provide guidance to program management office personnel for implementing Air Force quality requirements as they apply specifically to software.

Computer Program Development Plan

A data item description (DID) for a "Computer Program Development Plan (CPDP)," DI-S-30567A, 22 February 1978, was recently issued by the Air Force System Command. The DID calls for the bidder/contractor to include tasks associated with software quality assurance in the preparation of the CPDP.

OBSERVATIONS AND CONCLUSIONS

Requirements for software quality and quality management derive principally from the recent DOD system acquisition management policy for computer resources expressed by DODD 5000.29. There are several policy requirements of DODD 5000.29 which should have the effect of improving software quality, while at the same time reducing overall cost. These requirements, and their anticipated impact on software quality, are:

1. Managing software as an element or subsystem of major importance over the system life cycle. This should cause software to surface as a separately identifiable subsystem during acquisition of the total defense system. Improved management visibility should lead to improved management control, including control of software quality.

2. Formalizing both the identification of life cycle computer resource planning factors, and the establishment of related guidelines, via a Computer Resource Plan. This plan should serve the Government project manager as the vehicle for inclusion of planning for software quality management over the system life cycle.

3. Managing software as configuration items. This should pave the way for more consistent and uniform Government and industry application of the configuration management discipline to computer program configuration items. For each CPCI, it should facilitate separately identified development and product specifications, contract line items, work breakdown structure elements, price, schedule, design reviews, qualification test, configuration audits, and acceptance.

4. Identifying computer resource risk areas and a resolution plan in the decision coordinating paper (DCP) for DSARC review. This should help reduce Government authorization of development efforts involving computer programs which have performance requirements with an unacceptable likelihood of achievement.

5. Validating software requirements prior to DSARC II. This should help assure that computer program development specifications completely and accurately reflect requirements allocated from the Type A system specification, and that there is an adequate basis for subsequent development, test, and acceptance of the computer programs.

6. Establishing software development milestones, and measuring attainment against these criteria. This should provide a timely and more objective basis for Government monitoring and assessment of contractor performance during software development. It should help assure that software quality requirements are being achieved on-going, and complement testing for their achievement at the end.

120

Various computer resource management plans (CRMPs) have been prepared under guidance of DODD 5000.29, AFR 800-14, and DARCOM-C 702-4. The quality requirements planned for in these CRMPs generally are being incorporated in contracts. The emphasis on improving the quality (completeness, clarity, consistency) of computer program development specifications will establish a more objective basis for designing-to-meet-requirements during the subsequent development contract phase. The development of techniques and automated quality assurance tools for inspecting and testing computer programs during development, test, and evaluation will improve the quality of the delivered computer program product.

Resolution of the controversy regarding differences in terminology, concepts, and meanings for hardware and software is fundamental to effective implementation of DOD software quality policy. Uniform and consistent Government and industry understanding and application of software quality management will not be fully realized until this problem is resolved.

For example, MIL-STD-109B, "Quality Assurance Terms and Definitions," 4 April 1969, which is mandatory for use by all DOD components, does not use the term software or computer program. While many of the terms apply to software, such as material or item, many do not.

Some contractors claim that it costs additional money to comply with the new requirements for software management, including quality management, which they are seeing more frequently in recent requests for proposals. They contend that pricing it in the proposal makes them noncompetitive. This could be the case on a company's first or second attempt; but that is merely the inherent cost for learning how to use any new or improved technique. Learning improved management approaches for higher quality software at the same or lower cost is part of the competitive environment.

The conclusion is that contractors cannot afford *not* to implement appropriate software quality management, if they intend to remain competitive. Project managers are being presented with higher bids from contractors who claim the excess is the cost to comply with the new software quality management requirements. The project manager needs two irrefutable arguments. One is for his boss, to justify the extra funding. If that doesn't work, the other is for his contractor, to justify that it isn't needed.

Companies complying with the new requirements can be expected to deliver software of higher quality and lower cost than their competitors. Recent studies indicate that costs due to deficiencies can surpass the costs for a quality program.

ACKNOWLEDGMENTS

In preparing this article, material from the listed publications was used extensively. The author expresses his appreciation to the numerous individuals who contributed to the wealth of valuable information in these publications.

References

Circular No. A-109, *Major Systems Acquisition,* 5 April 1976. Executive Office of the President, Office of Management and Budget.

OFPP Pamphlet No. 1, *Major System Acquisitions, A Discussion of the Application of OMB Circular No. A-109,* August 1976. Executive Office of the President, Office of Management and Budget, Office of Federal Procurement Policy.

DODD 5000.29, *Management of Computer Resources in Major Defense Systems,* 26 April 1976.

DODD 5000.3, *Test and Evaluation,* 11 April 1978.

DODD 4155.1, *Quality Assurance,* 9 February 1972.

DODD 4120.21, *Specifications and Standards Application,* 9 April 1977.

DODI 4155.19, *NATO Quality Assurance,* 6 June 1978.

Defense System Software Management Plan, 19 March 1976. Management Steering Committee for Embedded Computer Resources.

Defense System Software FY 79-83 Research and Development Technology Plan, September 1977. Office of the Director of Defense Research and Engineering.

Embedded Computer Resources and the DSARC Process—A Guidebook, 1977. Defense System Acquisition Review Council.

Charter for the Joint DARCOM/NMC/AFLC/AFSC Commander's Joint Policy Coordinating Group on Computer Resource Management, 6 December 1977. Joint Logistics Commanders.

Reliability Standardization Document Program Plan, 10 March 1977. Department of Defense, Defense Materiel Specifications and Standards Office (DMSSO)/Joint Logistics Commanders (JLC) Documentation Task Group.

MIL-STD-721, *Definitions of Effectiveness Terms for Reliability, Maintainability, Human Factors and Safety.*

Joint DOD Services/Agency Regulation Configuration Management, 1 July 1974.

MIL-S-83490, *Specifications, Types and Forms,* 30 October 1968.

MIL-STD-490, *Specification Practices,* 30 October 1968.

MIL-Q-9858A, *Quality Program Requirements,* 16 December 1963.

MIL-S-52779 (AD), *Software Quality Assurance Program Requirements,* 5 April 1974.

DOD-STD-480A, *Configuration Control—Engineering Changes, Deviations and Waivers,* 12 April 1978.

MIL-STD-881A, *Work Breakdown Structures for Defense Materiel Items,* 25 April 1975.

7. Department of Defense Software Quality Requirements

Armed Services Procurement Regulation, 1976.

Defense Supply Agency Handbook 8200.1, *Defense In-Plant Quality Assurance Program,* August 1976.

Army Information Management, AR 18-1. Department of Army Automation.

Management of Computer Resources in Army Defense Systems, AR 70-XX, 28 December 1977. (Draft)

Circular DARCOM-C 702-4, *Army Defense Systems Software Control During the Production and Deployment Phase,* 28 March 1978. U.S. Army Materiel Development and Readiness Command.

MIL-STD-1679 (Navy), Draft, *Weapon System Software Development,* 22 May 1978.

TADSTAND 9 *Standard Tactical Digital System Software Quality Assurance Testing Criteria.* (Draft)

NAVSEAINST 4855, Draft, *Computer Software Product Quality Program of the Naval Sea Systems Command.*

AFR 800-14, *Acquisition and Support Procedures for Computer Resources in Systems,* Volume II, 26 September 1975.

ARCMDR 74-1, *Procurement Quality Assurance Program,* 3 January 1977.

AFCMD Regulation 800-1, *Contract Management Engineering,* 6 April 1978.

AFCMD Pamphlet 800-2, *Contract Management Engineering Guide,* 20 April 1978.

MIL-STD-483 (USAF), *Configuration Management Practices for Systems, Equipment, Munitions, and Computer Programs,* 31 December 1970.

Software Acquisition Management Guidebook: Software Quality Assurance, August 1977. United States Air Force.

Airborne Systems Software Acquisition Engineering Guidebook for Quality Assurance, November 1977. United States Air Force.

Computer Program Development Plan (CPDP), DI-S-30567A, 22 February 1978. Air Force Systems Command.

MIL-STD-109B, *Quality Assurance Terms and Definitions,* 4 April 1969.

DODD 5010.19, *Configuration Management,* 7 April 1970.

DODI 5010.21, *Configuration Management Implementation Guidance,* 29 January 1969.

DODD 5000.1, *Major System Acquisitions,* 18 January 1977.

DODD 5000.2, *Major System Acquisition Process,* 18 January 1977.

PART TWO

Concepts of Software Quality

CHAPTER 8

An Introduction to Software Quality Metrics

JAMES A. McCALL

INTRODUCTION

Life cycle management of large-scale software systems has been increasingly emphasized in recent years. This emphasis is due primarily to the unexpected high costs that have been experienced during the life of most systems. These high costs have not necessarily been related to the systems' inability to perform their intended functions, but instead can be attributed primarily to the high costs of maintenance, transferring the systems to another environment, interfacing the systems to other systems, and upgrading the systems. Examples of these situations have been well documented in the literature [1,2,3,4,5,6].

These high costs result from characteristics of software that do not necessarily relate to the correctness of the implementation of a function or how reliably the function operates, but instead relate to "how well" the software is designed, coded, and documented with respect to maintaining, transferring, modifying, etc., the software. This "how well" is a major aspect of software quality. This situation identifies a weakness in how the requirements of software system developments are defined currently. Emphasis is placed on the functions that must be performed, the schedule in which the system must be produced, and the cost of producing the system. Little or no attention is given to identifying what qualities over the life cycle the software system should exemplify. There are two major reasons for this focus. First, the initial operation of the system, how correctly and reliably the system performs, is always important to the sponsor of a development. It provides the first test of not only how well the developer has done, but also how well the sponsor has done in specifying, monitoring, and controlling the development. (Cost and schedule are obvious concerns since the system usually must be developed in a constrained period of time and within a constrained budget.) Second, no standard definition or identification of what qualities the acquisition manager should consider has been available. No mechanism has existed which would allow an acquisition manager to quantitatively specify the quality desired and then to measure how well the development was progressing toward the desired quality. The little consideration given quality to date generally has been very subjective and not followed up by measurement or assurance activities.

The illusiveness of a concise definition of software quality in part can be attributed to the fact that software production is still in its infancy. Until the last few years, the production of software was viewed as an art rather than an engineering discipline. The fact that software was viewed as an abstraction, having no physical presence to measure, contributes to this black box concept. Modern programming practices have greatly impacted this point of view by introducing significantly more management understanding and visibility into the software production process.

The potential life cycle cost savings of a standardized concept of software quality and a mechanism for specifying and measuring software quality are substantial considering the large portion of life cycle costs attributed to the qualities mentioned previously. The subject of this chapter and the next is a concept of software quality metrics and their application in a quality management program [7].

THE CONCEPT OF SOFTWARE QUALITY

The concept of software quality described in this chapter is based on eleven quality factors grouped according to three orientations or viewpoints with which an acquisition manager interacts with a delivered software product. These three orientations, which relate to life cycle activities associated with the end product, are product operation, revision, and transition. The factors are conditions or characteristics which actively contribute to the quality of the software. They are all acquisition manager-oriented characteristics. They have

FIGURE 1. *Allocation of software quality factors to product activity*

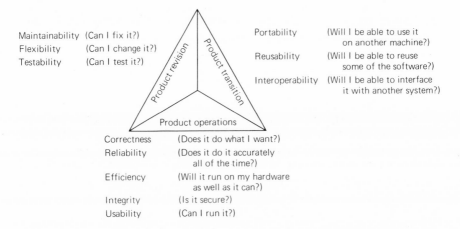

Maintainability (Can I fix it?)
Flexibility (Can I change it?)
Testability (Can I test it?)

Portability (Will I be able to use it on another machine?)
Reusability (Will I be able to reuse some of the software?)
Interoperability (Will I be able to interface it with another system?)

Correctness (Does it do what I want?)
Reliability (Does it do it accurately all of the time?)
Efficiency (Will it run on my hardware as well as it can?)
Integrity (Is it secure?)
Usability (Can I run it?)

TABLE 1. Definition of software quality factors

Correctness	Extent to which a program satisfies its specifications and fulfills the user's mission objectives.
Reliability	Extent to which a program can be expected to perform its intended function with required precision.
Efficiency	The amount of computing resources and code required by a program to perform a function.
Integrity	Extent to which access to software or data by unauthorized persons can be controlled.
Usability	Effort required to learn, operate, prepare input, and interpret output of a program.
Maintainability	Effort required to locate and fix an error in an operational program.
Testability	Effort required to test a program to insure it performs its intended function.
Flexibility	Effort required to modify an operational program.
Portability	Effort required to transfer a program from one hardware configuration and/or software system environment to another.
Reusability	Extent to which a program can be used in other applications—related to the packaging and scope of the functions that programs perform.
Interoperability	Effort required to couple one system with another.

129

been defined so they can be related to a cost to perform the activity characterized by the factor or to the cost to operate with a specified degree of quality. The relationship of the factors to the three orientations or product activities is shown in Figure 1. The questions in parentheses provide a relevancy or brief interpretation of the factors to an acquisition manager. The formal definitions of the factors are provided in Table 1.

This conceptualization of factors in software quality provides a framework for the acquisition manager to quantify concerns for the longer life cycle implications of a software product. For example, if the acquisition manager is sponsoring the development of a system in an environment in which there is a high rate of technical breakthroughs in hardware design, the portability of the software should take on an added significance. If the expected life cycle of the system is long, finding and fixing errors as effectively as possible (maintainability) becomes a cost-critical consideration. If the system is an experimental system where the software specifications will have a high rate of change, flexibility in the software product is highly desirable. If the functions of the system are expected to be required for a long time, while the system itself may change considerably from time to time, reusability is of prime importance in those modules which implement the major functions of the system. With the advent of more networks and communication capabilities, more systems are being required to interface with other systems and the concept of interoperability is extremely important. All of these considerations can be accommodated within the framework established.

THE CONCEPT OF SOFTWARE QUALITY METRICS

The above quality factors represent a management-oriented view of software quality. To introduce a dimension of quantification, this management orientation must be translated into a software-related viewpoint. This translation can be accomplished by defining a set of criteria for each factor. These criteria further define the quality factor and help describe the relationships between factors since one criterion can be related to more than one factor. The criteria are *independent attributes* of the software, or the software production process, by which the quality can be judged, defined, and measured. These attributes are shown in Figure 2. The factors are identified in ellipses and the criteria are identified in rectangles. The definitions of these criteria are provided in Table 2.

FIGURE 2. *Relationship of criteria to software quality factors*

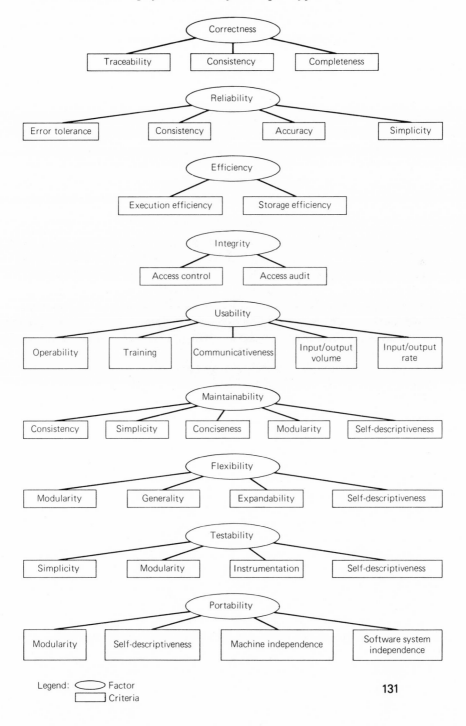

Legend: ⬭ Factor
▭ Criteria

FIGURE 2. *Continued*

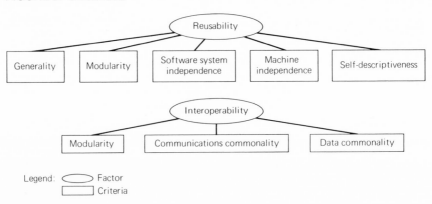

Quality metrics can be established to provide a quantitative measure of the attributes represented by the criteria. The hierarchical nature of the framework established, involving the factors, criteria, and metrics, allows for and facilitates expansion and refinement as further experience with these concepts is gained and as the software development technology advances. New metrics, criteria, and even factors may be identified as relevant to the needs of project management. This hierarchy is depicted in Figure 3.

The measurements, represented by the quality metrics, to be described below can be applied during all phases of development to provide an indication of the progression (quality growth) toward the desired product quality. The earlier in the life cycle the metrics are applied, the more "indicative" these metrics will be. Obviously, if a design specification is of high quality, but poorly implemented, the resulting software product will not be a high-quality product. Successive application of metrics during the development phase helps prevent that type of situation from developing. This overall concept is shown in Figure 4.

TYPES OF METRICS

The metrics discussed in this chapter are predictive-type measures. The subsequent chapter describes utilization of these metrics as an acceptance-type measure, as an additional tool for an independent verification and validation effort, and for predictive assessments during development. There are other reported efforts which are using metrics for attacking the problem in the form of acceptance tests, which can be used to assess the quality of a delivered product [8,9].

TABLE 2. Criteria definitions for software quality factors

Criterion	Definition	Related Factors
Traceability	Those attributes of the software that provide a thread from the requirements to the implementation with respect to the specific development and operational environment.	Correctness
Completeness	Those attributes of the software that provide full implementation of the functions required.	Correctness
Consistency	Those attributes of the software that provide uniform design and implementation techniques and notation.	Correctness Reliability Maintainability
Accuracy	Those attributes of the software that provide the required precision in calculations and outputs.	Reliability
Error Tolerance	Those attributes of the software that provide continuity of operation under non-nominal conditions.	Reliability
Simplicity	Those attributes of the software that provide implementation of functions in the most understandable manner. (Usually avoidance of practices which increase complexity.)	Reliability Maintainability Testability
Modularity	Those attributes of the software that provide a structure of highly independent modules.	Maintainability Flexibility Testability Portability Reusability Interoperability
Generality	Those attributes of the software that provide breadth to the functions performed.	Flexibility Reusability
Expandability	Those attributes of the software that provide for expansion of data storage requirements or computational functions.	Flexibility
Instrumentation	Those attributes of the software that provide for the measurements of usage or identification of errors.	Testability
Self-Descriptiveness	Those attributes of the software that provide explanation of the implementation of a function.	Flexibility Maintainability Testability Portability Reusability

TABLE 2. Continued

Criterion	Definition	Related Factors
Execution Efficiency	Those attributes of the software that provide for minimum processing time.	Efficiency
Storage Efficiency	Those attributes of the software that provide for minimum storage requirements during operation.	Efficiency
Access Control	Those attributes of the software that provide for control of the access of software and data.	Integrity
Access Audit	Those attributes of the software that provide for an audit of the access of software and data.	Integrity
Operability	Those attributes of the software that determine operation and procedures concerned with the operation of the software.	Usability
Training	Those attributes of the software that provide transition from current operation or initial familiarization.	Usability
Communicativeness	Those attributes of the software that provide useful inputs and outputs which can be assimilated.	Usability
Software System Independence	Those attributes of the software that determine its dependency on the software environment (operating systems, utilities, input/output routines, etc.).	Portability Reusability
Machine Independence	Those attributes of the software that determine its dependency on the hardware system.	Portability Reusability
Communications Commonality	Those attributes of the software that provide the use of standard protocols and interface routines.	Interoperability
Data Commonality	Those attributes of the software that provide the use of standard data representations.	Interoperability
Conciseness	Those attributes of the software that provide for implementation of a function with a minimum amount of code.	Maintainability

134

8. An Introduction to Software Quality Metrics

FIGURE 3. *Software quality framework*

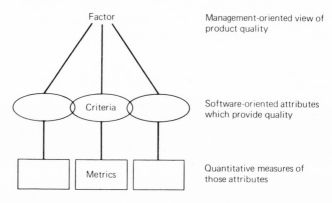

Factor — Management-oriented view of product quality

Criteria — Software-oriented attributes which provide quality

Metrics — Quantitative measures of those attributes

FIGURE 4. *Concept of software metrics*

Development			Evaluation	Operation
Requirements	Design	Code	Test	Operation Revision Transition

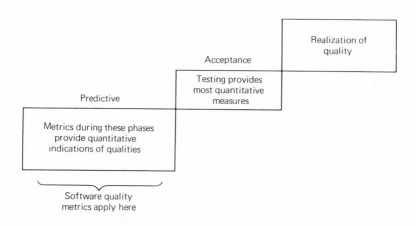

Realization of quality

Acceptance

Testing provides most quantitative measures

Predictive

Metrics during these phases provide quantitative indications of qualities

Software quality metrics apply here

The relationship between predictive- and acceptance-type metrics has not yet been clearly established. Acceptance-type metrics can be viewed as a validation of the predictive metrics. Additional research and experience in this area are required to formally establish the relationships.

The predictive metrics are oriented toward software available during the development phase. Software includes the source code, documentation including requirements specifications, design specifications, manuals, test plans, problem reports and correction reports, and reviews. Since the documents generated during software development vary between projects, the metrics related to documents are based on the existence of certain information regardless of the document in which it exists.

There are essentially two types of predictive metrics. The first type, like a ruler, is a relative quantity measure. The second type is a binary measure which determines the existence or absence of an attribute. The metrics presented in this chapter were chosen to be language-independent. The units of the metrics are important to avoid ambiguity and also to obtain a meaningful measure. The following rule was used in selecting the units of a metric: *The units of the metric are the ratio of the number of actual occurrences to the number of possible occurrences.* Once stated, this rule seems obvious, yet many studies have failed because they did not comply with this rule, resulting in poor correlation between the criteria and the factor.

An example of a relative quantity metric is the complexity measure which is applied during design to a design chart and during implementation to the source code. The metric is based on path flow analysis and variable set/use information along each path. A variable is considered to be "live" at a node if it can be used again along that path in the program. The complexity measure is calculated by summing the "liveness" of all variables along all paths in the program. The "units" rule is applied by dividing this measure by the maximum possible complexity of the program, i.e., all variables live along all paths [10].

An example of a binary measure is a checklist that is used to assess if a design document is complete. Each item in the checklist requires a score be given depending on the existence (1) or absence (0) of specific information. The metric is a normalized summation of scores for the checklist items.

These two examples are shown in Figure 5 in the form of a metric data collection worksheet which is used to record measurements. The worksheet identifies the phase or phases during which the measurement is taken and whether it is a relative quantity measure (value column on worksheet) or a binary measure (yes/no on worksheet). The

FIGURE 5. *Example metrics*

Factor(s): Reliability, maintainability, testability

CRITERION/ SUBCRITERION	METRIC	REQMTS		DESIGN		IMPLEMENTATION	
		Yes/No 1 or Ø	Value	Yes/No 1 or Ø	Value	Yes/No 1 or Ø	Value
Data and control flow complexity	SI. 3 Complexity measure (by module, see para. 6.2.2.6)						
	System metric value: $\dfrac{\text{Sum of complexity measures for each module}}{\text{\# modules}}$						

Factor(s): Correctness

CRITERION/ SUBCRITERION	METRIC	REQMTS		DESIGN		IMPLEMENTATION	
		Yes/No 1 or Ø	Value	Yes/No 1 or Ø	Value	Yes/No 1 or Ø	Value
Completeness	CP. 1 Completeness checklist:						
	(1) Unambiguous references (input, function, output).						
	(2) All data references defined, computed, or obtained from an external source.						
	(3) All defined functions used.						
	(4) All referenced functions defined.						
	(5) All conditions and processing defined for each decision point.						
	(6) All defined and referenced calling sequence parameters agree.						

137

metrics can be applied manually by utilizing the worksheet with the corresponding narrative descriptions of the measures or, in many cases, can be applied automatically with appropriate support software. In these two examples, the complexity measure is calculated by an existing software support system [11] and the completeness checklist could be automated if a formal requirements specifications or design language was used [12].

VALIDATION OF THE CONCEPT

The hierarchical framework presented above supports the simple, understandable, logical relationships of the components of the software quality concepts. It also supports the mathematical formulation and validation of the relationships between the metrics and the quality factors.

At various times during a software development, a set of metrics can be applied to available review material, documents, and code. When the metrics are applied, the resulting measurements can be viewed as an n-tuple $(m_1, m_2, m_3, \ldots, m_n)$. Each element, m_i, of this n-tuple represents a quantitative measure of the system with respect to a specific metric or software attribute.

Certain subsets of this n-tuple relate to specific software quality factors. For example, the subset $(m_1, m_2, \ldots, m_k)$ may contain the metrics applied during the design phase which relate to maintainability. This relationship is a function relating the measurement tuple to a rating of the specific quality factor: $f(m_1, m_2, \ldots, m_k) = r_M$, where r_M is a rating of the maintainability of the software. The definitions of the quality factors support the concept of a rating, e.g., the rating for the quality factor, maintainability, would be in terms of the amount of effort required to maintain the software.

The metric n-tuple has considerable value from a quality management viewpoint. An analogy can be drawn with the set of indicator lights in an airplane cockpit. If a particular indicator light flashes, this immediately identifies a specific characteristic which is beyond acceptable limits or has reached a level at which specific attention should be focused on that characteristic. There may be a sound reason for the indicator to be flashing, not necessarily resulting from an underlying problem, but a justification should be established. Beyond this indicator-light type of function, the formal relationships can be used for evaluation and prediction [13, 14].

The relationships between the metrics and the ratings of quality were derived by applying the metrics to the software products from several past large-scale command and control software developments, establishing the ratings of quality from several years of operational history, and performing a multivariable linear regression. The resulting functions took the form: $r_f^p = a_0 + a_1 m_1 + a_2 m_2 + \ldots + a_k m_k$, where r_f^p is the predicted rating of quality factor f, given the measurement k-tuple $(m_1, m_2, \ldots, m_k)$ and the a_i are the regression coefficients derived from the regression analysis. The relationships derived were validated in a command and control environment with a limited sample.

To illustrate the process used, an example of the analysis of one metric, the design structure measure, with respect to maintainability will be described. The metric was applied to the modules in System A and a rating of maintainability was calculated for each module by the following formula:

$$r_M^i = 1/\left(\frac{MD_i}{n_i}\right)$$

where MD_i = total number of man-days expended on fixes to module i, and n_i = total number of fixes to module i.

The rating of maintainability, r_M, then is based on the average number of man-days expended to make a fix to the software. As a result of performing a linear regression on the set of modules, where the rating of maintainability is the dependent variable and the metric value is the independent variable, a coefficient was derived as follows: $r_M = .48\ m_i$. This is shown in Figure 6. To validate this relationship, the same measurements were taken from another system, B, and plotted. If they fell within the 90 percent confidence interval, the relationship was considered validated. The ultimate use of this derived function is as a predictor of the quality of the system at some point early in the development. Based on the validation, a level of confidence in the predictions can be established.

The total set of metrics, most of which are applied during several phases of the development, consists of 25 measurements taken during requirements, 108 measurements taken during design, and 157 measurements taken during implementation. Up to 50 percent of these measurements can be collected automatically by software support tools that exist today.

Multivariate relationships were established for the quality factors and metrics which are appropriate to the command and control environment utilized for the initial study effort. The validation efforts have demonstrated significant correlations between several metrics and their related quality factors. The sample has not been large enough

FIGURE 6. *Design structure measure relationship to maintainability*

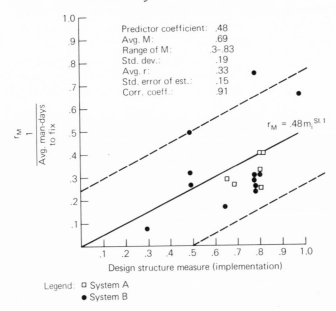

Legend: □ System A
● System B

nor diverse enough to claim the relationships are generally applicable. However, the methodology and the results of the analyses are valuable to project management [15].

CONCLUSIONS

In establishing the metrics, every attempt was made to utilize the work and experience of others. The first published effort formally establishing metrics appears to have occurred in 1968 [16]. In that paper seven major attributes were identified and a few metrics were established. The metrics and attributes were specifically oriented toward aerospace applications. More recent efforts have expanded the number of quality factors or attributes [17, 18, 19] and the applications to which the concepts apply [20, 21, 22, 23]. Many detailed studies of specific qualities and metrics have also been subsequently pursued [24, 25, 26].* All of these efforts dealt with source code metrics. Additionally, some efforts have described design document inspections [27]. The concepts described in this chapter are an extension of all

---

*A more exhaustive list of references can be found in reference 7.

these previous efforts. The extensions have been in the areas of providing a management-oriented view of software quality, quantifying the metrics, establishing metrics which specifically relate to the various quality factors, and applying automation to the metric collection even at the early phases of development.

The software quality metrics established and the methodology for their application are a step toward a more disciplined engineering approach to software quality assurance. The metrics provide a mechanism for quantitatively specifying the level of quality required in a software product. They also provide a consistent, quantitative means for the inspection of documents, review material, and code delivered during a software development.

The concept established is management oriented and based on simple, concise relationships for ease of use, and forces a life cycle management viewpoint. The metrics are oriented toward an early indication of poor quality so that efforts to correct problems can be made early in the development effort.

The fact that many of the metrics lend themselves to automatic application means they can be used objectively, consistently, and cost-effectively. Because benefits can be derived from the concepts and methodology now, even as the relationships are being refined through experience and validation in other environments, the next chapter provides a discussion of how to apply these software quality metrics in a quality management program.

References

1. *Proceedings of a Symposium on the High Cost of Software,* September 1973.
2. "Government/Industry Software Sizing and Costing Workshop—Summary Notes," USAFESD, October 1974.
3. "Findings and Recommendations of the Joint Logistics Commanders," Software Reliability Working Group, November 1975.
4. Lieblein, E. "Computer Software: Problems and Possible Solutions," CENTACS USAECOM Memorandum, November 1972.
5. Myers, G. *Software Reliability: Principles & Practices.* New York: John Wiley and Sons, Inc., 1976.
6. Myers, W. "The Need for Software Engineering," *Computer,* February 1978.
7. McCall, J.; Richards, P.; Walters, G. "Factors in Software Quality," 3 vols., NTIS AD-A049-014,015,055, November 1977. (Produced under contract F30602-76-C-0417 with the Air Force Systems Command Electronics Systems Division and Rome Air Development Center.)
8. Gilb, T. *Software Metrics.* Cambridge, Mass.: Winthrop Publishers, Inc., 1976.

9. Light, W. "Software Reliability/Quality Assurance Practices," *Proceedings from the Software Management Conference,* AIAA, 1976.

10. Richards, P. and Chang, P. "Localization of Variables: A Measure of Complexity," GE Technical Information Series 76CIS07, December 1976.

11. Richards, P. "Developing Design Aids for an Integrated Software Development System," *Proceedings of Computers in Aerospace Conference,* AIAA, 1977.

12. Tiechroew, D. "PSL/PSA: A Computer-Aided Technique for Structured Documentation and Analysis of Information Processing Systems," Proceedings of the 2nd International Conference on Software Engineering, IEEE, 1976.

13. Walters, G. and McCall, J. "The Development of Metrics for Software R&M," *1978 Proceedings of the Annual Reliability and Maintainability Symposium,* January 1978.

14. McCall, J.; Richards, P.; Walters, G. "Metrics for Software Quality Evaluation and Prediction," *Proceedings of Second Summer Software Engineering Workshop,* NASA/Goddard Space Flight Center, September 1977.

15. McCall, J. "The Utility of Software Quality Metrics in Large-Scale Software System Development," *Second Software Life Cycle Management Workshop,* August 1978.

16. Rubey, R. and Hartwick, R. "Quantitative Measurement of Program Quality," *Proceedings of 23rd National Conference,* ACM, 1968.

17. Boehm, B. et al. *Characteristics of Software Quality.* New York: North Holland Publishing Co., 1978.

18. Halstead, M. *Elements of Software Science.* New York: Elsevier Computer Science Library, 1977.

19. Kosarjo, S. R. and Ledgard, H. F. "Concepts in Quality Software Design," NBS Technical Note 842, August 1974.

20. PATHWAY PROGRAM — Program Quality Assurance for Shipboard Installed Computer Programs, Naval Sea Systems Command, April 1976.

21. Myers, G. J. *Reliable Software Through Composite Design.* New York: Petrocelli/Charter, 1975.

22. Abernathy, D. H. et al. "Survey of Design Goals for Operating Systems," Georgia Tech, GITIS-72-04, 1972.

23. Elshoff, J. "Measuring Commercial PL/1 Programs Using Halstead's Criteria," SIGPLAN Notices, May 1976.

24. Bell, D. E. and Sullivan, J. E. "Further Investigation into the Complexity of Software," Mitre, MTR-2874, June 1974.

25. Dunsmore, H. and Gannon, J. "Experimental Investigation of Programming Complexity," *Proceedings of ACM/NBS Sixteenth Annual Technical Symposium,* June 1977.

26. McCabe, T. "A Complexity Measure," *Proceedings of the 2nd International Conference on Software Engineering,* IEEE, 1976.

27. Fagan, M. "Design and Code Inspections and Process Control in the Development of Programs," IBM TR 00-2763, June 1976.

CHAPTER 9

Application of Metrics to a Software Quality Management (QM) Program

GENE F. WALTERS

INTRODUCTION

With the increasing complexity of the software systems being developed today and the requirement to develop them within a short schedule, there is greater emphasis than before on a strong quality management program. In such a program it is essential that we know how to specify and measure software quality so that we can ensure the system meets our overall life cycle objective. It is important not only from the system performance point of view but also in cost.

The role of the manager in a software quality program is important throughout the entire development phase of a program. The impact of the manager's decisions during this phase will be felt not only during operation and maintenance but also during future acquisitions that interface with the system or that incorporate existing software from the current development.

This chapter addresses how both the acquisition manager and the development program manager can identify which quality factors are important and how metrics of these factors can be applied in the software quality management program. (The acquisition manager and the development program manager titles throughout this chapter refer to the organizations rather than the persons, per se.) This approach of applying metrics is based upon the concept of software quality and of the associated metrics described in the previous chapter.

PRINCIPLES IN SPECIFYING SOFTWARE QUALITY

In the acquisition of a new system, especially where software is a sizable portion of it, a major problem of the procuring organization is how to identify which software qualities are important and then how to specify them in the form of requirements.

As the system evolves during development, the need arises to determine how well those requirements are being satisfied. If there are but a few indicators of the software quality until the acceptance test, then obviously, it is too late to perform any major rework and it would be prohibitively expensive.

Each software system is unique in its software quality requirements relative to specific levels of quality. There are basic system characteristics which affect the quality requirements and each system must be analyzed for its fundamental characteristics. Examples of these fundamental characteristics and the associated quality factors are:

Characteristic	Quality Factor
Human lives affected	Reliability
	Correctness
	Testability
Long life cycle	Maintainability
	Flexibility
	Portability
Real-time application	Efficiency
	Reliability
	Correctness
Classified information processed	Integrity
Interrelated with other systems	Interoperability

After the initial evaluation by the acquisition manager to reflect an estimate of the relative importance of the quality factors, the manager is faced with two sets of trade-offs. One set reflects the trade-offs between quality factors, and the other, which is perhaps the more important, reflects the trade-offs of cost versus quality.

The underlying basis or justification of measuring software quality is predicated upon the cost or additional resources required to compensate for poor quality during the life cycle. For example, there is a cost associated with a specified quality rating relative to maintainability. If that cost exceeds the estimated maintenance cost that will be incurred during operation, the acquisition manager may well reduce the required software quality rating for maintainability. Of course, this example is simplistic in that other considerations are not taken into account, such as the reduced operational effectiveness of a system that is more difficult to maintain.

All quality factors should be examined from a cost perspective to show the cost of not having the quality later in the development phase and after program acceptance. In considering all the factors, the life cycle implications of the system should be considered. Table 1 identifies when the quality factors can be measured, the life cycle implication of the quality factors, and the relative cost to provide these factors.

The other set of trade-offs that should be considered are the interrelationships among the factors. Table 2 can be used as a guide in determining these relationships. Some factors are synergistic, where others are in conflict. The following examples show how the factors are related:

Maintainability vs. Efficiency—optimized code, incorporating intricate techniques and assembly language, typically provides problems to the maintainer. Using modular high-level code to increase the maintainability of a system usually increases the overhead, resulting in less efficient operation.

Integrity vs. Efficiency—the additional code and processing required to control software or data access usually lengthen the run time and require additional storage.

Interoperability vs. Integrity—coupled systems allow for more avenues of access and different users who can access the system. The potential for accidental access of sensitive data is increased as well as the opportunities for deliberate access. Often, coupled systems share data or software, which compounds the security problem as well.

STEPS TO SPECIFY QUALITY

The preceding section described the principles used by the acquisition manager in specifying the quality of the software product. The steps outlined in this section are a more formal approach to this role related to the life cycle of the program.

145

TABLE 1. The impact of not specifying or measuring software quality factors

Factors \ Life-cycle phases	Development			Evaluation	Post-development			Expected cost saved:
	Reqmts analysis	Design	Code & debug	System test	Operation	Maintenance	Transition	cost to provide
Correctness	✓	✓	✓	X	X	X		High
Reliability	✓	✓	✓	X	X	X		High
Efficiency		✓	✓		X			Low
Integrity	✓	✓	✓		X			Low
Usability	✓	✓		X	X			Medium
Maintainability		✓	✓			X	X	High
Testability		✓	✓	X		X	X	High
Flexibility		✓	✓			X	X	Medium
Portability		✓	✓			X	X	Medium
Reusability		✓	✓				X	Medium
Interoperability		✓			X		X	Low

Legend: ✓—where quality factors should be measured
X—where impact of poor quality is realized

TABLE 2. Relationships between software quality factors

Factors	Correctness	Reliability	Efficiency	Integrity	Usability	Maintainability	Testability	Flexibility	Portability	Reusability	Interoperability
Correctness											
Reliability	O										
Efficiency											
Integrity			□								
Usability	O	O	□	O							
Maintainability	O	O	□		O						
Testability	O	O	□		O	O					
Flexibility	O	O	□	□	O	O	O				
Portability			□			O	O				
Reusability		□	□	□		O	O	O	O		
Interoperability			□	□					O		

Legend: If a high degree of quality is present for one factor, what degree of quality is expected for the other:

O   = High
□   = Low
Blank = No relationship or application dependent

Briefly, the steps are:

1.a *Identify and assign relative importance to factors* — In preparing a request for proposal (RFP) or system requirements specification (SRS), the acquisition manager should identify and assign a relative importance to each of the critical quality factors.

1.b *Cost-to-implement* vs. *life cycle cost savings trade-off* — The acquisition manager should evaluate the cost to provide the quality versus the resulting expected cost saving in later phases of the program. Based upon this trade-off for each factor, the relative importance should be revised if necessary.

1.c *Trade-off among factors* — The impact of the interrelationships among the critical quality factors should be examined and the relative importance of the critical factors re-evaluated. The resultant set of critical factors at this step will be those stressed in the requirements.

1.d *Provide definitions of factors* — Once the critical qualities have been identified and the priorities assigned, they should be included in the RFP or SRS along with the definitions of the factors. The developer should be required to respond to how the software will be developed to exhibit the qualities specified.

1.e *Provide detailed description of factor related to application* — Wherever possible, as much detailed explanation of the reason for specifying the factor should be included with the definition for each quality factor. For example, if portability is a major concern to the acquisition manager, as precise a description of portability as possible should be included. The types of environments to which the system might be transported should also be specified.

To be more specific, the acquisition manager should define the factors the software should possess. Each quality factor is then defined in terms of attributes whose presence in the software enhances the characteristics represented by the quality factor. To further define the quality requirements, the following additional steps would be employed:

2.a *Identify critical software attributes required* — Having identified the critical quality factors, the acquisition manager then identifies the related critical software attributes which are required. For example, to stress the importance of maintainability, the following software attributes would be identified as required in the RFP or SRS: (1) consistency, (2) simplicity, (3) conciseness, (4) modularity, and (5) self-descriptiveness. The precise definitions should be included in the RFP or SRS.

2.b *Request developer to provide plan to achieve attributes* — The acquisition manager should request the software developer to define in his plan how he will provide the required software attributes for each quality factor.

Further refinement of the approach can be accomplished by specifying the particular metrics to be applied. This requires precise statements of the level of quality that will be acceptable for the software. The mechanism for making the precise statement for any quality factor is a rating for that factor. The dependent variable for the ratings is the effort or cost required to perform a function such as to correct or modify the design or program. To apply this refinement the acquisition manager would follow these additional steps:

3.a *Specify rating for each quality factor* — After identification of the critical factors, the specific performance levels or ratings required for each factor should be specified. For example, a rating for maintainability might be that the average time to fix a problem should be five man-days or that 90 percent of the problem fixes should take less than six man-days. This rating would be specified in the RFP. To comply with this specification, the software would be required to exhibit those characteristics which, when present, give an indication that the software will satisfy this rating. These characteristics are measured by metrics which are inserted into a mathematical relationship to obtain the predicted rating.

3.b *Identify specific metrics to be applied*—The specific metrics should be identified which will be applied to various software products to provide an indication of the progress toward achieving the required level of quality.

EXAMPLE IN SPECIFYING QUALITY

To illustrate how the acquisition manager specifies quality, let us look at one particular application, software for an aircraft computer to provide flight control. In performing the first step of software quality factor analysis (1.a through 1.e as identified earlier), the acquisition manager must have a good understanding of the functions performed by the flight control computer and its role with respect to the operation of the aircraft.

Of all the quality factors, three are clearly more important. They are correctness, reliability, and efficiency. Even though it may be desirable to have the other software quality factors, the emphasis to be placed upon them is far less.

The benefits of requiring the correctness and reliability quality factors to be high with respect to cost-to-implement vs. life cycle cost impact is greater than for the efficiency factor. This in large part is due to the marginal gain in efficiency with increased effort after a certain point.

Since some of the quality factors may reinforce each other or may be in conflict, it is important to understand these relationships at the time of quality specification. In the case of the flight control computer, correctness and reliability are both likely to be high, whereas efficiency is not significantly dependent upon the other two.

After the acquisition manager has evaluated the flight control system with respect to the software quality factors, definitions of the factors and how they relate to the application should be provided. For example:

149

Definitions

Correctness—Extent to which a program satisfies its specifications and fulfills the user's mission objectives.

Reliability—Extent to which a program can be expected to perform its intended function with required precision.

Efficiency—Amount of computing resources and code required by a program to perform a function.

Reason for factors in application:

Correctness—System is man-rated.

Reliability—System is man-rated. High cost to replace read-only memory to correct latent errors.

Efficiency—Real-time constraints. Cost of hardware across many units. Size, power, weight constraints.

In the second step (2.a and 2.b) the acquisition manager specifies the software attributes. For the three factors identified, the software attributes are traceability, consistency, completeness, error tolerance, accuracy, simplicity, storage efficiency and execution efficiency. The definition of each would be provided in the specification to the development program manager along with the requirement for the developer to establish a plan on how he will ensure the software product will have these attributes.

In the third step (3.a and 3.b) the acquisition manager specifies in detail the desired or acceptable software quality rating and the metrics that will be applied to determine them.* For example, the ratings for a flight control system may be:

Required Rating for Correctness:

Measured at the time of requirements review—0.8
Measured at the time of preliminary design review—0.8
Measured at the time of critical design review—0.9
Measured at the time formal test starts—0.9
Measured at the time of acceptance test—0.99

Required Rating for Reliability:

Measured at the time of requirements review—0.8
Measured at the time of preliminary design review—0.8
Measured at the time of critical design review—0.9
Measured at the time formal test starts—0.9
Measured at the time of acceptance test—0.99

*At the current time few of the metrics have been validated to use as an acceptance criteria for the software product. However, they could be used as a basis for an incentive fee. See the chapter on "Software Acceptance Criteria."

Required Rating for Efficiency:

Measured at the time of requirements review — 0.7
Measured at the time of preliminary design review — 0.7
Measured at the time of critical design review — 0.7
Measured at the time formal test starts — 0.7
Measured at the time of acceptance test — 0.8

The ratings computed prior to the acceptance test are predictive and provide a coarse probability of the likelihood the product will contain the required quality to the level specified. The acquisition manager would provide the detailed definitions of the metrics used in computing the rating. Examples of those definitions were described in the previous chapter.

Since the metrics have had limited application at this time and little data has been gathered to validate the metrics in such areas as portability, interoperability and reusability, the acquisition manager at this time would best be advised not to levy requirements for meeting specified quality levels, but instead specify the relative importance of the quality factors as development guidelines. As has been pointed out in previous investigations [1, 2], the likelihood of achieving design goals such as efficiency is high when they are made explicit at the beginning.

APPLYING SOFTWARE METRICS DURING DEVELOPMENT

The metrics are quantitative measures of the software attributes which are necessary to realize certain quality factors in the software. The metrics provide an indication of the progression toward the achievement of a high-quality end product. At the time of acceptance testing, specific quality tests can be defined to evaluate the level of quality attained in the product.

The metrics that have been presented can be applied to products currently provided during a software development. They may be applied by: (1) acquisition manager to delivered products, (2) development program manager and reported to the acquisition manager in summary form during reviews, (3) development quality assurance personnel, or (4) independent quality assurance contractor for the acquisition manager.

In applying metrics it is important to use existing control mechanisms, i.e., reviews, status reports, documentation delivered during development, and the program source code. The current purpose of these controls is to evaluate the schedule and cost performance and to determine the functional correctness of the software being developed. The quality metrics are applied to these same control vehicles to provide an indication of the quality of the software product being developed. This concept is illustrated in Figure 1. Corresponding to three levels of specifying software quality, the measurement can be performed at three levels of detail.

The first level of measuring software quality involves applying the metrics to the software products as they are being produced. Different sets of metrics are applicable to products developed during the requirements analysis, design, and coding phases. The use of the metrics in this manner insures a formal and consistent review of each software product. The steps to be followed for this level of measurement are:

1.a *Apply the subset of metrics that apply at each phase*—The subset of metrics which relate to the identified critical quality factors and software attributes and are applicable to that phase of development should be applied to the available software products. For example, during the design phase, metrics could be applied to design specifications, interface control documents, test plans, minutes and materials prepared for reviews, etc.

1.b *Overall subjective evaluation*—A subjective evaluation of how well the software is being developed with respect to the specific

FIGURE 1. *Software development process control*

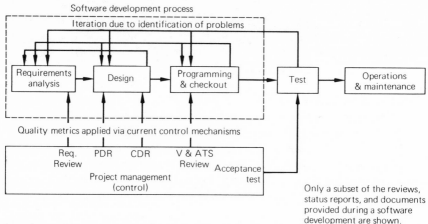

Only a subset of the reviews, status reports, and documents provided during a software development are shown.

Legend:

Req. Review — Requirements review
PDR — Preliminary design review
CDR — Critical design review
V & ATS Review — Validation and acceptance test
                specification review

quality factors can be made based on the inspection of the software products using the metrics.

The second level of detail utilizes experience gained through the application of metrics and the accumulation of historical information, taking advantage of the quantitative nature of the metrics. The values of the measurements are used as indicators for evaluation of the progress toward a high-quality product. The additional steps for this level of detail are:

2.a *Evaluate low metric scores*—After the metrics are applied to the available software products, the values are obtained and evaluated. If particular modules receive low scores, they can be individually evaluated for potential problems. If low metric scores are realized across the system, an evaluation should be made to identify the cause. It may be that a design or implementation technique used widely by the development team is at fault. Corrective action such as the enforcement of a development standard can then be introduced.

2.b *Analyze the variance of scores*—Further analysis can be conducted. An examination of the metric scores for each module in a system will reveal which metrics vary widely. Further examination will reveal if this variation correlates with the number of problem reports or with historical variances in performance. This sensitivity analysis identifies characteristics of the software, represented by the metrics, which are critical to the quality of the product. Quality assurance personnel should place increased emphasis on these aspects of the software product.

2.c *Evaluate scores against thresholds*—Threshold values may be required. A simple example is the percent of comments per line of source code. Certainly, code which exhibits only one or two percent measurements for this metric would be identified for corrective action.

The most detailed level of applying metrics involves predictive equations. Currently, generally applicable predictive equations are not available. However, as more project information is gathered to derive the equations, the following steps would appear to be appropriate:

3.a *Apply normalization function*—To illustrate the procedure, assume a normalization function has been developed for the factor, flexibility. The normalization function, applicable during the design phase, relates measures of modular implementation to the flexibility of the software. The predicted rating of flexibility is in terms of the average time to implement a change in specifications. The normalization function is shown in Figure 2. The measurements associated with modular implementation are taken from design documents which reveal if input, output, and processing functions are mixed in the same module, if application and machine-dependent functions are mixed in the same module, or if processing is data-volume or data-value limited. As an example, assume the measurements were applied during the design phase and a value of 0.65 was measured. Inserting this value in the normalization function results in a predicted rating for flexibility of 0.33, as identified by point A in Figure 2. If the acquisition manager had specified a rating of 0.2, identified by point B, it indicates that the software development is progressing well with respect to this desired quality. By analyzing the variance associated with this normalization function, Figure 3 shows that the acquisition manager has an 86 percent level of confidence that the flexibility of the system will be better than the specified rating.

3.b *Determine corrective action to be taken*—The comparison of the predicted rating with the specified rating provides a more quantitative indication, with an associated level of confidence, of how well the software development is progressing toward achieving the specified levels of quality. Corrective action based upon further analysis would be in order if the predicted rating was lower than the specified rating.

FIGURE 2. *Normalization function for flexibility during design*

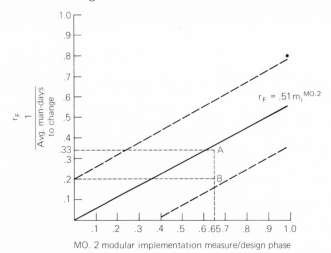

MO. 2 modular implementation measure/design phase

$r_F = .51 m_i{}^{MO.2}$

FIGURE 3. *Determination of level of confidence*

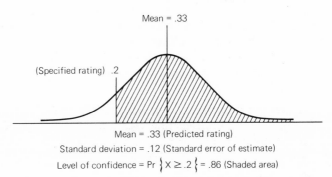

Mean = .33 (Predicted rating)
Standard deviation = .12 (Standard error of estimate)
Level of confidence = Pr $\left\{ X \geq .2 \right\}$ = .86 (Shaded area)

Even though steps 3.a and 3.b may not currently be appropriate for the acquisition manager to apply, the development program manager can certainly use them as another technique in a quality assurance program.

METRICS AS AN AID DURING AND AFTER ACCEPTANCE

Currently, the emphasis on acceptance testing is to ensure the required functions are performed correctly and meet specified performance criteria. However, with the emergence of a more comprehensive set of software metrics, the acquisition manager will be able in the future to specify acceptable levels of quality for increasing the effectiveness of the software and reducing the life cycle costs.

At the time of acceptance, we have three sets of software quality measures available for the products developed. Sets exist for each phase, namely, requirements preparation, design, and implementation/test. Since the software product consists not only of the computer program itself, but also the supporting documentation, there can be an acceptable level for each set. For example, if the metrics for the requirements and design documentation are relatively low, corrections and enhancements are likely to be difficult and therefore costly in the long run. In applying the metrics at acceptance, it is necessary to recompute the metrics for the requirements and design documentation, as any revisions or redesign are likely to be reflected in the latest versions. If the changes have been clearly indicated, the task of recomputing the metrics should be relatively easy.

The application of metrics at the time the software is accepted has potential long-term benefits by providing information for making future decisions concerning the product. Metrics can aid in answering the following typical questions:

Once the software is accepted and placed in operational use, how reliable and maintainable is the product going to be? The metrics for these factors will estimate the availability of the system in which the software resides and the expected effort required to fix latent errors.

If after the software is developed and used operationally, a new computer is acquired, how costly will it be to convert the software? If the metric value for portability is not sufficiently high, a redesign and development may be the most cost-effective solution.

If software is now in operation and the mission requirements are changed to accommodate new capabilities, are there any characteristics of the software that would increase the cost for modifying the software? Is the software flexible enough so that few enhancements are necessary?

If a software package has been developed for one application, how much of this package is salvageable for another? For example, a telemetry data management system is developed for an earth satellite. Using the same computer, are there any characteristics that are likely to make the task difficult using the existing software as a base for supporting another satellite?

SUMMARY

Over the past several years the interest in software metrics to evaluate the quality of the software product has increased because of the recognized high life cycle costs and low reliability associated with many of the recent systems. Even though software metrics are in their infancy, the current framework as described in the preceding chapter and the preliminary methodology outlined here provide a more quantitative approach to estimating the quality of and its impact on software throughout the life of the program.

Presently, there has been insufficient validation of the metrics to permit an acquisition manager to specify the "total quality requirements" that must be met for the software to be accepted. However, they can and should be used as an aid in evaluating the quality of the software product as it is being developed so that any recommended redesign can be initiated early to minimize both schedule and cost impacts. It is expected that the use of automated tools to collect and report on the metrics will increase. As this occurs, the application of metrics in a quality management program will become more prevalent.

References

1. Weinberg, G. M. *The Psychology of Computer Programming.* New York: Van Nostrand Reinhold Co., 1971, pp. 126–132.
2. Weinberg, G. M. "The Psychology of Improved Programming Performance," *Datamation,* November 1972.

CHAPTER 10

Software Acceptance Criteria

JOHN D. COOPER and
MATTHEW J. FISHER

INTRODUCTION

Subsequent to normal software development and its validation by the developer, the customer must be prepared to accept the product. This usually occurs when the customer judges that a particular version of the program exhibits a level of quality such that the software can be placed in the operational environment with reasonable confidence that it will perform effectively. To provide confidence that the software meets specified performance requirements, the user normally institutes acceptance testing. The basis for this testing is the set of performance requirements given the developer through contractual means at the outset of the development. A necessary condition is that the performance and quality requirements can be adequately quantified. This quantification leads into the realm of acceptance metrics or, more commonly, acceptance criteria. This chapter is concerned with two such acceptance criteria: endurance and adaptability. To the authors' knowledge, these are the only software acceptance criteria presently slated for contractual use.

THE CRITERIA

Based on a system's life cycle, it has been found that the largest portion of the total software costs arises during the deployment phase where a disproportionate share of resources is needed to maintain the computer programs. The two quality factors that possess the greatest potential for reducing the maintenance costs for software are reliability and flexibility. The resources expended for error correction are obviously less when errors do not exist. As reliability increases, the number of software errors decreases and thus the associated maintenance costs are reduced accordingly. Further, one may assert that when requirements change or errors are discovered, software which is flexible will impose a lower total cost to modify than will software which is inflexible. It is profitable, therefore, to concentrate upon increasing both the reliability and the flexibility of software. The discussion which follows concentrates on acceptance criteria which test for software *reliability* in terms of operational *endurance* and for software *flexibility* in terms of *adaptability*.

ENDURANCE

Endurance is that attribute of a program related to its ability to operate continuously over the time interval for which it was designed. Good endurance is indicative of two software qualities: it will operate for the period of time required in the operational environment; and that one particular class of serious errors has been reduced to a reasonable acceptance level. Also, the program's reliability can be said to have been increased since it will operate more as expected.

Historically, the lack of a quantifiable or measurable means for aiding in the computer program acceptance decision has been a perplexing problem in the software development/acquisition process. The attribute of software reliability called "endurance" can be used as one indicator of a program's acceptability. The fact that it is, to some degree, measurable provides some relief to the acceptance problem by yielding one criterion upon which to base the decision either to accept or reject the delivery of a new computer program.

In order to measure a program's endurance it must be subjected to a test specifically designed for that purpose. It is most economical when the endurance test is conducted as an adjunct to normal program acceptance testing. In some sense, the endurance test may be viewed as a take-home final exam. The next few sections will discuss some of the more significant aspects of testing and measuring program endurance.

Endurance Test Design

Before we discuss the design of an endurance test, we should first point out that the endurance test *is not* the *total* acceptance test. It merely tests the stamina of a program. It does not test for many of the other important acceptance criteria such as satisfaction of the performance requirements (other than period of operation), all other quality factors, adequacy and accuracy of documentation, human factors, etc. The following items should be taken into account when designing an endurance test:

Establish definitions — some of the terms not to be overlooked are types and categories of errors, fault, program stop, program reload, restart, and patches.

Develop a test plan based on the performance requirement's specification.

The test should be conducted in the ultimate operational hardware and environment.

The test should contain periods when the program is stressed to and beyond its limits. The author of the test plan must know what and how to stress the program.

The duration of the test should, as a minimum, span the total designed period of operating time. The only exceptions are if the program is job oriented, then it should run to completion; if it is a continuous, nonterminating system, then the test should run for no less than 25 hours.

All integrated and interfaced systems and subsystems should be in operation throughout the total test.

The amount of allowable degradation must be defined. The system's reaction to the failure of some peripheral or interfacing system must also be defined.

The computer programs to be tested should be those under formal configuration management and targeted for delivery.

All programs to be tested should be so identified.

The requirements for the endurance test should be made a binding part of the acquisition contract.

Endurance Test Conduct

To continue in the same vein, the items listed below should be considered for and during conduct of the endurance test:

A test specification is essential.

The test should be conducted by an independent, unbiased third-party organization.

Initial system setup, premission, and postmission periods should not be counted as part of the test duration.

The program should be subjected to a full range of inputs including illegal and abnormal or unexpected ones.

Care should be taken to insure that all functions and interfaces are exercised.

The test period should include the hour "midnight" or be 25 hours long to insure proper handling of the clock rolling over the various other types of time-related wrap-arounds.

While the program is being stressed, attempts should be made to exceed every data rate, transfer rate, storage area, and processor time availability.

The program should not be stopped until the scheduled test completion.

Any invocation of an auto-recovery feature, if available, should be counted as a program stop or failure.

Failure to satisfactorily complete the entire test for any reason should require that the full test be repeated.

Endurance Measurement

The first measure for endurance, a binary one, is obvious — the program either completed the endurance test without stopping or it did not. This pass/fail measurement should not be taken lightly. It is not as easy as it might seem at first. Ask yourself, *honestly,* how many programs do you know that could withstand 25 hours of continuous antagonistic abuse with no work-arounds allowed and every operation/usage strictly by the book? There are a lot of programs in the operational phase of their life cycle that could not pass such an endurance test, nor could very many of the programs still under development.

The pass/fail metric can be applied universally. To expand the scope of endurance measurements beyond that entails more subjective and program-unique metrics. A great deal depends on how well one can define things, especially the types and categories of errors. Very important are the terms and conditions of the stress portions of the test. A good way to remove the subjectiveness and at the same time expand the endurance metrics is to increase the list of pass/fail criteria (must be well defined) beyond just stops/failures. This forces the measurement back into the binary form. With a little thought and planning it should be relatively easy to tailor an endurance test for your system. The important thing is to give it a try.

Endurance Beyond Acceptance

The use of endurance testing should not be confined to the acceptance process. Before the final exam it can be used by the developer as a rehearsal and as a gauge to adjudge progress. If a program passes an endurance test at the time of acceptance, surely it should be able to again pass it anytime during its subsequent operational phase. This is especially valuable for use after program modifications and enhancements. The endurance test at program acceptance then forms a baseline to be measured against for the remainder of its lifetime.

The endurance test should be viewed as only a "yardstick," one way to measure a program. In the same sense as the yardstick, it is not possible to tell everyone who, how, or when to use it. It is merely one criterion for helping to measure one software quality attribute.

ADAPTABILITY

The second acceptance criterion that will be considered is adaptability. This criterion measures the ease with which a computer program can be revised by adding, changing, or deleting source statements. While many factors influence the ability to modify a program, adaptability is directed primarily at the design or structure of the program. For example, well-structured, modular programs normally exhibit a relatively high degree of adaptability. On the other hand, monolithic programs, with tightly coupled procedures, exhibit poor adaptability. This occurs because the design of modularized programs tends to isolate the impact of revisions, while highly coupled programs tend to distribute the effects of changes throughout the code. The various design aspects for adaptability have been addressed in the literature. The immediate concern, however, is not in the design, but in measuring the adaptability once the program has been developed. (This is not to imply that quality personnel should not assess, estimate, and influence program adaptability throughout the software development.) The thrust here is to find an approach to the quantification of adaptability, i.e., a quantification scheme which can be employed as a contractual instrument for acceptance of the software.

Characteristics of Adaptability

The ease with which a computer program can be modified is a consequence of numerous characteristics, both external and internal, to the program structure. Table 1 gives only a partial list of these characteristics which are identified by the letters C_1, C_2, . . . C_N.

External to the program structure, the concern may be with the amount of reserve core available to incorporate additions or future modifications into the program. Obviously, this condition is not a characteristic of software quality. Instead, it is a hardware constraint which has only an indirect bearing upon the adaptability. However, the software designer must be aware of this constraint. In fact, the designer may compensate for the limitation by making the program more storage efficient, the usual result being a lowering of adaptability.

A second external consideration is the amount of duty cycle available to the designer. This again is basically a hardware constraint or characteristic that can have a significant indirect effect upon software adaptability especially in real-time control systems. If a particular software modification requires more time than that available, the software will have zero adaptability with respect to that change. As with memory capacity, the software designer may be able to compensate by making the program more time efficient.

A timing problem internal to the program is the use of time-dependent code to establish iteration rates for real-time systems. Changes to the iteration rate may necessitate adding or subtracting many instructions distributed throughout the code, thereby making it difficult to modify the program.

Of a more direct consequence to adaptability and of much more importance to the present discussion is the modularity of the computer program, specifically the coupling of the program modules one to another. For programs where coupling between modules is high, adaptability is usually low. On the other hand, when modules are loosely coupled and perform independent functions, program adaptability is normally high.

TABLE 1

	Adaptability characteristics
C_1	Percent memory uncommitted
C_2	Percent cycle time uncommitted
C_3	Time-dependent code
C_4	Module coupling
C_5	Data/control flow
C_6	Number of program statements
$\vdots$	
C_N	

Module coupling has been explored by Myers [1]. He notes the following types of coupling:

Content coupled — if one module directly references the contents of the other

Common coupled — if two or more modules reference the same global data structure

Externally coupled — if two or more modules reference the same global data item

Control coupled — if one module explicitly controls the function of another

Stamp coupled — if two or more modules reference the same nonglobal data structure

Data coupled — if one module calls another module, and all inputs to and outputs from, the called module are data item parameters

Depending upon the type of system involved, the characteristics discussed above — reserve memory, reserve timing, time-dependent code, coupling, and others — assume various degrees of importance. For example, real-time control systems are normally affected more by timing considerations than by reserve memory. When measuring adaptability, then, those characteristics pertinent to a particular system must be stressed.

Quantification Schemes for Adaptability

Consider a modularized program that is to be revised. For the moment let us concentrate on observing only one module within that program. A proposed revision may produce several problems for the software designer. For example, the revision may require more memory than is available, or by changing the module, code revisions external to the module must be introduced. In fact, all the characteristics associated with adaptability, e.g., memory reserve, spare duty cycle, coupling, etc., may be affected. The problem becomes one of quantifying the effects on these characteristics as a result of the changes. Given the particular module revision, how does this change manifest itself in the code, timing, data, and documentation? What is the effect on each characteristic produced by the change and how can this effect be quantified? Once a quantification scheme is defined for each characteristic, these schemes can be combined to give an overall adaptability rating for that module. To illustrate, consider that the effects of the various characteristics are symbolized by the letters C_1, C_2, C_3, $\ldots$ C_N

where C_1 is the quantification scheme (an equation or expression) for the *effect* of memory reserve, and C_2 a second quantification scheme for the *effect* of spare duty cycle, and so on. The adaptability factor for the module would be some combination of these expressions. The adaptability factor for the ith module, AF_i, can then be expressed as the function, f, of the effects of each characteristic:

$$AF_i = f(C_1, C_2, C_3, \ldots C_N)$$

The obvious question is how to develop or define a quantification scheme for each characteristic. What equation or mathematical method do we use to quantify the effect of memory reserve, timing, coupling, etc? Before addressing this difficult problem, it should be pointed out that the above approach can be extended to the total software system simply by combining all the module adaptability factors. Thus, the system adaptability AF_s is a function F of the module factors

$$AF_s = F(AF_1, AF_2, \text{-------} AF_m)$$

where m is the number of modules.

Adaptability for Module Coupling

The fundamental question remains of how to define a quantification scheme for the adaptability characteristics. At present, very few such schemes exist, and it may even be impossible to develop schemes for some of the characteristics.

The process can be explained with the aid of Figure 1, which illustrates that requirement changes have caused a revision of the input/output (I/O) module for a particular program. The I/O module may increase or decrease in size and complexity to incorporate the new requirements. In the figure it is shown to expand slightly with M_{si} as the

FIGURE 1. *Example of adaptability measurement*

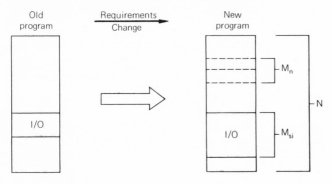

number of lines of code in the new module. The total number of lines of code in the new program is shown as N. More significantly, however, the figure symbolically indicates (by three dashed lines) the lines of code labeled M_n. M_n represents those lines of code, external to the I/O module, that must be changed to accommodate the change of the I/O module. These lines of code are indicative of the amount of coupling between the I/O module and the remainder of the program. Concentrating simply on coupling effects, one can reduce the quantification scheme for adaptability to that for coupling:

$$AF_i = f(C_1, C_2, \ldots C_N) \longrightarrow f(C_4)$$

where C_4 is for module coupling and i is the module to be changed. In the example above, the ith module would be the I/O module. Remembering this example, one can proceed by defining a quantification scheme for coupling. A typical scheme is given by the following expression:

$$AF_i = \frac{N - M_{si} - M_n}{N - M_{si} - M_n} \times 100$$

where the variables were defined in connection with Figure 1. The system adaptability is given by:

$$AF_i = \left(\prod_{i=1} \frac{AF_i}{100} \right) \times 100$$

It should be noted that these equations form only one set of equations for adaptability and that they are for module coupling only. The total expression for adaptability would be much more complicated.

Adaptability Test

The test for adaptability can be divided into two parts: a design walk-through and a measurement. Both parts depend upon a selection of revisions to the computer program. The following discussions outline the use of these revisions to determine adaptability.

Prior to contract award, a list of changes to the computer program is proposed. The proposed changes should be selected from those that are most representative of future expected changes. With this list, the developer can attempt to satisfy, in his design, the adaptability needed for customer acceptance. In order to mutually agree on the changes, both the developer and the user must begin to think about the ultimate software architecture. This planning lends visibility to the software very early in its development. The proposed program revisions should be selected to stress the program for its adaptability. Candidate revisions should be of various sizes and complexities.

WALK-THROUGHS. For each selected program change, the developer is required to walk-through the computer software with the customer, indicating where changes must be made to satisfy new requirements. In effect, the developer must treat these hypothetical revisions as if he were given a new contractual requirement, estimate the changes to existing software, and calculate the adaptability. The sequence of analysis which must be followed is:

1. System requirements analysis
2. Functional analysis
3. Hardware/software requirements
4. Estimated impacts on lines of code
5. Adaptability estimate computation

If properly carried out, these walk-throughs yield several benefits:

1. The developer must demonstrate his approach to implement a change to the user. To a large extent, the developer learns how good his software actually is since he is forced to walk-through a complete system design for each change. The user gains additional insight into the software and how to make changes.
2. During the walk-throughs, both the computer program and its documentation are scrutinized; the documentation is the means by which the developer and user agree to the impacts of revisions.
3. On the basis of the reports of these walk-throughs, the developer has, to some degree, guaranteed the cost of that particular change to the user. Costs for similar changes can be determined by extrapolation from the selected test cases.

MEASUREMENT. The second part of the adaptability test consists of actually making one of the software changes that had been examined during the walk-throughs. In this way true measurements of adaptability (instead of estimates determined during the walk-throughs) can be made. At first, it may appear that this procedure, i.e., making program changes, is an expensive way to calculate adaptability. Fortunately, the solution to this problem may not be that costly. For example, in a current DOD system, the contract requires six different computer programs in which the only differences were for the timing, formatting, and output parameters. This circumstance provided an effective vehicle for adaptability testing. If such a convenient situation does not exist, it can be created by withholding or separating a requirement from the initial design and then adding it later on in the development. If done properly, such an artificial requirement change can become effective.

SUMMARY

The criteria upon which software acceptance is judged should be contractually binding and be derived from requirement specifications. Contractual requirements are the prime instruments through which the acquisition manager can influence the software design and development. The manager must, therefore, insure that adequate specifications for quality are included and that those requirements are stated in a way that can be tested.

This chapter has concentrated upon two acceptance criteria or metrics: endurance and adaptability. These criteria were developed to provide user baseline tests for the quality factors of reliability and flexibility, respectively. If these baseline tests are properly structured, they also give the user a good indication of what to expect when the software is placed in an operational status.

With proper control, it may be possible to combine both the endurance and adaptability tests. This can occur if software failures resulting from the stress test are corrected under strict surveillance of the user. The corrections of the failures would then represent the test input or requirements for the adaptability.

The acceptance criteria examined here are only examples. They do not represent final solutions to the problems of acceptance metrics for reliability and flexibility. However, the approaches taken here appear to be feasible and practical. It is hoped that the discussions stimulate further research to expand and standardize the criteria.

Reference

1. Meyers, Glenford J. *Software Reliability Principles and Practices.* New York: John Wiley and Sons, Inc., 1976.

CHAPTER 11

The Applicability of Hardware Reliability Principles to Computer Software

NORMAN F. SCHNEIDEWIND

INTRODUCTION

It is tempting to apply hardware reliability, maintainability, and availability techniques to software due to the large body of literature and techniques which have been developed in this area. The application of hardware reliability to software is also attractive because hardware techniques have been successful, as evidenced by its use in space programs. It is shown that, in general, hardware reliability concepts and methods are not applicable to software reliability and that new concepts and analytical techniques are needed to accurately represent the unique characteristics of software.

IMPORTANCE OF TIME IN HARDWARE RELIABILITY

The passage of time is central to hardware reliability. After an initial debugging period, the reliability of a hardware system decreases with increasing time in the hardware reliability model. The reason for this property is that probability of failure increases with increasing operating time. This probability characteristic is the result of random stress accumulation during the useful life of a system and by deteriora-

171

tion during the wear-out phase. The life of a system may be divided into three phases: burn-in or debugging phase, useful or operational life, and wear-out phase. During these phases the failure rate $Z(T)$ is decreasing, constant, and then increasing, respectively. When failure rate is plotted against time, as shown in Figure 1, the characteristic "bathtub curve" is produced. During burn-in, marginal components are identified and removed from the system; thus the failure rate decreases and reliability improves because a smaller percentage of marginal components remain. However, the improvement in reliability is limited by the occurrence of chance failures which are characteristic of the second phase, or useful life of a system. The failure rate during this period is a constant λ, as shown in Figure 1. During this period the failure rate is independent of time, and its reciprocal is equal to m, the mean time between (or to) failures. The useful life is the only phase of system life during which it is valid to use m as a measure of reliability, since during the other two phases the failure rate is a function of time and its reciprocal is not equal to mean time between failures.

During the useful life phase, stress accumulations (e.g., thermal stress causing insulation breakdown or changes in electrical conductivity) occur at random and exceed the design strength of a component, i.e., failures do not cluster around some preferred time. Randomness implies that events occur at unpredictable moments and with irregularity. Over equal time periods of sufficient length, approximately the same number of failures will occur. These chance failures cannot be eliminated by good debugging techniques and maintenance practices. No one can predict when chance failures will occur; however, their fre-

FIGURE 1. *Failure rate vs. time*

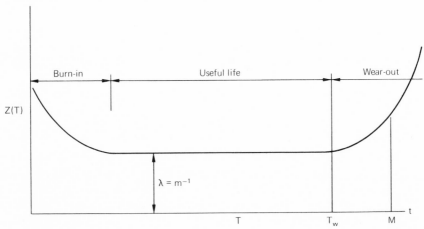

quency of occurrence can be reduced by good engineering and the use of redundancy [1]. The general solution to the reliability equation yields the expression $R(t) = \exp(-\lambda t) = \exp(-t/m)$, when the failure rate is equal to the constant λ. Thus the use of the exponential reliability law is only valid during the useful life of a system. The exponential reliability function is shown in Figure 2a.

It is important to distinguish between operating time t, a period of system use, and equipment life T. Equipment life is long relative to operating time. It is composed of all operating times plus scheduled and unscheduled maintenance and nonuse times. As T approaches T_W (time that wear-out phase begins), as shown in Figure 1, the failure rate begins to increase. This increase marks the beginning of the wear-out phase. This rise will be pronounced for mechanical equipment but will increase much less rapidly for electronic equipment. In this case

FIGURE 2. *(a) Exponential reliability function vs. operating time; (b) Normal reliability function vs. operating life*

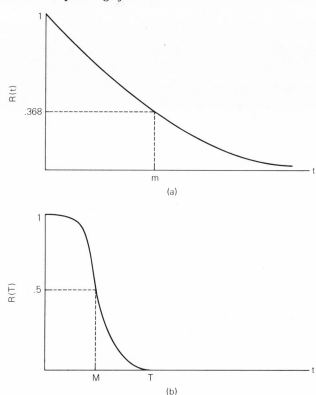

the rise will signify component aging rather than wear-out. Failures in this phase do not occur at random; there is a clustering of failures around the mean life M. The normal distribution has been found to provide a good representation of the wear-out phase of system life. The normal reliability function

$$R(T) = (\delta \sqrt{2\pi})^{-1} \int_{T}^{\infty} \exp(-x^2/2)\, dT$$

where $x = (T-M)/\sigma$, is shown in Figure 2b [1]. Notice that exponential reliability is a function of t and has the single parameter λ, while normal reliability is a function of T and has the two parameters M and δ. Thus, whether the concern is with reliability during an operating period t or with reliability during later life T, time is the key variable in hardware reliability. In short, there are more opportunities for misfortune the longer equipment is operated.

APPLICABILITY OF TIME IN SOFTWARE RELIABILITY

The foregoing hardware reliability concepts are not totally applicable to software reliability. If we plot detected software errors against time (calendar time, cumulative labor development time, or cumulative equipment operating time), we observe the pattern of Figure 3. Like hardware, there will be an initial period of rapid error detection, followed by some stabilization of the error rate. Unlike hardware, however, there will be no wear-out phase. Perturbations may be introduced by design changes to the software and to a lesser extent by software maintenance. Design changes may produce major jumps in error

FIGURE 3. *Software errors detected vs. time*

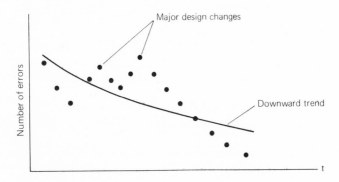

rate due to the initial debugging of new modules. Corrections made during maintenance may introduce new software errors. In general there is a long-term downward trend of error detection (decreasing error rate) but with transient increases (or decreases) in error rate as a result of design and maintenance activity.

There is a fundamental difference between hardware and software as far as the interpretation of the time variable is concerned. In hardware reliability the passage of time is associated with a failure event, i.e., an accumulation of stresses is reached which causes a component to fail. An error in software, on the other hand, was made by the programmer or exists because of an incorrect specification. The passage of time is related to error detection and not to error occurrence; the errors which are detected were made at a previous time. The amount of time (labor or machine) involved in error detection and the probability of error detection are a function of test time, type of test, and choice of test data because these factors determine which part of a program will be exposed to testing and to the possible detection of errors on a particular program path.

OTHER SOFTWARE RELIABILITY DIFFERENCES

It was mentioned previously that hardware has, or is assumed to have, a constant failure rate during its useful life. This is not the case for software. The software error rate and the time between software errors are not constant because of the highly variable factors mentioned in the previous paragraph. Mechanical hardware units exhibit a time between failures which is normally distributed during the wear-out phase (a clustering of failures around the mean life) accompanied by an increasing failure rate. In contrast, software has an indefinite life; in general, it continues to improve with continued testing and use (decreasing error rate), but this trend may be temporarily reversed if major modifications are undertaken.

In hardware reliability there is a dichotomy of events between survival and nonsurvival and between failure and no failure. Software errors are finer grained, ranging from minor clerical mistakes to major errors in logic. Thus, a discussion of software errors and error rates is meaningful only when the type of error and severity are specified. The different error categories are associated with different degrees of reliability such as fully operative, total failure, partially operative (works with certain data), degraded operation, etc.

When hardware components fail, they are usually replaced with working units and the failed units are discarded or repaired off line. A software module with an error cannot be replaced with a good unit; it must be fixed. (An exception to this procedure is the use of fault-tolerant software where an alternate module—one programmed to achieve the same result as the primary module but using a different algorithm—is employed.) When a failed unit is replaced in hardware, an identical unit is used as the replacement. This is not applicable in software, of course, because a copy of the defective program would also be defective. Thus it is necessary to either fix the defective module or replace it with an alternate module which was developed by a different programmer or uses a different algorithm. Obviously, the latter method is the only way to achieve software redundancy; however, the use of redundant modules, as in fault-tolerant software systems, has only been used in high-reliability, real-time applications.

HARDWARE MAINTAINABILITY AND AVAILABILITY

Important aspects of good hardware maintainability are preventive maintenance (identification and replacement of marginal components), operational testing (check-out performed prior to a mission), spare parts provisioning, and the use of diagnostic routines to identify marginal and defective components. These procedures contribute to the reduction of emergency maintenance time, as measured by the mean time to repair r. The debugging phase lasts for the duration of the burn-in period. This action contributes to the improvement of reliability by increasing m. A measure of the time that a system operates without error as a fraction of scheduled operating time is $A = m/(m + r)$, where A defines system availability and $m = \lambda^{-1}$ [1].

MAINTAINABILITY AND AVAILABILITY FOR SOFTWARE

It is customary to think that preventive maintenance and premission testing do not apply to software because it is assumed that once software has been produced, tested, and shown to be "satisfactory," there is no need for field testing because no events will occur between the time of producing the software and its operational use to cause software errors. This is a naive view because one or more of the following could occur: undocumented or unauthorized changes to the software, changes in input data or data base, changes to the hardware or operating system, or changes in operating procedure. Therefore, both preventive maintenance testing and premission testing should be performed on a selective basis. The former would be used to stress critical

176

parts of the software with high input rates and complex sets of input data; the latter would be used in conjunction with hardware readiness checks to ensure the correct functioning of the primary software prior to a mission.

Debugging lasts for the life of software and is not limited to its initial life as in the case of hardware. The reason for this is the inevitable changes that are made to the software in order to improve it and adapt it to new operational requirements.

Unlike hardware, duplicate software units cannot be employed to provide a supply of "spare parts" for replacement purposes, because the "spare" would be defective. If replacement of software is used, it must be with a differently programmed unit which produces the same result as that attempted by the replaced unit.

Although availability is a general expression that can be used as a measure of available system time under any operating condition, it would be incorrect to use $m = \gamma^{-1}$ in the expression $A = m/(m + r)$ (mtr) for software availability because the software error rate is not a constant. Both m and r are highly variable for software. Because of this variability, it is very difficult to predict software availability, i.e., sample data taken at time t to predict m and r at time $t + 1$ will be unrepresentative of m and r at $t + 1$. Therefore, software availability computations are usable for historical purposes only.

HARDWARE FAILURE-DETECTION TECHNIQUES

Hardware failure-detection techniques generally involve the observation of incorrect binary outputs (voltages) when correct binary inputs (voltages) are applied to a circuit. Detection of marginal components involves the observation of incorrect voltage levels in a circuit. The difference between the two is that with the former, the electrical value of the component has changed to the extent that a desired binary 1 is now read as a binary 0, or vice versa, and with the latter the electrical value has changed to the point where it lies outside the range for correctly representing a 1 or 0, thus leading to ambiguity in signal interpretation. Intermittent signal values are the plague of hardware maintenance personnel because of the inability to properly measure the incorrect signal value due to its transient nature.

Fault isolation involves setting up a series of tests (application of given binary inputs) in order to isolate or identify a failed component by virtue of its producing incorrect binary outputs when correct binary inputs are applied. This procedure involves the application of the Boolean logic equations, which govern the operation of the suspected circuits, in such a way that each test of a series of tests eliminates additional circuits as the possible source of the fault until a test is reached where the binary output indicates the location of the fault conclusively.

Hardware error detection techniques rely extensively on the infant mortality property of hardware components. That is to say, it is expected that a high percentage of the marginal components will fail in early life due to the transient voltage spikes induced by power-on and power-off operations. Exclusive of transient effects, just the presence of full voltage applied to some components will cause early failure.

SOFTWARE ERROR-DETECTION TECHNIQUES

One reason hardware debugging is easier and more successful than software debugging is that hardware signal relationships can be represented in a binary format. This property reduces the ambiguity of testing. Software testing, on the other hand, is fraught with ambiguity and cannot be entirely represented by binary or Boolean relationships. Certain software functions cannot be conveniently represented by Boolean equations. Examples of this are memory to memory transfer, iteration count, numerical precision, data base updating, search operations, and input-output transfers. For testing purposes these functions could only be classified as binary if the outcome of the function is defined to be successful or unsuccessful. However, outcomes arranged on a continuous scale are of interest, such as number of words correctly transferred, number of key words correctly located, number of correct data base updates, etc. Thus, software testing is infinitely more complicated than hardware testing. This complexity has led to the development of structured and modular programming; this approach is aimed at error avoidance by means of good programming methods [2]. In other words the strategy is to minimize the need for testing.

The lack of binary representation of software functions makes fault isolation, in the formal sense as used in hardware, very difficult. For one thing, the input values used for testing cannot be represented binarily. "Isolation" must proceed in bigger jumps and less precisely than with hardware. A specific set of input values is used to force a traversal down a particular path of the program in the hope that the instructions associated with an observed error can be identified. Little is known about good testing procedures; this is an area of active research. However, many software practitioners agree that partitioning a program into its paths or execution sequences is a good testing strategy. This is particularly appropriate when the program has been well structured. Then it is easy to identify each construct (If, Then,

Else) or path with a specific set of input data values for the purpose of devising tests. When an error occurs, it is easier to associate an error with a path than in the case of an ill-structured program.

Early mortality and burn-in phase concepts do not exist to a significant extent in software, because faulty software will not necessarily be identified in the early life of the software. There is nothing inherent in the operation of software which would force the failure of "marginal components." The occurrence of an error is largely a function of the selection of test data, if testing, or operating conditions (output requirements), if performing production work. This situation suggests the use of saturation testing, involving the use of complex sets of input data, including extreme values, in an attempt to force errors which may be present.

CONCEPTS AND TECHNIQUES FOR SOFTWARE RELIABILITY

It has been mentioned that structure is important as a technique for designing programs in order to minimize error commission during programming. In a broader sense, structure, or its related attribute complexity, can be used by management as a quantitative control of program production and as a means of devising testing strategies [3,4,5,6]. In order to use these techniques, it is necessary to represent a program as a directed graph [7]. This is not difficult to do since a directed graph has some properties in common with a flowchart and, if a decision table is used to represent program logic rather than a flowchart, the decision table can be readily translated to a directed graph. Once a program is represented as a directed graph, the structural properties (number of paths) can be used as measures of program complexity. Management can use these measures to prevent excessive program complexity. This is desirable because it has been demonstrated that there is a strong relationship between complexity and number of errors, error-detection time, and error-correction time [8]. Computer programs are available for computing complexity values from the definition of a directed graph.

Management can also use complexity measures as a means of allocating resources to testing, i.e., personnel and computer time are allocated in proportion to the complexity of a series of programs which are to undergo testing. Since test resources are limited, it is desirable to optimize their use. Complexity measures provide a quantitative basis for this management decision. In the past, intuitive notions of complexity have been used in some organizations to manage programming and testing. Number of statements has been the most frequently used quantitative measure of programming and debugging difficulty. Although number of statements is significantly correlated with programming errors and difficulty of testing, it is inadequate for conveying all aspects of complexity (structure).

This has been a brief introduction to the concept of program structure as a means of improving and controlling software reliability. The interested reader is referred to the references given in this section for details. An important aspect of software reliability which has not been covered is the effect of quality of specifications on quality of software. In this area, as in the case of programming, structure is the key, as evidenced by the recent activity in the field of structured design.

SUMMARY

Although time is critical to hardware reliability, it is of little importance to software reliability. Other characteristics of hardware reliability, such as burn-in, constant failure rate and wear-out, are also not applicable to software reliability. It has also been shown that hardware maintainability and availability concepts, such as replacement of failed units with spare parts, have no counterparts in the software world. On the other hand, operational testing, when tailored to the characteristics of software, has as much validity for software as for hardware. The inability to express software functions in the form of Boolean equations prevents the use of fault isolation techniques as used in hardware maintenance. Partitioning of programs into paths for testing and error analysis purposes is the more appropriate technique for software. Finally, the structure of software is a key consideration for improving and controlling software reliability.

References

1. Bazovsky, Igor. *Reliability Theory and Practice.* Englewood Cliffs, N.J.: Prentice-Hall, 1961.
2. Dijkstra, Edsger W. "Notes on Structured Programming," in *Structured Programming.* New York: Academic Press, 1972.
3. Bradley, G. H.; Green, T. F.; Howard, G. T.; and Schneidewind, N. F. "Structure and Error Detection in Computer Software," *Proceedings, AIEE Conference,* 1975, pp. 54–59.
4. Green, T. F.; Schneidewind, N. F.; Howard, G. T.; and Pariseau, R. "Program Structures, Complexity and Error Characteristics," *Computer Software Engineering,* Polytechnic Institute of New York, 1976, pp. 139–154.

5. Schneidewind, N. F. "The Use of Simulation in the Evaluation of Software," *Computer,* IEEE Computer Society, April 1977, pp. 47-53.
6. McCabe, T. J. "A Complexity Measure," *IEEE Transactions on Software Engineering,* vol. SE-2, no. 4, December 1976, pp. 308-320.
7. Chan, Shu-Park. *Introductory Topological Analysis of Electrical Networks.* New York: Holt, Rinehart and Winston, Inc., 1969.
8. Schneidewind, N. F. and Hoffman, H. M. "Experiments in Software Error Data Collection and Analysis," *Proceedings of the Sixth Texas Conference on Computing,* University of Texas at Austin, November 1977, pp. 4A1-4A12.

PART THREE

Practices for Software Quality Management

CHAPTER 12

Design Practices to Effect Software Quality

LAWRENCE J. PETERS

INTRODUCTION

Quality is a property of software which is designed in rather than added as an afterthought or infused via programming standards. Like beauty, quality is in the eye of the beholder. It resists serious attempts at quantification. A variety of software design methods and practices [1] have been publicized which are purported to ensure quality software. But these are primarily directed at localized technical issues related to the execution of an assumed overall plan directed at quality software. What are these higher-level issues and how may they be addressed in such a way as to encourage quality software? This chapter will discuss management approaches which will encourage the design of quality software.

COMPONENTS OF SOFTWARE QUALITY

Software quality is often thought of as consisting of a number of "ility's." For example, extensibility, understandability, etc. [2]. In this discussion, the perspective will be from the standpoint of the following software quality components:

Maintainability—the degree to which the structure and organization of the software system is externalized. Particularly important is the design rationale behind this structure.

Efficiency—the degree to which the software design matches the minimal or optimal design for this algorithm.

Extensibility—the level of coherence exhibited by each individual portion of the software such that it can be enhanced or its functions added to with no more than local impacts.

Reliability—the apparent degree to which the design is responsive to the user's requirements—not only meet his requirements as perceived by the designer but as perceived by the user himself.

Although a causal link between these quality elements and design practices has not been rigorously proven, it is intuitively obvious that "good" designs will result in software which exhibits these qualities. Several software design methods have been promoted [3,4,5,6] which claim to produce such "good" designs. But only one has provided any help to the designer in assessing how "good" his design is [3]. If, however, the use of a design method alone were sufficient to ensure quality software, then why is there still much concern? More than a method alone is needed.

IMPEDIMENTS TO QUALITY SOFTWARE

The act of design has been characterized by at least one design theorist as being "wicked" [8]. The thrust of this characterization was that designers (and those directing their efforts) are in the disquieting position of not having a well-defined, sequential set of steps to perform. Instead, it is not always clear how one is to proceed nor even where to proceed to. On another level, those managing the process have even less direction. Several important sources of difficulty exist. These are discussed in the text which follows.

Levels of Issues

Not all design issues have the same scope of effect or implications with respect to software quality. However, the fact that there are two major classes of design issues is often overlooked. One class of issues relates to the overall architecture of the system. The other class relates to the structure and operation of individual elements within the system. Failure to recognize and address both classes results in systems whose architecture is poor but whose individual components are outstanding, and vice versa.

186

Clearly, localized detailed design issues are easier to deal with and less frustrating than larger, system-level issues. For example, is it easier to discuss screen formats for an interactive graphics system or the appropriate philosophy on which to base the system architecture?

Changing Requirements

Much of this "wickedness" of software design comes from the fact that the problem we are attempting to solve is changing while we are solving it. Some of these changes come from the refinement of the designer's understanding of the problem, while others come from changes in the problem statement itself. Both result in destabilizing the design activity with the predictable result that overall quality is reduced.

The linking of problem elements also reduces the manageability of requirements definition and change. For example, the classic problem of program size and execution time demonstrates the difficulty of modifying one requirement without affecting the other.

A higher-level issue remains, however: Can the requirements for a software system be specified without the prior existence of a model or conceptual notion of the system? The existence of such a model implies that some rudimentary design work has taken place.

Inflexible Approach

With pressures from management, peer groups, and salesmen from professional education firms, many organizations have adopted specific design methods. These have been used, in many cases, with religious zeal. However, many of the software design problems an organization addresses may not be well suited to the method the company has adopted. This can result in force fitting the problem to the solution approach.

REALIZING DESIGN QUALITY POTENTIAL

The previous paragraphs discussed some of the common impediments to attaining quality software. These imply some solutions. The topics to be presented next are merely approaches and not intended as specific rules, since the details of given situations and a given company will dictate an individualized course of action.

The key factor to keep in mind is that the facets described below are something of a shopping list. The items selected from the list must be chosen with the characteristics of the user, customer, developing organization, and individual contributors in mind.

Design Integrity

The perception of quality by an observer depends largely on the structure and organization presented to him. But, more importantly, the level of organization perceived is a function of the degree to which the various elements of the system are linked together via an overall theme. The observer may not even be consciously aware of the theme but its absence will be obvious. In a book on software engineering [9] the critical need for conceptual integrity in software systems is pointed out. What this translates into for software is the need to:

    a. Prudently define the architecture of the system.
    b. Externalize this process and subject it to close scrutiny by colleagues and other project members.
    c. Consciously organize the discernible parts of the system and review/revise this organization early on.

When reviewing a design, the overall theme on which it is based should be obvious. The key question to be answered is, why? That is, why did the designer(s) configure the system that particular way? Some of the more familiar answers to this type of inquiry by reviewers include:

It is the "best."
It is the only one we could come up with under the circumstances.
It is similar to one we read about.
We built something like this before.
The equivalent of, " . . . no reason for it, we just did it that way."

Some of the less familiar answers to such queries include:

This architecture is designed to provide three levels of controlled system degradation without catastrophic loss of service.

Modularization has been designed to facilitate introductions of new features planned for next year.

This scheme maximizes the use of existing application software.

Software quality is more than what is in the eye of the beholder. Instead, the key issue is what will management (or customer) settle for. Insisting that the architecture of a system, or even a small portion of it, be justified produces new insights and nuances about the system. Experience has shown that such insight reduces errors and inefficiencies as well as improves other qualities of the product.

Rationalize Design

The need to externalize the large or architectural decisions should not be confused with the need to externalize the small or local issues. The latter relate to decisions on how detailed requirements will be met. Several approaches are possible but only a relative few have a rationalized basis. In this case, rationalized basis refers to the overall guidelines employed in meeting detailed requirements. Such guidelines are referred to as rationales. Many approaches to software design have been published but only a relative few include a rationale. They all include useful techniques. An approach which consists of techniques and a unifying rationale by which these can be employed is referred to as a method [1]. Examples of software design rationales include:

Data structure holds the key to effective software design [4,5].

Data flow is the key to successful software design [3,10].

Examples of techniques include:

Iteratively refining the design in a stepwise fashion [6].

Use of specialized graphics such as bubble charts [10], data structure diagrams [4,5], and specialized flow diagrams [11].

The advantage of a method over a technique may not be obvious. In trivial design tasks, almost anything will do. This stems from the fact that the boundaries of the problem are such that it can be mentally "surrounded" with relative ease. The course to a solution is clear. Success is assured. However, more complex problems are not surroundable. It is often not apparent how one is to proceed. In these latter instances, techniques alone provide no guidance. Methods, on the other hand, provide enough guidance at a high level to focus attention on the more critical issues. They capture the "what" and, in principle, the "how," the details of "how" being left to the user. Clearly, methods are more effective at addressing complex design problems.

Know Your User

Most of us have been involved with at least one software tool or system which failed because of user dissatisfaction. The system may have been elegant in its use of modern programming practices but was rejected. Why? In most cases, the user did not perceive the system as meeting his needs. Whether it did or not is unimportant. A number of design-related methods are available which can be effective in addressing this problem.

189

The development and maintenance of a user model begins during the analysis and requirements definition phases. It can be as simple as a few flow diagrams with accompanying text or as involved as a complete model of the customer's operation.

The goal is to maintain an externalized form of how the user is viewed. Present this to the user and encourage him to comment on its accuracy. Where they have been employed, user models have resulted in benefits which include:

The realization by the user that the designer(s) cares about his problem and recognition that the user is best qualified to comment on it.

A rudimentary understanding of how the system works.

An acceptance of the system without serious reservations, since surprises are few and the user identifies with its configuration since he has had a hand in it.

What does a user model look like? Several methods [10,12,13,14] are available which can act as a means of answering this query. Basically, a user model is a depiction of the data, relationships, and activities within which the user (and the proposed system) functions. It captures those necessary environmental factors which allow the designer to determine that what he is designing is well suited and effective.

Match Problem and Solution

A tacit assumption made by those who promote one method or technique or another is that it will work on every problem encountered. For example, we don't see statements like, "If your problem does not look like this, don't use my method." Remember, each method or technique is directed at an idealized "typical" sort of problem. It is based on the author's experience and biases. They may not be the same as those needed on a given project.

Don't be afraid to invent! In a recent unscientific survey conducted by this author of users of certain widely publicized design methods, it was found that those interviewed were reluctant to divulge their design documents. Each of these designs was based on a particular method that the organization or company had received training in. When these people were "pressed" about their hesitation, they confided that they did not employ the method quite the way it was supposed to be. They modified it to suit such factors as:

Characteristics of the problem
Personnel involved

Customer-imposed constraints
Management fiat
Schedule/cost considerations
Computing resource constraints

What they did was really software engineering. They composed an effective approach to solving their problem. This composition consisted of known elements and some that were invented extemporaneously.

An example of the kinds of characteristics needed to match problem and solution method [1] is shown in Figure 1.

One additional suggestion regarding the suitability of a particular approach to your problem is to examine the types of examples used by authors to demonstrate the use of the method or to relate experiences with it. Do these sample problems look anything like yours? Are they even close?

Externalize Design Decisions

If a design is viewed as containing some strange or mysterious nuances, it will likely be changed or judged to be of poor quality. Quality software must meet user needs. It may not be something that would be gladly published by some academic journal, but it works effectively. This means the design was tailored, where necessary, to meet a unique set of requirements and environmental constraints. The basis for some of these subtleties in the design are not always obvious to the casual reviewer. Sometimes they may not even be obvious to the designer himself. Often, habits are formed and retained unconsciously.

The use of peer group reviews [15] of code and designs has been advocated for some time. The main advantage is to force the designer to consciously "walk through" the design and identify any "fuzzy" thinking that may be present. Certainly, peers will help to identify problems, but externalizing design decisions takes the design of quality software out of the realm of magic and into the experience base of other designers.

Define Design Objectives

The effectiveness of the software being designed can be the result of an accident or a conscious act. This effectiveness is often the primary means by which the customer views software quality. But other, more technical factors also exist which relate to quality. Often, the target that was aimed at when design activity began gets obscured by detailed issues and frenetic activity.

191

FIGURE 1. *Areas of application of software design methods**

Method	Specialized graphics	Defined procedure(s)	Training support	Tutorial documents
1. *Structured design*	use structure charts for system architecture	an iterative framework which guides the solution development	two courses offered by Yourdon, Inc.	book by Yourdon & Constantine; book by G. J. Myers
2. *The Jackson methodology*	tree-like charts for data structures	loosely defined guidelines to address various problems	two-week course offered through Infotech	book by Jackson (challenge to read) presented via examples
3. *Logical construction of programs*	use Warnier chart for data structure	well-defined set of procedures at all levels of detail	incorporated in a course offered by Infotech	book by J.-D. Warnier
4. *Meta-stepwise refinement*	use a tree diagram for program structure	high-level guidelines for the basic steps	no formal offerings	book by H. F. Ledgard
5. *Higher order software*	structured flowcharts for control structure	mostly theoretical discussion(s) with limited operational details	by arrangement with Higher Order Software	no formal text, several papers in journals

Method-Attribute

	Requirements traceability	Known experience base	Compatibility with other techniques/schemes	Area of application	Evaluation (quality) criteria
1.	designer's responsibility	up to 5 years experience within firms like IBM & Hughes	usable with any module design strategy	systems whose data flow can be communicated graphically	a well-defined set of design heuristics
2.	designer's responsibility	early versions available since 1972 with emphasis on business application	usable with other data structuring methods	business & other systems with well-understood data structure(s)	verify compliance with basic assumptions
3.	designer's responsibility	extensive use throughout Europe & other foreign countries	procedural nature would limit compatibility	business & other systems with well-understood data structure(s)	verify compliance with basic assumptions
4.	designer's responsibility	primarily limited to theoretical developments	would benefit from design evaluation criteria	applications with well-understood, stable requirements	no specific guidelines
5.	potentially available through an analyzer	proposed application on NASA Space Shuttle program	would benefit from design guidelines	applications with high reliability requirements	primarily automated analysis of design

The concept of defining objectives or quality targets for the design to hit is not a new one. But often, objectives are not stated in a measurable, concise, and disciplined manner. This makes the evaluation of a system subjective, but, more importantly, design activity meanders since no clear goals are in sight. Objectives which can be clearly defined as goals contain at least three necessary elements:

    a. A statement of the problem, or problem element, addressed.

    b. A statement of the objective of the design solution phrased so as to be measurable.

    c. A statement of the criterion or measurement mechanism by which the attainment of the objective can be measured.

For example, a high-level objective may be stated as follows:

Problem: The response time for seat-availability queries is too high.

Objective: Reduce response time for such queries.

This translates into what is perhaps the most common objective of software systems, "improve customer service." How will we know if this objective is ever met? A restatement may improve matters:

Problem: The response time for seat-availability queries is averaging 5 seconds. This is approximately 2 seconds too high.

Objective: Reduce average response time for seat-availability queries by at least 2 seconds.

Measurement criterion: Response time is defined as the elapsed time from depression of the enter key until the entire response appears on the screen given the hardware environment is functioning properly and the query rate does not exceed n queries per second . . .

The above is measurable. It may, in fact, have all the appearances of a requirement. It is a requirement — one on which the design can be tested and measured. Such statements tend to focus design activity toward externalized, quality-oriented goals.

An example of a form which could be employed to make use of this technique is shown in Figure 2. Note that the numbers of primary objectives should be kept manageably low; for instance, seven or less would be advisable.

An additional benefit of defining objectives is that test cases and performance limitations are being defined as well. This provides the code-testing activity with a measurable indication of what the code was intended to do. The advantage of this lies in the fact that basing testing on what is in the code tests the code to see that it does what it does—

FIGURE 2. *Sample design objectives form*

Priority	Problem	Objective	Measurement criterion	Test case no.
Two Levels: Primary & Second-ary	Simple state-ment of problem addressed.	These state-ments must be measurable.	Specific descrip-tion of how user will know the ob-jective has been met.	This may alternately be used to identify the section(s) in the test plan which re-late to this objective.

Each of the above is required for all objectives.

not what it was intended to do. Thus, employing measurable objectives can close the gap between the design and the resulting code.

CONCLUSIONS

The quality of a software product is a function of several unquantifiable variables. The design practices employed to attain a desired quality (qualities) or acceptance level must be engineered to quantify the form quality takes in each instance. Not all the techniques discussed here are suitable in every software design effort. Thus, there is no single key to successful production of quality software. Rather, the key to success must be fashioned to suit the "lock." Although there exists underlying concepts, as discussed here, which aid in fashioning such keys, success is an individualized phenomenon.

References

1. Peters, L. J. and Tripp, L. L. "Comparing Software Design Methodologies," *Datamation*, vol. 21, no. 11, November 1977, pp. 89–94.
2. Boehm, B. et al. *Characteristics of Software Quality*. TRW Series on Software Technology. New York: North-Holland Publishers, Inc., 1978.
3. Stevens, W. P.; Myers, G. J.; and Constantine, L. L. "Structured Design," *IBM Systems Journal*, 2, 1974, pp. 115–139.
4. Warnier, J. D. *Logical Construction of Programs*. Leiden: H. E. Stenfert Kroese B. V., 1974.
5. Jackson, M. A. *Principles of Program Design*. New York: Academic Press, 1975.

6. Wirth, N. "Program Development by Stepwise Refinement," *Communications of the ACM,* vol. 14, November 4, 1971, pp. 221-227.

7. Rittel, H. W. J., as described in *Basic Questions of Design Theory,* Bazjanac, V., editor. New York: American Elsevier Publishing Co., Inc., 1974.

8. Peters, L. J. and Tripp, L. L. "Is Software Design Wicked?" *Datamation,* vol. 22, no. 6, June 1976, pp. 127-136.

9. Brooks, F. P., Jr. *The Mythical Man-Month.* Reading, Mass: Addison-Wesley Publishing, 1975.

10. Yourdon, E. and Constantine, L.L. "Structured Design." New York: Yourdon, Inc., 1975.

11. Peters, L. J. and Tripp, L. L. "Design Representation Schemes," *Proceedings of the MRI Symposium on Software Engineering,* 1977.

12. Stevens, S. A. and Tripp, L. L. "Requirements Expression and Validation Aid," Proceedings of the Third International Conference on Software Engineering, 1978.

13. Ross, D. T. and Brackett, J. W. "An Approach to Structured Analysis," *Computer Decisions,* September 1976, pp. 40-44.

14. DeMarco, T. "Structured Analysis and System Specification." New York: Yourdon, Inc., 1978.

15. Weinberg, G. M. *The Psychology of Computer Programming.* New York: Van Nostrand Rheinhold, 1971.

CHAPTER 13

Programming Practices for Increased Software Quality

JOHN R. BROWN

INTRODUCTION

It is safe to say that there has been great progress toward an improved software engineering discipline during the past decade. It is safe because nearly everybody wants to believe it is true, and it is very difficult to find evidence to dispute the claim. It is also difficult to find supporting evidence despite (1) our intuition, (2) much data collection in the last few years, (3) the fact that some of the newly introduced modern programming practices came about as cures for serious software production ailments, and (4) substantially increased attention to the cost and quality of producing complex software.

A few important attempts to measure our progress have been made. This chapter focuses primarily on one such recent attempt sponsored by the U.S. Air Force at Rome Air Development Center (RADC). Several years ago RADC initiated six studies aimed at evaluating the extent of improvement achieved by selected contractors through the application of differing programming practices. These studies were accomplished by Boeing Computer Services, Computer Sciences Corporation, Martin-Marietta, System Development Corporation, TRW, and Sperry Univac [1,2,3,4,5,6]. RADC initiated the studies by formulating and stating the following hypothesis:

Rules governing software development, if rigorously defined and applied, and supported by modern techniques and tools, make possible the production of higher quality software at lower than usual cost.

Each contractor was subsequently expected to identify and examine available evidence to assess the impact of modern programming practices on systems development and attempt to confirm and (where possible) quantify the hypothesis. The references provide elaborate detail on the objectives, approaches, activities, and findings of the individual studies; there is no need nor intent to report in similar depth here. It is the intent to concentrate on general study conclusions which are common to most of the contractors and to summarize these results. We hope to show also that there is much yet to be done in the progressive evolution of a truly improved software engineering discipline and, in fact, that the evolution itself will require a highly disciplined approach if needed improvements are to be achieved within the next decade.

EVOLUTION OF MODERN PROGRAMMING PRACTICES (MPP)

The emergence of a discipline of software engineering has been more of a happening than an accomplishment. In fact, the only proven engineering technique applied to the establishment of improved modern programming practices (MPP) is the well-known practice of trial and error.

There are, of course, many problems that have plagued software development over the years. People seeking to invent and use disciplined approaches to software engineering have done so primarily to reduce or completely eliminate the problems and their often serious consequences. The complete list of such problems is long, but some of the more typical include:

Cost overrun
Poor visibility of development status/problems
Unreliability
Hard to maintain (brittle)
Poor requirements
Inefficient use of resources
Schedule overrun
Loss of project control
Lack of conclusive testing
Poor documentation

The practices invented to address these problems both singly and in limited combinations make up a much longer list of techniques, tools, procedures, concepts, and organizational approaches than the list of sample MPP identified and described here:

REQUIREMENTS ANALYSIS AND VALIDATION TOOLS: Automated aids and techniques which support the precise definition/specification of software requirements and further aid in verification of the completeness and consistency of the contents of the specification prior to design. Examples are the Computer Aided Requirements Analyzer (CARA), Systematic Activity Modelling Method (SAMM) and automated SAMM Interactive Graphics System (SIGS), the Structured Analysis and Design Technique (SADT), and the Software Requirements Engineering Methodology (SREM).

PROJECT MANAGER CONCEPT: An organizational aspect of software development which stresses total responsibility and authority of a single individual, the project manager, to lead a team of qualified individuals in application of varied skills required to accomplish the goals of the project. A key responsibility is to separate and delegate responsibilities and authority to other members of the team, thus focusing project manager attention to general, long-term project direction, financial/schedule planning and control, and interaction with the customer and other external interfaces.

TOP-DOWN DESIGN: An approach to both the formulation and presentation of a design solution which involves an initial statement of problem/solution at the highest possible functional level, followed by successive elaborative design iterations which decompose, refine, and more fully define component functions and all functional interactions. Techniques used to illustrate designs as they evolve top down include hierarchical charts, call trees, and SAMM, SADT and Hierarchy plus Input-Process-Output (HIPO) diagrams.

INCREMENTAL DEVELOPMENT: The identification, design, coding, and testing of functionally meaningful subsets (i.e., increments) of the overall software system wherein each increment (1) is a self-sufficient, executable, and testable portion of the complete software capability and (2) adds to or builds upon the preceding increment.

ENFORCED PROGRAMMING STANDARDS: The establishment and enforcement of standard programming practices and strict rules to direct the efforts of developers in the production of code and documentation which meets or surpasses adopted standards. This includes definition of certain practices which must be followed, identification of other practices which are not permitted, and active review process to ensure compliance with the rules and achievement of the standards. Typical practices are standard methods for structuring programs, use of program commentary, naming conventions, data initialization requirements, sharing of data by multiple program components, format and ordering of statement labels, modularity requirements, and restricted use of certain control statements such as GO TO.

FORMAL SPECIFICATION AND ANALYSIS OF REQUIREMENTS: A highly systematic approach to the preparation, communication and evaluation of requirements during early stages of project activity. Includes (1) development of a formal document, usually in accordance with a prescribed specification standard of format and content; (2) performance of in-depth analyses of the specified requirements, often with support of simulation and other techniques aimed at demonstrating reasonableness of performance characteristics and exploring alternatives; and (3) performance of a comprehensive requirements specification review and conducting one or more formal review meetings as necessary to investigate and resolve problems and permit baselining of an approved, official specification.

PHASED PRODUCTION APPROACH: A systematic, formalized approach used most often in producing large-scale software systems. The development process is viewed as a sequence of distinct but strongly connected phases such as requirements definition, preliminary design, detailed design, implementation, test, and operations and maintenance. In actual practice the development process may involve repetition of some phases and iterative completion of phases in combination, e.g., where preliminary design analyses lead to further refinement and more detailed specification of requirements and vice versa.

IN-PROCESS DOCUMENTATION: The generation, maintenance and review of a single source document in keeping with an established "document-as-you-go" policy. Preparation of the document (or notebook or folder) is initiated very early in the development activity. The document is incrementally completed as the contents become available, including all pertinent development and test information (requirements, design data, code, flow diagrams, test plans, test results, etc.). Often the document contains a cover sheet specifying a detailed development plan (i.e., programmer estimates of completion dates for intermediate milestones) and providing a means for indicating actual completion dates and review events to depict the status of each software unit.

200

INDEPENDENT TESTING: The performance of formal testing by a team of testing specialists which is organizationally separate from the group or groups responsible for software design, code, debug and development testing. Test team activities include analysis of software requirements; planning; preparation and performance of tests; review of test results for satisfaction of requirements; identification, reporting, and analysis of discrepancies between expected and actual performance; and, re-testing after discrepancies are resolved and fixes made by the developers.

SOFTWARE DEVELOPMENT AND TEST TOOLS: The general practice of making extensive use of automated tools for differing purposes and at various stages throughout the software development process. Popular tools include simulators, data base definition/construction aids, flow-charters, static data flow analyzers, test monitors, editors, coding standards auditors, cross-reference aids, comparators, and test data generators.

FORMAL SOFTWARE CONFIGURATION MANAGEMENT: The establishment and adherence to formal management principles, policies, and procedures specifically calling for rigorous review and acceptance of contractual and internal baselines and supported by formal procedures and techniques for (1) configuration identification and documentation, (2) configuration change evaluation and status accounting, (3) change control, and (4) configuration verification. Configuration management calls for identification of a series of baselines and ensures that appropriate care be taken to maintain control of change in the transition between baselines throughout the development process.

FORMAL INSPECTION OF DESIGN AND CODE: A formal practice of conducting independent and unbiased reviews to permit assessment of the quality of software products, most often design documentation and source code. Includes formal inspection techniques such as peer group critiques and walk-throughs, quality assurance reviews and audits, and design reviews.

INDEPENDENT SOFTWARE QUALITY ASSURANCE: The establishment and adherence to a systematic approach oriented toward achievement of specific, desired software qualities. Generally involves creation of an independent team with responsibility and authority to define and conduct quality reviews of all software products as necessary to determine and ensure that acceptable quality levels are reached prior to delivery. Typical software quality assurance tasks involve definition and enforcement of standard programming practices; planning and conducting a comprehensive program of reviews, audits, and inspections spanning all software products, analysis and identification of customer quality requirements; support to and witnessing of independent testing; and, often, direction of software configuration management and discrepancy reporting activities.

EGO-LESS PROGRAMMING: A team approach to software development which stresses the combined team contribution (through systematic, continuous collaboration and coordination of team member efforts) while de-emphasizing (i.e., depersonalizing) the individual contribution. The team jointly designs the program modules, individuals code them, and all team members review and approve each module, thus achieving a total team responsibility sense of ownership for the program.

CHIEF PROGRAMMER TEAM: A highly structured team approach to software development. Team members generally include one chief programmer who designs and develops critical program components and directs efforts of all team members; one or more back-up programmers who work on less critical components; and a clerk or librarian responsible for general administrative functions, programming support, and day-to-day configuration management tasks.

STRUCTURED PROGRAMMING: A practice that has been at times defined as "top-down development with chief programmer teams aided by the program support library," but actually refers to the restricted use of limited control structures in the coding of a program, in particular the "sequence," "if-then-else," and "do-while" constructs. Most structured coding standards also permit use of the "do-until" and "case" constructs. The coding of programs in accordance with the standard is often facilitated by a structured programming language and preprocessor which translates to a source language appropriate for the target computer.

PROGRAM SUPPORT LIBRARY: A practice involving creation and use of a central facility for storing and handling all computer program development information. The support library concept often includes a broad range of informal configuration management, administrative, and technical development support functions and is staffed with both personnel and tools appropriate for such tasks.

BASELINING OF REQUIREMENTS SPECIFICATION: The development, review, customer acceptance, and documentation of the software requirements specification to be used as a formal, approved baseline for subsequent phases of software development. The formal baselining event usually occurs just after completion of the requirements specification and considerably before the first software design review. The baseline serves as evidence of a mutual understanding and written agreement as to proper interpretation of mandatory provisions of the requirements specifications which are the basis for software end-item acceptance.

The manner in which MPP have evolved suggests that there is some extent to which the full range of problems can be combatted by an equally full set of MPP. Unfortunately, we have had very little insight into the actual effectiveness of applied practices and have had difficulty answering questions such as:

Has the evolution of modern, innovative methods had a significant, favorable influence on software cost and quality?

If so, how much?

Are some methods "better" than others?

Can a "best" combination of methods be found?

MEASURING THE VALUE OF MPP

Historically, the Air Force, specifically RADC, has played an important part in the establishment of many of these modern practices. Several years ago RADC, in seeking to more fully support evolution of truly worthwhile practices, decided it was time to make a serious effort to answer the above questions and contracted for the six MPP studies mentioned previously. This set of studies was one of the first serious and comprehensive attempts to evaluate the impact of MPP. For this reason, each contractor was given a good deal of latitude with respect to the study approach taken and the particular practices evaluated. Nevertheless, there was a fair amount of commonality (in a generic sense) among those practices chosen, and relatively general agreement among contractors concerning some important study findings. One area of surprisingly strong general agreement was in the overall relative magnitude of the positive impact of practices on cost and quality issues. Generally speaking, the following pattern was observed:

Highest impact practices

Formal specification and analysis of requirements
Top-down, rigorous design methodology

Next highest impact practices

Phased, incremental production approach
In-process documentation
Development and test tools

Next highest impact practices

Independent testing
Enforced programming standards

In addition to the preceding relative ranking of the importance of practices, the study contractors found other specific points of agreement as well, namely:
Software requirements must be identified and baselined prior to implementation.

If software requirements are not baselined and controlled:

There is no way to tell what the software is supposed to do.
There is no way to tell if the software does what it should.
Talk of productivity is baseless and clouded with uncertainty.

Requirements should be defined (at least in part) by an organization independent from the implementers.

Requirements are commonly misunderstood.

Standardization, whether applied to data, to program, to interfaces, to documentation format and content, to naming conventions, or any other facet of software, has a positive, beneficial effect on configuration management, conservation of resources, and reduction of errors.

Quality must be designed into software; it can't be tacked on by testing.

Rushing software development and taking shortcuts usually results in lower rather than higher quality and productivity.

It is important in testing to demonstrate that a program meets its requirements and to exercise all of the code.

Project reviews for customer involvement and for visibility and control are essential.

For meaningful measures of project progress, critical project events and recognizable milestones must be defined.

Changes to baselined and formally controlled products should be permitted only after careful analysis of cost and schedule impact.

Structured programming is many things to many people; the discipline associated with uniform adherence to structured design and coding standards has resulted in higher quality software; all in all, structured programming has not been a panacea for software production ills as many promised.

Greater emphasis (e.g., more thorough analysis, extensive research, detailed review, and broader participation) in requirements and design phases leads to significant reductions in both the frequency and seriousness of problems with software throughout the life cycle.

Another especially general study finding was that all of the modern programming practices were evaluated to have a substantial positive impact on the production of software of higher than usual quality, but the assessments of MPP impact on cost were mixed. There are several reasons for this outcome, the most noticeable being the diverse definitions of "cost" used by the different contractors. For instance, some studied the impact of MPP on initial system development cost, others studied life cycle development cost, and yet others examined MPP in the context of the total system life cycle including long-term operations and maintenance. In fact, some negative cost impact was reported in some cases where the cost of implementing a practice (including automated tool development, documentation, training, etc.) was not prorated over either the total life cycle of a major software system or a number of different applications. For the most part, however, the studies at least strongly suggested that MPP, if properly implemented and carefully applied, should have (and in most cases have had) a positive life cycle cost payoff. Especially important elements of the implementation and application of MPP which bear strongly on their ultimate impact include:

Completeness of definition
Consistency of application
Severity of the problem being addressed
Timeliness of introduction into the project environment
Tailoring to needs of the actual users

RESEARCH AND DEVELOPMENT OF MPP

Completion of the MPP evaluation studies has helped, as expected, to determine both the nature and the magnitude achieved to date of an increased software engineering discipline. As was initially hypothesized, the results indicate that important progress toward an improved software production technology and methodology has been made. They clearly indicate, however, that there is still much more room for further improvement. For example, much has been done to directly combat critical quality problems and where existing practices are being applied regularly, the overall influence (although perhaps not measured precisely) is strongly felt to be substantial and positive. However, there are numerous on-going projects both large and small for which there has been limited (if any) use of powerful practices when and where they are clearly needed. This points up several vital avenues of research and development yet to be seriously undertaken. The first area of need is in research required to formalize and generalize some of the more widely useful and established practices. This research must concentrate on human engineering of tools, techniques, and procedures if we expect to achieve more widespread, cost-effective use of improved practices. We must also investigate and provide for the acquisition and application of specialized tools and must find ways to transfer all kinds of practices (not just the automated tools) from one environment to another.

Another broad area of important research and development is in the study and constructive definition of modern programming environments. Significant progress in this area will require much supporting work in development of:

Standardized software engineering definitions and terminology and valid measures of the impact of practices.

Better (e.g., more direct) techniques for assessing and predicting practice impact.

Rational and reliable approaches for selection of certain practices to meet the specific needs of a particular project and/or programming environment.

A third extremely important area of investigation is in the extension and refinement of existing practices as necessary to fully address other continuing and critical production problems. It seems clear that as time goes by, systems become more complex and critical, more and more people become involved, and the need for more people-to-people communication increases. In light of the rising cost of both people and communications, we can avoid losing the ground we have fought so hard to gain only if we see to it that current practices are refined and, if necessary, reoriented to specifically address the likely people-to-people communication problems of the future.

In summary, future progress toward more effective MPP will depend largely upon research and development in areas of:

Methods for increasing the ready availability of practices for newly identified applications and making the practices easier and more natural to use.

Study, definition, and construction of modern programming environments which offer flexible selection of appropriate practices for differing types of production efforts.

Continued study of new and better MPP to cope with persistent critical issues including software reliability, maintainability, and, above all, life cycle software cost.

MODERN PROGRAMMING PRACTICES — THE FUTURE

The above-mentioned areas of MPP research and development are very important. Perhaps even more important to ultimate MPP effectiveness, however, is the basic approach taken to further the evolution of the practices. In this regard, we can learn a great deal from the general MPP study results which stress the high value of (1) formal definition, baselining, and control of requirements, (2) top-down design, and (3) a phased, incremental production approach. That is, the same kind of systematic formalism, rigor, and production control that has effectively improved the development of software can and should be applied (with similar success) to the formulation of the MPP of the future. In much the same way that we have learned that we build better software at less cost when we begin with an agreed-to understanding of what it's supposed to do (i.e., the requirements), we certainly should be able to implement better modern practices based upon a clear specification of need for an improved software engineering discipline. The more definitive the need, the more likely we will know what manner of impact to expect (e.g., higher reliability at slightly increased cost, easier to maintain but somewhat less efficient, etc.) and the easier it will be to measure the impact and thus determine how well the practice satisfies the requirements for it. Quite possibly the difficulty encountered in evaluating and quantifying the impact of MPP in past efforts will be lessened as more formal treatment of MPP requirements is achieved.

Another serious problem which has limited the effectiveness of MPP has been an almost total lack of coordination present in the parallel definition and implementation of practices which are ultimately applied to the same system development. Only rarely do we find a pair of practices which smoothly interface; more often we see that they in some way detract from the potential positive benefit of each other. A partial solution to this problem can come from top-down design wherein the possible combinations of practices are considered and strict attention is given to the design of a fully integrated set of practices which are more mutually supportive than we have seen in the past. Even more progress can be made in this direction through a phased, incremental approach to MPP development. This approach would encourage the quest for an improved software engineering discipline to tackle the most critical needs first, followed later by those which are more icing on the cake. In addition there would be an opportunity and responsibility to incrementally evaluate the effectiveness of individual practices and combinations and, where actual impact falls short of that desired, redesign and refine as necessary.

All in all, we are simply suggesting that we should apply modern programming practices to themselves — that is, to live up to good, known standards as we search for and set new ones.

References

1. Brown, J. R. *Impact of MPP on System Development,* TRW Final Technical Report No. RADC-TR-77-121, May 1977.
2. Black, R. K. E.; Katz, R.; Gray, M. D.; and Curnow, R. P. *BCS Software Production Data Final Technical Report,* No. RADC-TR-77-116, March 1977.
3. Prentiss, Nelson H. Jr. *Viking Software Data,* Martin Marietta Corp. Final Technical Report No. RADC-TR-77-168, May 1977.
4. Branning, W. E.; Erickson, W. A.; Schaenzer, J. P.; and Willson, D. M. *Modern Programming Practices Study Report,* Sperry Univac Final Technical Report No. RADC-TR-77-106, April 1977.
5. Perry, G. H. and Willmorth, N. E. *An Investigation of Programming Practices in Selected Air Force Projects,* System Development Corp. Final Technical Report No. RADC-TR-77-182, June 1977.
6. Carter, S.; Donahoo, J.; Farquhar, R.; and Hunt, J. *Software Production Data,* Computer Sciences Corp. Final Technical Report No. RADC-TR-77-177, July 1977.

CHAPTER 14

Software Quality Assurance Tools and Techniques

DONALD J. REIFER

INTRODUCTION

The high cost and poor quality of computer software have become subjects of major concern to governmental and industrial managers. The National Bureau of Standards has estimated that the federal Government expends over $5 billion annually on software and that the accumulated federal investment in software exceeded $25 billion in 1976. [1]. Commercial firms spend a large proportion of their gross sales on data processing including software. Yet, the literature is filled with horror stories attributing large cost overruns and significant system failures to poor software management and quality control practices. These problems are compounded by the cost of errors made by operational software. In a recent report, the General Accounting Office identified software errors that resulted in transactions that have cost taxpayers millions of dollars [2]. This situation, if not rectified, will probably get worse as society's dependence on digital computers, including microprocessors, increases in the next few years.

Many software practitioners recognize these problems exist and are attempting to do something about them. The first steps they are taking in their attack on the problem are aimed at introducing sound management and engineering practices to the art of computer programming. Some of these quality management combatants are drawing from traditional product assurance experience to develop *new assurance technology* for computer software. The objective of this chapter is to explain how modern tools and techniques support this new technology. We shall accomplish this goal by first developing categories for quality assurance tools and techniques (aids) and discussing example aids. Second, material on toolsmithing is provided. Finally, an assessment of the state of the technology is made and recommendations aimed at improving current practice are offered.

TECHNIQUES, TOOLS AND METHODOLOGIES

Experience has indicated that good techniques, tools, and methods must be employed to have a successful quality assurance program. Quality assurance is a service function created to provide management with the independent checks and balances it needs to control and assess product quality. Economic considerations are such that the quality assurance (QA) must accomplish its assigned task efficiently and at minimum cost to remain effective. Technical considerations are such that QA can only justify its role if it contributes directly to product development with minimal disruption and meaningful results. Both economic and technical considerations dictate that QA use proven tools to automate the techniques and methods it employs to accomplish its purpose.

For the purpose of this chapter, automation is defined as mechanizing methods using tools and techniques. Tools are computer programs used to aid the quality inspector in evaluation of the developer's computer program products or procedures. Techniques are procedures arranged to simplify the evaluation process.

Software quality assurance personnel employ the methods of inspection, analysis, demonstration, and test. Inspection confirms product or procedure compliance with stated requirements by examination. Analysis studies the product or procedure in detail in order to confirm an answer or results of a solution analytically. Demonstration provides tangible and visible evidence of compliance by making trial output acceptable for review and comparison against stated goals.

Quality assurance tools and techniques can be classified based upon the method they support. Table 1 lists available tools and techniques by category. The taxonomy is structured to minimize overlap between categories. It is not all inclusive and does not purport to be totally complete.

Let us now discuss each of the tools and techniques listed in Table

14. Software Quality Assurance Tools and Techniques

TABLE 1. Quality assurance tools and techniques

Class	Inspection	Analysis	Demonstration	Test

Tech-nique	Auditing
	Code inspection
	Design inspection
	Reviewing
		Analytical modeling
		Correctness proof
		Error-prone analysis
		Execution analysis
		Post-functional
		  analysis
		Simulation
		Standardization
		Static analysis
			Functional testing
			Walk-throughs
				Algorithm evaluation
				  test
				Correctness proofs
				Equivalence classes
				Functional testing
				Logical testing
				Path testing
				Simulation
				Stress testing
				Symbolic execution

Tool	Consistency checker
	Editor
	Requirements tracer
	Standards analyzer
		Accuracy study
		  processor
		Comparator
		Consistency checker
		Cross-referencers
		Data base analyzer
		Decision tables
		Dynamic analyzer
		Editor
		Flowcharter
		Hardware monitor
		Interface checker
		Interrupt analyzer
		Logic analyzer
		Simulators
		Software monitor
		Static analyzer
		Structure analyzer
		Timing analyzer
			Dynamic simulator
			Hardware monitor
			Software monitor
			Standards analyzer
			Test bed
				Automated test
				  generator
				Comparator
				Debugger
				Dynamic analyzer
				Dynamic simulator
				Flowcharter
				Hardware monitor
				Instruction trace
				Simulators
				Software monitor
				Test drivers, scripts
				Test-result processor

Sup-port tool (Com-mon)		Language processors Libraries MIS Standards Text editor		

1. We will begin by defining each tool and technique using a glossary. Then, we will relate each tool and technique with usual quality assurance activities. Finally, we will illustrate how each tool and technique supports the evaluation of software quality.

Techniques Glossary

The twenty techniques listed in Table 1 are defined in the following paragraphs. Table 2 illustrates which technique supports various quality assurance functions (the functions shown are representative functions for quality assurance as listed in MIL-S-52779,* Software Quality Assurance Program Requirements). Table 3 displays the degree of support each technique provides for assessing the properties of software quality in matrix form (the quality factors shown in the table are defined in chapter 8).

1. ALGORITHM EVALUATION TEST. A technique used to evaluate critical algorithm trade-offs (i.e., speed versus size versus precision) before the design is finalized. Often called "the hardest out first method," the technique creates a detailed design based upon trial coding results for key algorithms. The algorithms are often extensively exercised in a simulated environment to ensure mission requirements are satisfied.

2. ANALYTICAL MODELING. A technique used to express mathematically (usually by a set of equations) a representation of some real problem. Such models are valuable for abstracting the essence of the subject of inquiry. Because equations describing complex systems tend to be complicated and often impossible to formulate, it is often necessary to make simplifying assumptions, which may tend to distort accuracy [3].

3. AUDITING. A formal technique employed to examine and verify through inspection either the status of a program and its documentation or the adherence of project personnel to established procedures. Scheduled audits are normally contractually imposed and periodically held. Unscheduled audits are utilized at random intervals to assess compliance with quality requirements.

4. CODE INSPECTION. A disciplined technique used for inspecting the code and identifying errors. Participants have well-defined roles and criteria for evaluating the code. If errors are identified, the code is reworked. Follow-up procedures are used to ensure that the errors have been corrected [4].

5. CORRECTNESS PROOFS. A technique used to prove the correctness of programs using means similar to those employed to prove mathemati-

---

* See Chapter 7 for a more extensive description.

TABLE 2. Supporting techniques for quality functions

Function

Techniques	Quality planning	Work tasking	Configuration management	Testing	Corrective action	Library controls	Design standards	Documentation standards	Reviews and audits	Subcontractor controls
1. Algorithm evaluation test				×			×	×	×	×
2. Analytical modeling	×			×			×	×	×	×
3. Auditing		×	×	×	×	×	×	×	×	×
4. Code inspection									×	
5. Correctness proof				×						
6. Design inspection									×	
7. Error-prone analysis				×						
8. Equivalence classes				×						
9. Execution analysis				×						
10. Functional testing				×						
11. Logical testing				×						
12. Path testing				×						
13. Post-functional analysis				×			×			
14. Reviewing	×	×	×	×	×	×	×	×	×	×
15. Simulations				×					×	
16. Standardization	×	×	×	×	×	×	×	×	×	×
17. Static analysis				×					×	
18. Stress testing				×					×	
19. Symbolic execution				×						
20. Walk-throughs				×			×	×	×	×

TABLE 3. Technique effectiveness in assessing quality properties

Quality property

Techniques	Correctness	Efficiency	Integrity	Maintainability	Modifiability	Portability	Reliability	Testability	Usability
1. Algorithm evaluation test	M	M	L	L	L	L	H	M	M
2. Analytical Modeling	M	M	L	L	L	L	H	M	L
3. Auditing	H	M	M	H	H	M	H	H	H
4. Code inspection	M	L	L	M	M	M	H	M	M
5. Correctness proof	H	L	L	L	L	L	M	M	L
6. Design inspection	H	H	H	H	H	H	H	H	H
7. Error-prone analysis	M	H	L	L	L	L	M	M	L
8. Equivalence classes	M	M	M	L	L	L	H	H	L
9. Execution analysis	H	H	M	L	M	L	M	L	L
10. Functional testing	H	H	H	M	M	M	H	H	L
11. Logical testing	M	M	L	M	L	M	H	M	L
12. Path testing	M	L	L	L	L	L	H	H	L
13. Post-functional analysis	M	H	L	M	M	M	H	M	L
14. Reviewing	H	M	M	M	M	M	M	H	M
15. Simulation	H	H	H	H	H	H	H	M	H
16. Standardization	H	H	M	M	M	H	M	H	H
17. Static analysis	H	L	H	H	H	L	H	M	H
18. Stress testing	M	H	M	M	M	L	H	M	M
19. Symbolic execution	M	M	M	M	M	M	H	M	L
20. Walk-throughs	M	M	M	M	M	M	H	M	M

Legend: H — High effectiveness
M — Medium effectiveness
L — Low effectiveness

cal theorems. Axioms and theorems derived are used to establish the validity of the program with respect to a precise specification of its purpose. The most frequently used method is known as the inductive assertion or Floyd method [5]. Several approaches are being pursued. One approach seeks to demonstrate program correctness a priori by establishing the proof prior to implementation. Another approach uses an interactive system to prove correctness a posteriori [6].

6. DESIGN INSPECTION. A disciplined technique used for inspecting the design and identifying errors. Participants have well-defined roles and criteria for evaluating the design. If errors are identified, the design is reworked. Follow-up procedures are used to ensure that the errors have been corrected [4].

7. ERROR-PRONE ANALYSIS. A technique employed during coding to identify areas of the program that have required abnormally frequent correction and change. These areas can either be reworked or subjected to an extensive test effort [7].

8. EQUIVALENCE CLASSES. A technique used to automatically identify a complete set of test cases for a program. The set is interpreted in terms of inequalities involving program variables that define a set of conditions necessary for the particular program flow to actually occur. Some experience in the practical application of the technique has been reported [8,9].

9. EXECUTION ANALYSIS. A technique employed during test to investigate program behavior errors and to identify areas in the code that were either untested or not fully tested. The program is executed and statistics are collected. Test results and the statistics are then analyzed to insure that each interface, functional and test requirement has been correctly mechanized by the code.

10. FUNCTIONAL TESTING. A technique used to demonstrate that the software performs its specifications satisfactorily under normal operating conditions, computing nominally correct output values from nominal input values [10].

11. LOGICAL TESTING. A technique used to confirm that the code performs its computation correctly. Items validated by logical testing include arithmetic (i.e., precision, accuracy etc.), error handling, initialization, interfaces, and timing [10].

215

12. PATH TESTING. A technique used to confirm that certain test-effectiveness measures based on the program's control topology have been realized. The technique assures that a sufficient number of statements, branch paths, and subroutine calls have been exercised during program execution. It also helps identify a complete set of test cases for the program [11].

13. POST-FUNCTIONAL ANALYSIS. A technique employed after completion of functional testing to identify functionally weak areas in the program. The recorded test results are analyzed and the quality of the final product is determined [7].

14. REVIEWING. A technique employed to examine and verify through inspection either the status of a program and its documentation or adherence of project personnel to established procedures. Scheduled reviews are normally contractually imposed and periodically held [12]. Informal reviews are held frequently to assess in detail the technical adequacy of the software product [13].

15. SIMULATION. Simulation is the process of studying specific system characteristics by use of models exercised over a period of time and a variety of conditions for the purpose of evaluating alternatives, timing, system capacities, performance, and constraints within the confines of that system [14]. Simulation can be used by quality assurance throughout the life cycle. It can assist in evaluating conceptual trade-offs [15]. It can also be used to model the environment and provide realistic test inputs to a program being examined.

16. STANDARDIZATION. A technique used to create an authoritative model against which products and/or procedures can be compared in order to determine their quality. Software items for which standards can be easily established include documentation [16,17], languages [18,19], designs [20,21,22], and structured programming [23].

17. STATIC ANALYSIS. A technique employed during test to identify weaknesses in the source code. The syntax of a program is examined and statistics about it are generated. Items such as relationships between module, program structure, error-prone constructions, and symbol/subroutine cross-references are checked and violations of established rules are analyzed.

18. STRESS TESTING. A technique employed to confirm that the code performs its specifications satisfactorily under extreme operating con-

ditions, computing nominally correct output values from worst case input values (i.e., singularities, end points for the range of data, etc.).

19. SYMBOLIC EXECUTION. A technique that employs symbolic data to confirm that the software performs properly. Symbolic execution allows one to choose intermediate points in the test spectrum ranging from individual test runs to correctness proofs. Its results can be used to develop a minimum set of test cases [24,25].

20. WALK-THROUGHS. A technique used for reviewing the design or code and identifying errors. The responsible programmer discusses his product with his peers and solicits their constructive advice. Product modifications are then made at the discretion of the programmer to correct problems identified during the review [26].

Tool Glossary

The thirty-two tools listed in Table 1 are defined in the following paragraphs. For simplicity's sake, several of these tools are generalized to represent classes of tools (i.e., tool numbers 7, 17, 20, 22, 24, and 26). For the generalized case, several examples are provided. Table 4 illustrates which tool supports what quality assurance function. Table 5 displays the degree of support each tool provides for assessing the properties of software quality in matrix form.

1. ACCURACY STUDY PROCESSOR. A computer program used to perform calculations or assist in determining if program variables are computed with required accuracy. The processor accepts mathematical equations and data as inputs. It then uses the data as variables in the equations and solves them [27].

2. AUTOMATED TEST GENERATOR. A computer program that accepts inputs specifying a test scenario in some special language, generates the exact computer inputs, and determines the expected results. The NASA-developed Automated Test Data Generator (ATDG) serves as one example [28]. ATDG takes identified code segments, determines all possible logic transfers between those segments, defines a path through the module under test, and generates input data required to execute the selected paths. The General Electric automated software test driver serves as another example [29]. This program automates the process of test planning, test setup, test execution, and test analysis. Other generators are described in a recent report [30].

TABLE 4. Supporting tools for quality functions

Function

Tool	Quality planning	Work tasking	Configuration management	Testing	Corrective action	Library controls	Design standards	Documentation standards	Reviews and audits	Subcontractor controls
1. Accuracy study processor				X						
2. Automated test generator				X						
3. Comparator			X	X				X		
4. Consistency checker							X	X		
5. Cross-reference				X						
6. Data base analyzer				X						
7. Debugger				X						
8. Decision tables		X	X	X	X	X			X	X
9. Dynamic analyzer				X						
10. Dynamic simulator				X						
11. Editor				X						
12. Flowcharter				X			X			
13. Hardware monitor				X						
14. Instruction trace				X						
15. Interface checker				X						
16. Interrupt analyzer				X						
17. Language processor				X			X			
18. Libraries			X	X						X
19. Logic analyzer				X						
20. MIS		X	X	X	X	X				X
21. Requirements tracer			X	X	X				X	X
22. Simulator				X			X			
23. Software monitor				X						
24. Standards	X	X	X	X	X	X	X	X	X	X
25. Standards analyzer				X			X	X		
26. Static analyzer				X			X	X		
27. Structure analyzer				X			X			
28. Test bed				X						
29. Test drivers, scripts				X						
30. Test-result processor				X						
31. Text editor	X	X	X	X	X	X	X	X	X	X
32. Timing analyzer				X						

TABLE 5. Tool effectiveness in assessing quality properties

Quality Property

Tools	Correctness	Efficiency	Integrity	Maintainability	Modifiability	Portability	Reliability	Testability	Usability
1. Accuracy study processor	M	L	L	L	L	L	H	L	L
2. Automated test generator	M	L	L	L	L	L	H	H	L
3. Comparator	L	L	L	L	L	M	M	L	L
4. Consistency checker	H	L	L	L	L	L	H	M	L
5. Cross-reference	M	L	L	M	M	L	M	L	L
6. Data base analyzer	M	L	L	M	M	M	M	M	L
7. Debugger	M	M	L	L	L	L	H	L	L
8. Decision tables	M	L	M	L	L	L	M	M	L
9. Dynamic analyzer	H	H	L	M	M	L	H	M	L
10. Dynamic simulator	H	M	L	L	L	L	H	L	L
11. Editor	M	L	L	M	M	L	M	M	L
12. Flowcharter	H	L	L	M	M	M	M	H	H
13. Hardware monitor	M	H	L	L	L	L	H	M	L
14. Instruction trace	L	M	L	L	L	L	H	M	L
15. Interface checker	H	L	M	M	M	L	H	L	L
16. Interrupt analyzer	H	L	M	M	M	L	H	L	L
17. Language processor	H	M	M	H	H	H	H	H	H
18. Libraries	L	L	H	L	L	L	L	L	H
19. Logic analyzer	M	M	L	L	L	L	H	M	L
20. MIS	H	L	L	L	L	L	L	L	L
21. Requirements tracer	H	L	L	M	M	M	M	H	L
22. Simulator	H	H	M	M	M	M	M	M	H
23. Software monitor	M	H	L	L	L	L	H	M	L
24. Standards	H	H	H	H	H	H	H	H	H
25. Standards analyzer	H	L	M	H	H	M	M	M	M
26. Static analyzer	H	L	M	M	M	L	M	M	M
27. Structure analyzer	H	M	L	M	M	M	M	M	M
28. Test bed	H	H	H	H	H	H	H	H	H
29. Test drivers, scripts	M	L	L	L	L	L	H	H	L
30. Test-results processor	M	L	L	M	M	M	M	H	H
31. Text editor	M	L	L	H	H	L	L	H	H
32. Timing analyzer	H	L	M	M	M	L	H	L	L

Legend: H — High effectiveness
  M — Medium effectiveness
  L — Low effectiveness

3. COMPARATOR. A computer program used to compare two versions of the same computer program under test to establish identical configuration or to specifically identify changes in the source coding between the two versions [3].

4. CONSISTENCY CHECKER. A computer program used to determine (1) if requirements and/or designs specified for computer programs are consistent with each other and their data base and (2) if they are complete. The consistency checker computer program developed by TRW is an example [31].

5. CROSS-REFERENCE. A group of computer programs that provide cross-reference information on system components. For example, programs can be cross-referenced with other programs, macros, parameter names, etc. This capability is useful in problem-solving and testing to assess impact of changes to one area or another [3]. This capability should be provided in most compiler environments [32].

6. DATA BASE ANALYZER. A computer program that reports information on every usage of data, identifies each program using any data elements, and indicates whether the program inputs, uses, modifies, or outputs the data element. Any unused data is printed. Errors dealing with misuse and nonuse of data and conflicts in data usage are identified during the analysis [3].

7. DEBUGGER. Compile and execution-time check-out and debug capabilities that help identify and isolate program errors. They usually include commands or directives such as DUMP, TRACE, MODIFY CONTENTS, BREAKPOINT, etc. [3]. Some debuggers operate at the source level (e.g., SIMDDT for SIMULA 67, and COBDDT for COBOL on the PDP-10) and others at the object level with some additional source information (e.g., DDT for FORTRAN on the PDP-10) [33]. The following types of basic information are normally provided:

TRACE: A timed record of program execution and machine environment information.

DUMP: A record of selected portions of memory or register usage output after a specified point in the program's execution has been reached.

SNAP: A record of intermediate values of items captured during program execution.

BREAKPOINTS: A facility whereby the normal computation is interrupted and debugging activities commence execution.

220

8. DECISION TABLES. A mechanism used to represent information on program conditions, rules, and actions in tabular form that can be automatically translated to executable code by a processor. Decision tables are a tabular representation of the design which can be used to clarify the control flow of decision alternatives by presenting the information in a concise and understandable format [14]. A dated but useful survey of automated decision table processors is available [34].

9. DYNAMIC ANALYZER. A computer program that instruments the source code by adding counters and other statistics-gathering sensors and produces reports on how thoroughly the various portions of the code have been exercised after the augmented code is executed. Dynamic analyzers provide information useful for tuning, optimization, and test case design [3]. Many dynamic analyzers have been developed. Comparative analysis of several analyzers [35] and user feedback with such systems have been published [36].

10. DYNAMIC SIMULATOR. A computer program used to check out a program in a simulated environment comparable to that in which it will reside. Closed-loop effects between computer and environmental models are gained when the various models respond to inputs and outputs. The simulator allows the environment to be stabilized at a specific configuration for any number of runs required to observe, diagnose, and resolve problems in the operational program [3]. The Dynamic Test Station (DTS) being developed by the U.S. Air Force to support the test of the operational flight software for the F-16 fighter aircraft serves as an example [37].

11. EDITOR. A computer program used to analyze source programs for coding errors and to extract information that can be used for checking relationships between sections of code. The editor can scan source code and detect violations to specific programming practices and standards, construct an extensive cross-reference list of all labels, variables and constants, and check for prescribed program formats [3].

12. FLOWCHARTER. A computer program used to show in detail the logical structure of a computer program. The flow is determined from the actual operations as specified by the executable instructions, not from comments. The flowcharts generated can be compared to flowcharts provided in the computer program design specification to show discrepancies and illuminate differences [3]. Several flowcharters such as AUTOFLOW and FLOWGEN are commercially available. Several structured flowchart representations have been proposed [39].

221

13. HARDWARE MONITOR. A unit that obtains signals from a host computer through probes attached directly to the computer's circuitry. The signals obtained are fed to counters and timers and are recorded. These data are then reduced to provide information about system and/ or program performance (CPU activity, channel utilization, etc.) [40]. Several useful articles on using this tool have appeared in the literature [41,42].

14. INSTRUCTION TRACE. A computer program used to record every instance a certain class of operations occurs and triggers event-driven data collection. In some cases, this creates a complete timed record of events occurring during program execution [3]. Experience using traces to locate sources of nonrepeatable, intermittent malfunctions has been reported [43].

15. INTERFACE CHECKER. A computer program used to automatically check the range and limits of variables as well as the scaling of the source program to assure compliance with interface control documents [3]. Other computer programs have been developed to automatically verify that modularity rules have been followed [44].

16. INTERRUPT ANALYZER. A computer program that determines potential conflicts to a system as a result of the occurrence of an interrupt [3].

17. LANGUAGE PROCESSORS. Computer programs used to translate high-level or symbolic instruction mnemonics into computer-oriented code capable of being executed by a computer. Compilers, assemblers and meta-assemblers are example tools used for program development. Other language processors have been developed to support requirements generation and validation [45], design [46], and test [29]. Preprocessors have been developed to support implementation of modern programming techniques.

18. LIBRARIES. A collection of organized information used for reference or study. Many varieties of library systems can be implemented. Some manage the storage and distribution of the computer program in both source and object form. Others manage the computer program, its documentation and related test data (i.e., test cases, procedures, results). Programs which support their implementation are commercially available and include Applied Data Research's LIBRARIAN and International Business Machine's Program Production Library (PPL) [3]. The use of a library and its effect on productivity have been reported [47].

19. LOGIC ANALYZER. A computer program used to automatically reconstruct equations forming the basis of a program and to flowchart assembly language programs. One such program translates assembly language instructions into a machine-independent microprogramming language and builds the microprogramming statements into a network in which the flow of control is analyzed and equations are reconstructed [48].

20. MANAGEMENT INFORMATION SYSTEM. Consists of a computer-based information system (a particular combination of human service, material service, and equipment service) for the purpose of gathering, organizing, communicating, and presenting information to be used by individuals for planning and controlling an enterprise [49]. Several packages which serve as essential elements of a management information system are discussed with examples in a recent publication [50].

21. REQUIREMENTS TRACER. A computer program used to provide traceability from requirements through design and implementation of the software products. Traceability is characterized to the extent that an audit trail exists for the successive implementation of each requirement. The University of Michigan-developed Problem Statement Language/Analyzer serves as an example [51]. Experience using the Michigan and other similar systems has been reported [52].

22. SIMULATOR. A computer program that provides the target system with inputs or responses that resemble those that would have been provided by the process for the device being simulated. The simulator's function is to present data to the system at the correct time and in an acceptable format [3]. Several of the many varieties of simulators available are briefly described as follows:

Interpretive computer simulator: A computer program used to simulate the execution characteristics of a target computer (provides bit-for-bit fidelity with results that would be produced by the target machine) using a sequence of instructions of the host computer.

Peripheral simulator: A computer program used to present functional and signal interfaces representative of a peripheral device to the target system.

Statement-level simulator: A computer program used to simulate the execution characteristics of a target computer at the source instruction-level using a sequence of instructions on the host computer.

223

System simulator: A mechanization of a model of the system (hardware, software, interfaces) used to predict system performance over time.

23. SOFTWARE MONITOR. A computer program that provides detailed statistics about system performance. Because software monitors reside in memory, they have access to all the tables the system maintains. Therefore, they can examine such things as core usage, queue lengths, and individual program operation to help measure performance. Use of software monitors has been described in a recent publication [53].

24. STANDARDS. Procedures, rules, and conventions used for prescribing disciplined program development. Architecture and partitioning rules, documentation conventions, language conventions, configuration, and data management procedures, etc., are typical examples under this category [40].

25. STANDARDS ANALYZER. A computer program used to automatically determine whether prescribed programming standards and practices have been followed. The program can check for violations to standards set for such conventions as program size, commentary, structure, etc. [3]. The National Bureau of Standards-developed FORTRAN Analyzer serves as an example [54].

26. STATIC ANALYZER. A computer program used to provide information about the features of a source program. This type of tool examines the source code statically (not under execution conditions) and performs syntax analysis, structure checks, module interface checks, event sequence analysis and other similar functions. Several of the many varieties of static analyzers available are briefly described as follows:

Overlay analyzer: A computer program that examines the source program in order to determine mutually disjoint segments that can reside in the same area of memory at run time [33].

Units consistency analyzer: A computer program which analyzes the source code version of equations to assure that they consistently reference the global data base [55].

Usage statistics gatherer: A computer program that computes statistics based on the number of times various items appear in a source program [33].

27. STRUCTURE ANALYZER. A computer program used to examine source code and determine that structuring rules set for either the control or data structure, or both, have been obeyed. Typically, the

program parses an equivalent model of the control or data topology before commencing analysis [3].

28. TEST BED. A test site composed of actual hardware (hardware test site) or simulated equipment (software test site) or some combination. A hardware test site uses the actual computer and interface hardware to check out the hardware/software interfaces and actual input/output. The program execution is confirmed using actual hardware timing characteristics, but the output is limited and test repeatability is a problem. A software test site uses an instruction-level and/or statement-level simulator to model actual hardware. A software test site permits full control of inputs and computer characteristics, allows processing of intermediate outputs without destroying simulated time, and allows full test repeatability and good diagnostics. The Shuttle Avionics Integration Laboratory represents an elaborate hardware test bed [56] and the Software Design and Verification System (SDVS) represents a sophisticated software test bed [57].

29. TEST DRIVERS, SCRIPTS. To run tests in a controlled manner, it is often necessary to work within the framework of a "scenario" — a description of a dynamic situation. To accomplish this, the input data files for the system must be loaded with data values representing the test situation or events to yield recorded data to evaluate against expected results. These tools permit generation of data in external form to be entered into the system at the proper time [3].

30. TEST-RESULT PROCESSOR. A computer program used to perform test output data reduction, formatting, and printing. Some perform statistical analysis where the original data may be the output of a monitor [3].

31. TEXT EDITOR. A computer program used to prepare documentation and perform work-file edits (erase, insert, change, and move words or groups of words). The program requires a facility for on-line storage and recall of text units for inspection, editing, or printing [3].

32. TIMING ANALYZER. A computer program that monitors and prints execution time for all program elements (functions, routines, and subroutines). A more detailed description of the tool appears in the literature [48].

TOOLSMITHING

As we can ascertain from the previous two sections, the quality engineer has many tools and techniques at his disposal. One of the quality engineer's major tasks in developing an acceptable software quality assurance program for a specific project is to select those tools and techniques that will allow him to accomplish his functions in the most efficient and cost-effective manner. Selection assumes that the quality assurance organization has its methods and techniques codified in written form (i.e., usually as procedures in a manual), its tools developed and maintained under configuration control in a centralized library, and its sources for supplementing existing tools and techniques identified in case acquisition is warranted. Factors which impact selection and should be evaluated are listed in checklist form in Table 6 [58]. An evaluation guide for determining whether or not it is cost effective to develop new tools is included as Figure 1 [59,60].

The author believes that the tools and techniques displayed in Figure 2 represent the minimum set required to construct a responsive software quality assurance program. They provide for balanced coverage of the required quality assurance functions as illustrated in tables 2 and 4. They also provide for balanced assessment of the properties of quality software as illustrated in tables 3 and 5. Other tools and techniques may be added as the need arises so long as their costs can be justified in terms of the benefits derived.

SUMMARY

We have covered a lot of ground with regard to software quality assurance tools and techniques. Points are:

1. The quality assurance organization should utilize tools and techniques whose cost/benefits can be demonstrated and whose risk is acceptable.
2. The quality assurance organization should have a toolsmith whose sole responsibility should be the development and maintenance of written procedures and a tool library. Tools placed within the library should be qualified, documented, and placed under configuration control. Acquisition of new tools should occur only when they can be economically justified.
3. We can conclude from experience that tools and techniques improve final program quality. Before we can progress further, we have to have a better and more quantitative understanding of

226

TABLE 6. Factors impacting tool and technique selection

Factor	Evaluation criteria	Yes	No	Notes
Applicability	Is the tool or technique suited for the task? If not, can it be modified easily to do the job?			
Availability	Is the tool or technique ready for use? If so, can it be delivered to the customer in acceptable form if he desires it?			
Cost/Benefit	Can the use of the tool or technique be justified in terms of return on investment? If not, why use it?			
Experience	Has the tool or technique been used on other projects? If so, how many and with what results? If not, have adequate precautions been taken to manage the potential risk?			
Quality	Are the tools and techniques documented and is adequate user documentation available? Are the tools under configuration control? Have the tools been qualified formally? Have the tools been developed using modern programming techniques and a High Order Language (HOL)?			
Resources	Have the potential sizing and timing growth implications of tool use been factored into the decision?			
Risk	Have the risks associated with developing or using the tool or technique been quantified?			

FIGURE 1. Cost effectiveness evaluation guide for quality assurance tools and techniques

Cost analysis		Benefit analysis	

Cost analysis

1. NONRECURRING COSTS — Amount
   A. Analysis — $_____
   B. Program development — _____
   C. Program modification — _____
   D. Program purchase — _____
   E. Training — _____
   F. Installation & checkout — _____
   G. Support — _____
   H. Conversion — _____
   I. Other — _____

   TOTAL — $_____

2. RECURRING COSTS
   A. Computer time — $_____
   B. Clerical support — _____
   C. Program maintenance — _____
   D. Support — _____
   E. Other — _____

   TOTAL — $_____

3. Est. cost growth rate _____ %
4. Total cost (years) $_____

Benefit analysis

1. QUALITATIVE BENEFITS — CHECK
   A. Improved control — ( )
   B. Operations & reliability — ( )
   C. Customer service — ( )
   D. Safety — ( )
   E. Timeliness — ( )
   F. Accuracy — ( )
   G. Others — ( )

2. QUANTITATIVE BENEFITS — Amount
   A. One-time benefits — $_____
   B. Recurring benefits
      ° Material — _____
      ° Equipment — _____
      ° Labor — _____
      ° Computer usage — _____
      ° Program maintenance — _____
      ° Other — _____

      TOTAL — $_____

3. Est. benefits growth rate _____ %
4. Total benefits (years) $_____

Prepared by: _____

Approved by: _____

Reviewed by: _____

FIGURE 2. *Minimum set of tools and techniques*

Techniques	Tools
Auditing	Dynamic analyzer
Design inspections	Language processors
Reviewing	Standards
Standardization	Standards analyzer
Walk-throughs	Test bed

just what quality is and how you can measure it. Only then can we hope to make quality an integral part of the software systems we produce.

RECOMMENDATIONS

The following recommendations hopefully may prove controversial enough to stimulate the actions needed to improve the state of software quality assurance technology. These recommendations are based on the conclusions summarized in the previous paragraph and on past experience.

1. Standard terminology is needed in the field of software quality assurance. An attempt should be made to have committees develop standards under the auspices of either a professional society (e.g., the IEEE, NSIA, etc.) or the Government (e.g., the National Bureau of Standards, etc.).

2. A medium for software quality assurance information exchange is needed. An attempt should be made to create a special-interest group under the auspices of a professional society or an ad hoc committee. This group would encourage publication of user experience both pro and con in the professional literature. They would also work with the universities to establish appropriate educational training.

3. For all practical purposes, there are no pragmatic measures of and measuring techniques for software quality assurance. Very few new techniques and tools have been developed over the past few years to help the quality engineer. New technology is needed to advance the state of the art. A coordinated research and development program is needed to ignite the spark and improve current practice. This program should investigate new concepts and develop new tools and techniques.

229

4. The software quality assurance organization's role is similar to that of an internal auditor. Possibly, some of the techniques developed by the accounting profession can be adopted for use by the software discipline. An attempt should be made to create an ad hoc committee under the auspices of the professional societies to see if cross-fertilization is mutually beneficial. Auditability assumes that the software has been designed to be audited. Investigations aimed at developing appropriate design practices seem useful.

5. Inspections are a useful quality assurance technique. Quality personnel have used them effectively for many years. A key tool in inspections is statistics. Goods are sampled as they are being manufactured and statistical inference is used to determine quality. Software science is essentially statistical in nature. Research to determine if it could be effectively applied to determine software quality during program development should be initiated.

6. Quality assurance organizations basically serve the user. Yet, most of their tools and techniques provide little assistance in assuring usability. Renewed attention should be placed on making the quality assurance organization more responsible to the user. New tools and techniques are needed. Perhaps, some of the work being done in the area of human factors and man-machine interaction can be adopted for use by quality assurance.

ACKNOWLEDGMENTS

The author acknowledges the suggestions and criticisms provided by his many thoughtful colleagues at TRW. He thanks his wife and family for their patience and understanding.

References

1. Fife, Dennis W. *Computer Software Management: A Primer for Project Management and Quality Control,* U.S. Department of Commerce, National Bureau of Standards, Special Publication 500-11, July 1977.
2. General Accounting Office, *Problems Found with Government Acquisition and Use of Computers from November 1965 to December 1976,* Report to Congress, FGMSD-77-14, 15 March 1977.
3. Reifer, Donald J. and Trattner, Stephen. "A Glossary of Software Tools and Techniques," *Computer,* July 1977, pp. 52-60.
4. Fagen, M. E. "Design and Code Inspections to Reduce Errors in Program Development," *IBM Systems Journal,* no. 3, 1976, pp. 182-211.
5. Reynolds, C. and Yeh, R. T. "Induction as the Basis for Program Verification," *IEEE Transactions on Software Engineering,* vol. SE-2, no. 4, December 1976, pp. 244-252.

6. Good, D. I.; London, R. L.; and Bledsoe, W. W. "An Interactive Verification System," *Proceedings of the International Conference on Reliable Software*, IEEE, April 1975, pp. 482–492.

7. Tsui, Frank and Priven, Lew. "Implementation of Quality Control in Software Development," *Proceedings of the 1976 National Computer Conference*, AFIPS Press, 1976, pp. 443–449.

8. Miller, Edward F., Jr. "Program Testing: Art Meets Theory," *Computer*, July 1977, pp. 42–51.

9. Howden, William E. "Methodology for the Generation of Program Test Data," *IEEE Transactions on Software Engineering*, vol. SE-3, 1977, pp. 266–278.

10. Fairley, Richard E. "Tutorial: Static Analysis and Dynamic Testing of Computer Software," *Computer*, April 1978, pp. 14–23.

11. Reifer, Donald and Ettenger, Robert L. *Test Tools: Are They a Cure-all?* SAMSO-TR-75-13, 15 October 1974.

12. *TRW, Airborne Systems Software Acquisitions Engineering Guidebook for Reviews and Audits*, Report No. 30323-6006-TU-00, November 1977.

13. Freeman, Peter. "Toward Improved Review of Software Designs," *Proceedings of the 1975 National Computer Conference*, AFIPS Press, 1975, pp. 329–334.

14. Bratman, Harvey and Finfer, Marcia C. *Software Acquisition Management Guidebook: Verification*, ESD-TR-77-263, August 1977.

15. Reifer, Donald J. *A Structured Approach to Modeling Computer Systems*, SAMSO-TR-75-3, 30 August 1974.

16. MIL-STD-483 (USAF), *Configuration Management Practices for Systems, Equipment, Munitions and Computer Programs*, June 1971.

17. National Bureau of Standards, *Guidelines for Documentation of Computer Programs and Automated Data Systems*, Federal Information Processing Standards Publication 38, February 1976.

18. MIL-STD-1589 (USAF), JOVIAL (J73/I), 28 February 1977.

19. "Draft Proposed ANS FORTRAN, BSR X3.9, X3J3/76," *SIGPLAN Notices*, vol. II, no. 3, March 1976.

20. Stevens, W. P.; Meyers, G. J.; and Constantine, L. L. "Structured Design," *IBM Systems Journal*, no. 2, 1974, pp. 115–139.

21. Freeman, P. and Wasserman, A. I. *Tutorial on Software Design Techniques*, IEEE Catalog No. 76CH1145-2C, 1977.

22. Peters, L. J. and Trip, L. L. "Comparing Software Design Methodologies," *Datamation*, November 1977.

23. *Structured Programming Series*, USAF Rome Air Development Center, Vols. 1–15, July 1975. DDC Accession Numbers Follows:
"Programming Language Standards," AD-A016 771.
"Pre-Compiler Specifications," AD-A018 046.
"Pre-Compiler Program Documentation," AD-A013 255.
"Data Structuring," AD-A015 794.
"Program Support Library Requirements," AD-A003 339.
"Program Support Library Program Specifications," AD-A007 796.

"Documentation Standards," AD-A016 414.

"Program Design Study," AD-A016 415.

"Management Data Collection and Reporting," AD-A008 640.

"Chief Programmer Team Operations," AD-A008 861.

"Estimating Software Resource Requirements," AD-A016 416.

"Training Materials," AD-A026 947.

"Software Tool Impact," AD-A015 795.

"Validation and Verification," AD-A016 668.

"Final Report," AD-A020 858.

24. Darringer, John A. and King, James C. "Applications of Symbolic Execution to Program Testing," *Computer*, April 1978, pp. 51-60.

25. Howden, W. E. "Symbolic Testing and the DISSECT Symbolic Evaluation System," *IEEE Transaction on Software Engineering*, vol. SE-3, 1977, pp. 266-278.

26. Waldstein, N. S. *The Walk-Thru-A Method of Specification, Design and Review*, IBM Corporation Technical Report TR 00.2536, June 1974.

27. Logicon Technical Staff, *Management Guide to Avionics Software Acquisition: Volume IV — Technical Aspects Relative to Software Acquisition*, ASD-TR-76.11, vol. IV, June 1976.

28. Hoffman, R. H. "NASA/Johnson Space Center Approach to Automated Test Data Generation," *Proceedings of Computer Science and Statistics: Eighth Annual Symposium on the Interface,* available from UCLA, February 1975.

29. Panzl, David J. "Automatic Software Test Drivers," *Computer,* April 1978, pp. 44-50.

30. Trattner, S. *Tools for Analysis of Software Security,* Aerospace Corporation, ATR-77 2740-1, 15 October 1976.

31. Landes, Michael. "Consistency Checker," Summary, *Presentation at the International DOD/Industry Conference on Software Verification and Validation*, Rome Air Development Center, August 1976, p. 69.

32. Callender, E. D.; Feliciano, M.; and Jennings, L. D. *SAMSO Computer Language and Software Development Environment Requirements,* SAMSO-TR-290, 1975.

33. Felty, James L. and Roth, Martin S. *Software Support Tools,* Intermetrics Inc., IR-204-2, 15 October 1976, p. 13.

34. Couger, J. Daniel. "Evaluation of Business System Analysis Techniques," *Computing Surveys,* vol. 5, no. 3, September 1973, pp. 186-190.

35. DeWolf, J. Barton and Wexler, Jonathan. "Approaches to Software Verification with Emphasis on Real-Time Applications," *Proceedings of the AIAA/NASA/IEEE/ACM Computers in Aerospace Conference,* October 31-November 2, 1977, pp. 41-51.

36. Whipple, L. K. and Pitts, M. A. *User's Appraisal of an Automated Program Verification Aid,* AFAL-TR-75-242, December 1975.

37. Spanbauer, Robert N. (USAF). "The F16 Software Development Program," *Proceedings of Conference on Managing the Development of Weapon System Software,* Maxwell Air Force Base, Alabama, 12-13 May 1976, pp. 30-1 to 30-13.

38. Lanzano, B. C. *Program Automated Documentation Methods,* TRW Systems, TRW-SS-70-04, November 1970.
39. Nassi, I. and Schneiderman, B. "Flowchart Techniques for Structured Programming," *SIGPLAN Notices,* August 1973, pp. 12-26.
40. Reifer, Donald J. *Interim Report on the Aids Inventory Project,* SAMSO-TR-74-184, 16 July 1975.
41. Nutt, Gary J. "Tutorial: Computer System Monitors," *Computer,* November 1975, pp. 51-61.
42. Highland, Harold J. (ed.) *Computer Performance Evaluation,* U.S. Department of Commerce, National Bureau of Standards, Special Publication 401, September 1974.
43. Baum, J. D. and DiStefano, J. B. "Avionics In-Flight System/Software Test Tool — Anomaly Trace," *Proceedings of the Aeronautical Systems Software Workshop,* Dayton, Ohio, 2-4 April 1974, pp. 355-359.
44. Hamilton, M. and Zeldin, S. "Higher Order Software — A Methodology for Defining Software," *IEEE Transactions on Software Engineering,* vol. SE-2, no. 1, March 1976.
45. Bell, Thomas E.; Bixler, David C.; and Dyer, Margaret E. "An Extendable Approach to Computer-Aided Software Requirements Engineering," *IEEE Transactions on Software Engineering,* vol. SE-3, no. 1, January 1977.
46. Caine, Stephen H. and Gordon, E. Kent. "PDL—A Tool for Software Design," *Proceedings of the 1975 National Computer Conference,* AFIPS Press, 1975, pp. 271-276.
47. Baker, F. Terry. "Structured Programming in a Production Programming Environment," *IEEE Transactions on Software Engineering,* vol. SE-1, no. 2, June 1975, pp. 241-252.
48. *Poseidon MK88 Fire Control System Computer Program Verification and Validation Techniques Study, Volume III,* Ultrasystems Inc., Newport Beach, CA, November 1973.
49. Malcolm, Donald G. "Cost-Effective Management Information Systems," *Management Information Systems Short Course Notes,* Engineering 819.39, University of California at Los Angeles, May 1978.
50. Hardy, I. Trotter; Leong-Hong, Belkis; and Fife, Dennis W. *Software Tools: A Building Block Approach,* U.S. Department of Commerce, National Bureau of Standards, Special Publication 500-14, August 1977.
51. Teichroew, D. and Hershey, E. A., III. "PSL/PSA: A Computer-Aided Technique for Structured Documentation and Analysis of Information Processing," *IEEE Transactions on Software Engineering,* vol. SE-3, no. 1, January 1977, pp. 41-48.
52. Basili, Victor R. "A Panel Session — User Experience with the New Software Methods," *Proceedings of the 1978 National Computer Conference,* AFIPS Press, 1978.
53. Ramamoorthy, C. V. and Kim, K. H. "Software Monitors Aiding Systematic Testing and Their Optional Placement," *Proceedings of the 1st National Conference on Software Engineering,* IEEE Catalog No. 75CH0992-8C, September 1975.

54. Lyon, Gordon and Stittman, Rona B. *A FORTRAN Analyzer,* U.S. Department of Commerce, National Bureau of Standards, Technical Note No. 849, October 1974.

55. Herring, F. P. and Mabee, C. J. *Survey of Support Software for Operational Flight Programs and Avionics Integration Support Facility Software,* TRW Systems, Report 28675-6232-RU-00, May 1977.

56. Chambers, T. V. "Shuttle Avionics Integration Laboratory," *Proceedings of the AIAA/NASA/IEEE/ACM Computers in Aerospace Conference,* October 31–November 2, 1977, pp. 212–221.

57. Hollowich, Michael and Borasz, Frank. "The Software Design & Verification System (SDVS), An Integrated Set of Software Development and Management Tools," *NAECON '76 Record,* IEEE Catalog No. 76CH1082-7 NAECON, 1976, pp. 920–926.

58. *TRW, Airborne Systems Software Acquisition Engineering Guidebook for Quality Assurance,* Report No. 30323-6005-TU-00, November 1977.

59. Cardenas, Alfonso. *Management Information Systems Lecture Notes,* University of California at Los Angeles, Engineering 819.39, 1–5 May 1978.

60. Floyd, D. and Lipow, M. *Reliability: Management, Methods and Mathematics,* 2nd Edition. Redondo Beach, CA: Lloyd Lipow Publishers, pp. 512–514.

CHAPTER 15

Software Verification And Validation (V & V)

ROBERT O. LEWIS

V&V—ESSENTIAL ELEMENT OF SOFTWARE QUALITY MANAGEMENT

Few, if any, ancillary activities to the software development process offer as wide a range of influence and beneficial effects on software quality management as verification and validation (V&V). Conscientiously applied, V&V interfaces with and reinforces the entire development cycle and can continue to reduce unwanted perturbations and resulting costs well into the operational life of the system involved. No claims are made that V&V is the panacea for inadequate design or implementation, but rather it should be thought of as a preventive, helping to assess and ensure the general health and sufficiency of the software program to which it is applied.

Lack of Universal Understanding and Acceptance

Despite its rather wide application to many of the nation's more significant software development efforts over the past ten years, V&V remains an enigma to a relatively large group that includes a sizable number of software developers. No doubt this misunderstanding has emanated largely from incorrectly defined and applied programs that were called V&V but that were in reality either a portion of what the purist would describe as V&V or were simply misnamed. Thus, one of the major objectives of this chapter is to state, as unambiguously as possible, the precepts which must be satisfied if a program is to be defined as V&V. These ground rules are sufficiently broad in scope to accommodate all of the possible design and development variables, while providing a general framework for the selection and application of specific methods, tools, and techniques to match the particular job requirement. Thus, V&V should always be viewed as an adaptive process which is tailored to fit each application.

UNRAVELING THE ENIGMA

To formulate a robust definition of V&V, it is not enough to know what it is, but also what it is not. Thus, the statement of precepts will present arguments on both counts to promote understanding and discourage misconceptions.

Rule 1: V&V must be an independent, third-party activity.

Rule 2: V&V must be thought of as an overlay, not an integral part of the development cycle — an added value concept.

Rule 3: V&V must report to and owe its fundamental allegiance to the developing user agency, not the developing contractor.

Rule 4: Although it may share the development tools, V&V must provide its own tools and disciplines apart from those used in development.

Rule 5: Although somewhat flexible in terms of its starting point, V&V must *verify* each phase relative to itself and to its adjacent phases.

Rule 6: V&V must provide a means of *validating* all testable software performance requirements.

Failure to satisfy any one of the above rules, no matter how conscientiously the effort is applied, should result in renaming of the activity.

Supporting Arguments

Rule 1 must be considered in terms of available resources within the developer's sphere of influence. One obvious choice is to obtain a separate contractor who has a history of successful V&V programs, is not in any way involved with the hardware or software procurements, and who has no other conflict of or vested interest. A second choice is to obtain the services of a qualified organization from outside the developer's group and establish them in this role; however, this organization must be able to satisfy the other five rules.

Rule 2 is so stated to avoid the misunderstanding between the term "validation" as used in defining the second stage of the software acquisition life cycle and the term "validation" used in V&V. The differences are quite obvious. In the former case, validation is the conceptual proof that the preliminary system design is ready to proceed into full-scale development and is indeed a part of the overall development cycle and is not in any way associated with V&V. In the latter case, validation is a specific set of activities that occurs during testing (and integration on larger systems) to ensure that system and software performance and quality requirements are satisfied. Because V&V is characteristically an additional resource allocated to a development effort, it is thought of as an overlay which should never impede or interfere with the development effort. For lack of a better term, V&V is a piggyback activity that goes largely where the development program leads it.

Rule 3 dictates that the program management office (development/ user agency) serve as the buffer through which the V&V organization requests data and documents and reports its evaluation and analysis results back to the developing contractor. This rule maintains the proper V&V objectivity with the developer and prevents him from complaining that his efforts are diluted or impacted by interference from the V&V group. Conversely, it prevents too close a relationship from forming between the two groups which would compromise the adversary relationship.

Rule 4 implies that the organization selected to perform V&V has a defined methodology and a set of tools and techniques that are complementary, not identical, to those used by the developer. In this way, synergistic rather than redundant effects can be derived. This rule does not preclude the sharing of large-scale simulations and analysis aids provided by the developer which will tend to better distribute their cost over the entire program.

Rule 5 pertains to verification activities that are fundamentally the complementary activities aligned to the development cycle phases. For example, design verification parallels the design period; code verification parallels the coding period, etc. Because of this parallelism and the cost savings possible from early discovery of requirement and design problems, V&V should begin as early as possible in the development cycle. Although each phase of development and its corresponding V&V activities can be thought of as having a unique character, they are by no means autonomous and have to be considered a continuous flow transitioning from phase to phase. Thus, a comprehensive verification discipline maintains its perspective in terms of predecessor events and data, its current state, and by logical implications is able to predict ahead at least into the near term to forecast risks and suggest redirection of future effort. A methodology which refuses to support the concept of information flow and pooling of pertinent data beyond each phase boundary, looking at itself only as a series of distinctly different steps, is indeed poor.

Rule 6 is directed at validation activities which are test and demonstration oriented. Validation is essentially that part of V&V which looks back at the software requirements and determines through testing that they are (or are not) satisfied by the observable system performance indicators. The implication of validation is that the system will meet its operational life cycle design commitments.

These precepts are in themselves insufficient to define V&V, but rather are a means of authenticating or disqualifying a program. They have little to do with the quality and application of methodology; these are the subjects of the following sections.

EXPANDING THE DEFINITION OF V&V

Verification and validation (V&V) is the systematic process of analyzing, evaluating, and testing system and software documentation and code to ensure the highest possible quality, reliability, and satisfaction of system needs and objectives. This is accomplished in a series of steps which are interfaced with the development process. Figure 1 presents an overview of this relationship depicted in its simplest form and uses commonly accepted names for each box. It is acknowledged that various Government and industry groups may have their own names which differ from these, but, hopefully, the intent is so obvious that further clarification is not necessary.

Verification is the iterative process aimed at determining whether the product of each step in the software development cycle fulfills all the requirements levied by the previous step:

Does B fulfill requirements of A?

Does C fulfill requirements of B? (+ A implied)

Does D fulfill requirements of C? (+ A and B implied)

In this way, each phase provides a definitive, verified baseline for the next. Perturbations must be fed back to each previous phase during development to ensure integrity of the requirements-design-code-

FIGURE 1. *V&V and the software development cycle*

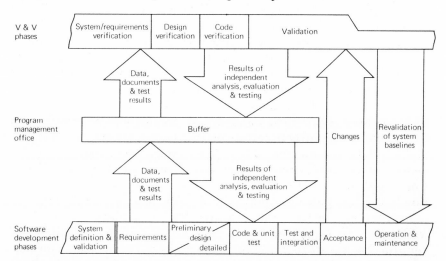

test chain. Any V&V methodology that does not support this feedback has serious shortcomings.

Validation is the process of executing the software package and comparing test results to required performance: Does D fulfill requirements of A? Comprehensive validation ensures that all software performance and quality requirements are adequately tested or observed and that the results can be repeated whenever necessary to support recalibration and rebaselining of the system after changes are installed. Thus, validation has no definite termination and can be used throughout the life of the system to maintain configuration and operational integrity.

Types of V&V

A number of adjectives have been used to describe the V&V process relative to its starting point in the software development cycle. Thus, the terms used herein are typical and nonsacred. For any V&V program that begins before or during the requirements phase, the terms "full, in-phase" V&V are appropriate. Conversely, if V&V begins during any subsequent phase of development, it can be neither of the preceding. The term "full" is dropped because all the influence the V&V group could and would otherwise have on the establishment and documentation of requirements becomes an after-the-fact retrospective activity, and cost savings from discovery of requirement imperfections are less than optimal. The term "in-phase" becomes immediately ambiguous since the first thing the V&V group must do is go back and verify the earlier phases (e.g., requirements). Once the V&V activity catches up and begins to run in sync with the development, the terms "partial, in-phase" V&V could apply, but are seldom used. Finally, there is an end-game V&V, somewhat characteristic of added test and integration resources, which is far less cost effective and requires the V&V group to perform much of its analysis in retrospect. It still requires limited requirements and design documentation analysis, but the emphasis shifts to concentrate on the results of testing and hence is highly validation oriented. Third-party independent testing and test analysis is certainly beneficial, but V&V is most effective and efficient when applied from the beginning of the development program, not simply the test phase. Application of V&V from the beginning will more than compensate the procurer for the dollars expended on V&V. Software error cost studies from a large number of sources all confirm that it costs 20 to 40 times more to fix a requirement error during testing than if it were fixed during production of the requirements document, hence the big payoff from full, in-phase V&V.

Some Qualifying Statements about V&V

The most controversial aspect of any discussion of V&V occurs whenever an attempt is made to detail the activities of each major phase. The three major things that make a concise, universal definition difficult are:

1. The nature of the software being developed — real or non-real time, scientific or business, highly algorithmic or logical, etc.
2. The uniqueness of the developing agency — peculiarities of specification trees, languages, coding practices, methods of testing, etc.
3. The V&V group's methodology — differences in emphasis, allocation of resources, tools, analysis techniques, products, etc.

Therefore, to avoid as much conflict and argument as possible, a minimum set of essential ingredients is given. Provided that these ingredients are present in the methodology, it becomes a matter of choice and tailoring of techniques to match the job parameters and customer desires. Thus, the descriptions of each V&V phase attempt to remain as generic and unambiguous as possible.

Three additional qualifications remain to be discussed before the detailed phase descriptions are presented:

1. A V&V phase called system verification can occur prior to requirements verification which concentrates upon all high-level system documentation including operations planning, the system specifications, trade-off studies, etc. Because of its similarity to requirements verification, its detailed description is omitted.

2. Design is quite often divided into a two-phase part of the cycle — preliminary and final, or high-level and detailed, or whatever anyone desires to call it to indicate the split. It has no significant impact on methodology and is consolidated in this chapter.

3. Few programs ever make a clean break between development phases. Overlaps and nonspecific transitions are, therefore, accepted as a reality of complex software development. Top-down structured software development practices cause many iterations between phases to occur as high levels are designed, coded, and tested to serve as the foundation for lower levels which repeat the process until the job is finished. The following guidelines have been established through experience to indicate that phase transitions have occurred.

   a. Normally, requirements verification continues from development contract award until the Part I (B5) computer program development specification is approved. This should be prior to, but can occur as late as, preliminary design review (PDR).

   b. Normally, design verification continues from the first availability of preliminary design material (usually as presented at PDR) through approval of the Part II (C5) computer program product specifications and the detailed design data to the start of coding (after critical design review [CDR]).

   c. Code verification includes the period covering actual coding and individual module (or unit) testing.

   d. Validation begins when groups of modules are combined into functionally testable groups and are usually turned over to a separate test and integration organization.

DETAILS OF EACH MAJOR V&V PHASE

Each V&V phase will now be addressed in detail, indicating the various functions and input/output information needed to perform these functions.

Requirements Verification

This V&V activity (Figure 2) examines the sources of the requirements, looks introspectively at the requirements themselves as stated in the associated documents, and attempts to look ahead at their impact on system/software design. The criticality and risks associated with each requirement are examined and those representing potential problems for implementation are given a high priority in terms of V&V resource allocation. A means of tracking the requirements must be established during this phase since the validation phase will ultimately use this information to check that the system performs as intended.

Since requirements are somewhat abstract and must be translated into software and hardware logical operations and algorithms during design, the use of automated verification tools is usually restricted to problem statement languages, correctness proofs, truth table exercises, and high-level simulations and models. The V&V contractor must consciously determine if such tools are worth their expense or if manual analytical techniques will serve just as well. Particular attention is given the testability of each requirement. In any case, the net product from the requirements verification phase should be a solid set of requirements documents essentially free of ambiguity, omission, and inconsistency. This goal is seldom realized in the real world and the anomalies and problems identified by this process are thus carried forward into the next phase as unresolved problems. However, this is not necessarily a weakness, since the identification process has brought them to light where particular attention can be given their solution during design.

A formal coupling between the requirements and design phases must be accommodated. Although this can take several forms, the V&V contractor usually utilizes an automated tool to first list, analyze, and then link the two together. Thus, each requirement is traced to a particular design element(s) and vice versa. This two-way relationship is very important in that it supports comparative analysis between phases.

Design Verification

This verification activity (Figure 3) examines the design of the software in terms of its logical integrity, ability to satisfy the requirements, mathematical operations, and timing (algorithms). Although there are many other items to be considered, such as data base design, control structures, task allocations and architecture, the most significant activities in this phase are based around the quality of the design documents and data. A different form of analytical tool can be em-

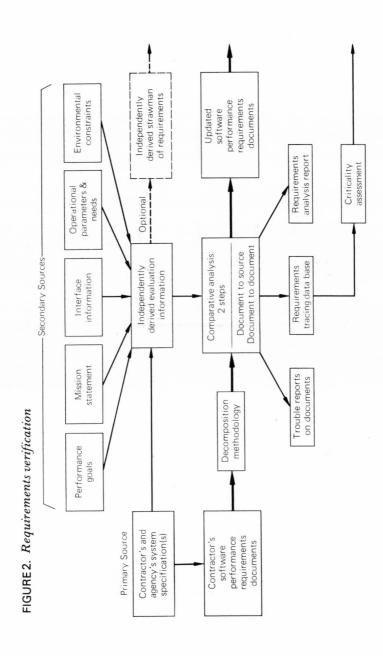

FIGURE 2. *Requirements verification*

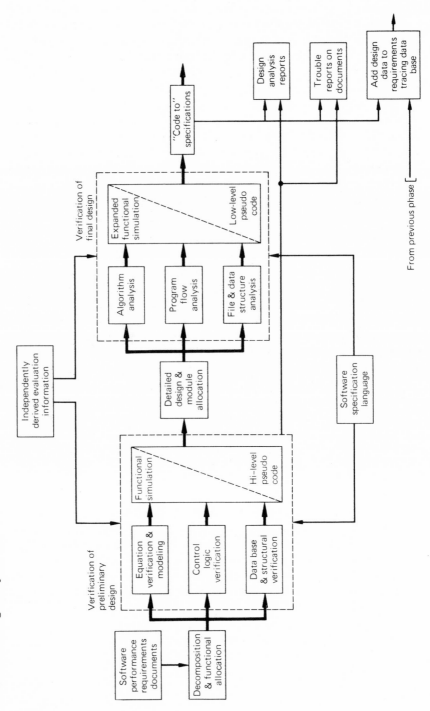

FIGURE 3. *Design verification*

ployed in this phase since the level of abstraction is further reduced from that of the requirements. Algorithms can be modeled and tested, logical flow can be simulated, special design languages can be used, data bases can be verified, constructs can be defined and the entire system is capable of being modeled, if desired. Because the detailed flow of data elements is described, overall timing and operational parameters can be examined analytically. This phase is usually viewed as two distinct parts, preliminary and detailed design.

After the design documentation reaches a point of sufficient definition and quality that coding can begin, a period of overlap may exist during which time two verification activities occur simultaneously — design and code verification. This is especially evident when top-down, structured programming techniques are involved. To appreciate this concept, recognize that coding begins at high levels while detailed design is still occurring at low levels. Iterations of this scheme occur until all levels are finally coded.

Code Verification

This V&V activity (Figure 4) begins when sufficient code exists to be examined analytically, either through inspection (code reading and such) or by automated analysis aids such as static and dynamic analyzers, standards enforcers, data base verifiers, etc. Often the analyst goes back to a model or simulation developed for design verification to compare it to the performance of a newly coded module. Equations coded for specific tasks are compared to baselined models to ensure the integrity of the implementation, etc. The programmer's testing to ensure error-free compilation and data base integrity (e.g., use of common variables) is considered part of coding, not testing.

Again, the automated tracing mechanism is used, this time to link particular elements of code to the design and requirements. This mechanism now synthesizes the first three development phases into a data stream. As significant portions of code are produced, the analysis environment takes on the form of testing, leaving behind the paper/calculator/modeling studies, and begins using more powerful tools such as emulators, code-level simulators, and, ultimately, the target computer. As this transition occurs, testing and integration begins. Again, this phase often has a vague starting point and is usually considered to be the point at which two or more modules already proven to be sane are integrated together and functionally tested by some form of driver.

Validation

Validation (Figure 5) parallels testing and integration. It begins

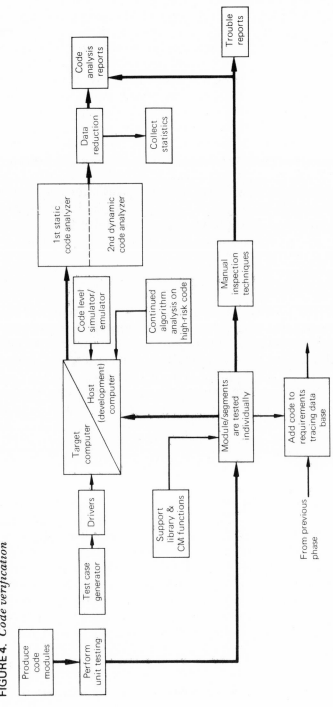

FIGURE 4. *Code verification*

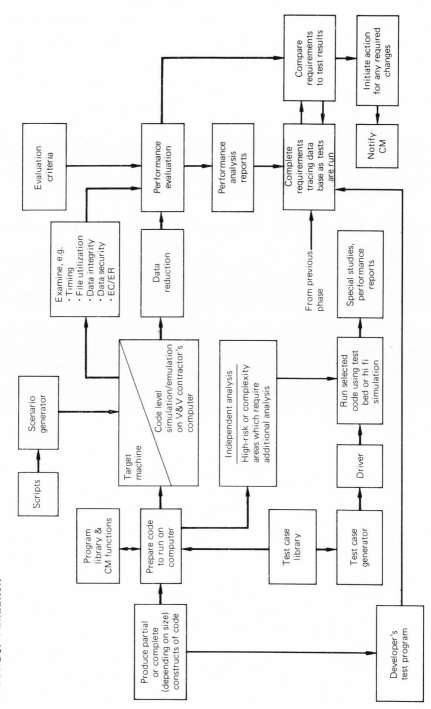

FIGURE 5. *Validation*

when sufficient amounts of code are present to perform validation of functional and performance requirements. Here the use of the requirements-to-design-to-code tracing mechanism pays off. This data base allows the V&V contractor to examine requirements with respect to particular tests intended to demonstrate them. Here the V&V organization divides its resources into two realms: (1) to monitor the developer's tests and (2) to perform independent tests often generated to go beyond those designed by the developer to try to "break" the system. By determining independently where the choke points and limits of the system are, the V&V group provides an important service to the procuring agency. He is able to say with confidence just how robust the system is and how well it can be expected to perform its mission even when unexpected problems occur.

The principal activities of validation are directed at assuring software quality. Through selected testing early in this phase, the testing can continue to use a host computer with simulations or emulations of the target computer, but ultimately no system can be truly validated by this type of testing and must finally use the hardware configuration of the production system for acceptance and operational testing.

The goal of validation is to say confidently that the observable and measurable quality of the system software meet (or exceed) their design goals. The requirements tracing tool is the mechanism through which this monitoring activity occurs. Thus, validation spreads back across the entire spectrum of development to ensure quality of the delivered software.

V&V IS ALSO MANAGEMENT SUPPORT

The degree of management support provided by the V&V organization is largely determined by the needs of the program management office and therefore varies widely even among similar programs. Since there are no predefined management mechanisms included in the generic V&V methodology except for software requirements tracing, the following list is considered typical of the services that a V&V organization could provide the program manager:

1. Independent status and resource monitoring
2. Configuration management support
3. Open item tracking
4. Program impact and cost evaluation
5. Change evaluation
6. Software reliability studies
7. Evaluation and quantification of documentation
8. Participation in reviews and committees

248

9. Collection and evaluation of development statistics
10. Software library maintenance
11. Ancillary planning and control mechanisms

There is no attempt to prioritize this list since the degree of need for support in a particular area self-defines the priority.

TYPICAL OUTPUTS OF A V&V PROGRAM

Because of the adaptive nature of V&V, there can be no predetermined list of products which are always generated on each and every program, but rather there are guidelines which suggest what might be expected. Assuming a full, in-phase V&V program, the list would probably include the following:

1. Risk and criticality study reports
2. Requirement analysis reports
3. Design analysis reports
4. Code analysis reports/data reduction
5. V&V test plans and procedures
6. Automated testing and analysis reports
7. Independently generated scripts and scenarios
8. Interface analysis reports
9. Model and simulation documentation and user reports
10. Error analysis and trouble reports
11. Independent evaluation of developer's test program
12. Reports of special studies (usually directed at high-risk areas)
13. Validated requirements data base
14. System performance analysis report

The philosophy behind the V&V products is to establish a pipeline through which informal communiques are passed quickly to the program manager with formal follow-up procedures to ensure that the problem and analysis reports include the disposition and status of all issues affecting the system. The style and presentation media selected for all reporting mechanisms must be chosen deliberately to provide high visibility and understanding. The products should be selected to provide a chronological history of the program, life cycle traceability and in-depth evaluation of each critical element of the program.

PLANNING FOR EFFECTIVE V&V

This subject alone could fill a textbook, and therefore discussion is limited to the more important issues which are treated in an abbreviated form:

1. Get started as early in the program as possible.
2. Produce a V&V plan, preferably as part of the proposal, live and work by it, and change and add to it when necessary.
3. Provide mechanisms which lock the V&V program to the developer's schedules and milestones.
4. Perform a criticality assessment, preferably as part of the proposal, which enables realistic resource allocations. (V&V cannot repeat everything the developer does; therefore, concentrate resources for highest program payoff.)
5. Select experienced V&V personnel for all key positions.
6. Perform conscientious tradeoffs between automated and manual analysis techniques.
7. Share the developer's models, simulations, and tools where possible to avoid costly and time-consuming parallel developments.
8. Provide additional models, tools, etc., where the development program is deficient. Share the results of analysis (via program management as buffer).
9. Provide management support mechanisms that contribute to the orderly control and coordination of V&V and development activities within the overall project.
10. Tailor the methods, tools, and techniques to suit the attributes of the system.

The last issue has so many facets that precise direction is difficult. Two examples can be used to illustrate the point. If the system being developed is real time, sensor driven and pushes the state of the art, the V&V activities would of necessity emphasize modeling and simulation, timing studies, scenario generation, extensive exercise-driven testing, performance measuring/monitoring, execution optimization, etc. Conversely, if the system is a management information system, then the emphasis shifts from algorithmic to logical operations, data base and I/O optimization, user interface control, data security, etc.

Some V&V planning is intuitive and some is based on painstaking analysis of all the known characteristics of the program and the system to be built. A key factor in V&V program effectiveness is to build in flexibility so that the V&V program can be redirected without massive replanning. This can best be accomplished by a combination of "soft" planning factors including contingencies and options, purposely nonspecific tasks such as special studies, independent testing that is fully defined only after the developer's testing is performed and points to areas which are not adequately tested or that fail to pass acceptance criteria, and by remaining at generic tasking levels where possible (e.g., design documentation review). Procurers should be aware that it is highly desirable not to attempt to lock the V&V contractor into an overly confining statement of work. The strategy that must permeate a V&V effort is that of problem-oriented tasking: discover and work to correct the deficiencies — do not try to take on the developer's job.

SELECTING APPROPRIATE V&V TOOLS

Software literature abounds with tool surveys, articles of the specific tools designed as cure-alls for particular types of software, development methodologies, special languages, new higher-order languages, etc. The space limitations of this chapter prevent any effective evaluation or critique thereof; however, it is possible to discuss what those tools and techniques are supposed to do — reduce or eliminate errors. Errors occur in two realms — specification or precoding and code. Specifications generally cover requirements and design almost exclusively, save only the modeling and simulation that include some software. Code covers all tangible evidence that can be exercised and tested. Therefore, two kinds of tools must be employed — those that assist in the analysis of the specification realm and those that operate upon or with the code.

A point that must be appreciated is that specification errors can be just as catastrophic as code errors. It should be noted that several studies, including one performed by the author in late 1975, disclosed that a little more than 60 percent of all errors occurring in a sample of 5 large software development programs were latent errors emanating from faults in the requirements and design documentation. When such a large number of errors is allowed to go undetected until testing, significant cost and schedule impacts occur.

In the same analysis the more than 4300 errors examined were arranged into classes and types. Out of the 76 error types determined to be a minimal set for identification, a subset of only 15 covered 85 percent of these errors. Table 1 is included to briefly describe the 15 error types of the specification errors. The most obvious conclusion that can be reached in terms of tool and technique selection is therefore to choose those which concentrate on the error types listed.

The same analysis also looked carefully at coding errors and disclosed that only 4 error types encompassed 76 percent of all implementation errors. Thus, the conclusions surrounding tool selection for testing code should be oriented toward trapping and correcting the error types shown in Table 2.

251

TABLE 1. Specification error types

Requirements Faults

Operating rules information inadequate or partially missing (largest contributor)

Performance criteria/information inadequate or partially missing

Ambient environment information inadequate or partially missing

System mission information inadequate or partially missing

Requirement incompatible with other requirements

89 percent of all requirements errors and omissions fall into these five categories

Design Faults

Processing

Erroneous logic or sequencing (largest contributor)

Required processing results inaccurate

Routine does not expect or accept a required parameter

Routine will not accept all data within allowable range limits

Validity checks are not made for I/O data

Recovery procedures are not implemented or are not adequate

Missing or inadequate required processing

85 percent of all design processing errors and omissions fall into these seven categories

Data

Erroneous or ambiguous values (largest contributor)

Erroneous or inadequate storage

Missing variables

89 percent of all design data errors and omissions fall into these three categories

TABLE 2. Code error types

Erroneous or inadequate decision logic or sequencing

Erroneous or inadequate arithmetic computations

Erroneous branching

Branching or other test done incorrectly

76 percent of all implementation errors and omissions fall into these four categories

NEW DIRECTIONS FOR FUTURE V&V PROGRAMS

Experience factors and hindsight strongly indicate that at least half the V&V resources should be expended during the precode phase of software development. This not only means an early start, preferably in phase with the developer throughout the program, but also requires the V&V organization to concentrate heavily on the specification deficiencies to ensure that no code is developed before the design is adequate and truly implementable. Then, during the code and testing phases, the V&V organization must share certain resources of the developer, provide tools and techniques which complement and augment the developer's, and should continuously strive to uncover the true performance bounds and limitations of the system. These goals can only be realized through a systematic, flexible methodology that at all times stresses the quality of the final products. By combining an effective V&V program with the other attributes of software quality management, a significant step can be taken toward the objectives of highly reliable software developed within cost and schedule constraints.

CHAPTER 16

Software Testing in Computer-Driven Systems

J. GARY NELSON

INTRODUCTION

A French meteorological satellite sends erroneous destruct signals to 72 of 141 high-altitude weather balloons [1]. The Ballistic Missile Early Warning System (BMEWS) mistakes the rising moon for a massive Soviet missile raid [2]. Both problems occurred because of computer software shortcomings. Consider the Strategic Air Command's Auto-mated Command Control System (SACCS 465L). One software error happened each day. About 95 percent of the SACCS 465L software delivered to SAC had to be rewritten [3].

Why did these critical problems go so long without discovery and correction? Because the state of the art in software testing lacked the sophistication to uncover them during the development test process; because proper testing that may have uncovered them early in the de-velopment cycle was either done poorly or not done at all.

The last 20 years have seen unprecedented technological advances in reduction of size and weight in computer hardware, plus improve-ment of the computer power per dollar. These advances have spurred the technical community into finding more and bigger jobs for the cheaper resources to do. The technology has gone from tubes/

transistors through integrated circuits to medium- and large-scale integrated elements. However, two decades ago, software was in an era when highly efficient programs which used little of the scarce and expensive computer hardware resources were sought . . . when the size and complexity of the programs could be handled by one good programmer . . . when the design of the software was largely left up to the programmer's art . . . when he *tested* his own product. We now see software moving toward an era when high efficiency is not the prime concern since computer hardware resources are not scarce nor expensive . . . when the software design is extremely complex . . . when self-documentation and readability of the code demand programming standards rather than individual programming style . . . when the only thing that programmer testing will show is that it works exactly as he programmed it.

From an economic perspective, it is predicted that in 1985, 95 percent of the total system development costs will be allocated for software [1]. If one combines these estimates with the fact that 34 to 50 percent of software development costs are devoted to check-out and test, it becomes obvious that software testing merits considerable attention. This chapter examines the complex processes of software testing emphasizing some of the more critical issues.

TESTING PRINCIPLES

Before we discuss specific testing methodologies, let us state some general philosophical principles that a developer or project manager must consider in establishing a viable and profitable test program. Some of these issues will be reexamined in more detail later in this chapter.

Integrated Test Planning

Software testing is not a one-time event. Adequate testing can only be achieved if it is performed throughout the development phase (and, to some extent, during the operational phase) of the system life cycle.

As was mentioned before, software problems still exist in often aggravating quantities through deployment and into operational utilization. Therefore, testing should be considered throughout the system's useful life. Please note that testing here connotes planned, disciplined, instrumented, and repeatable exercises of the system or some developmental test bed (or the requirements and specifications themselves) with the expressed purpose of determining some attribute or performance parameter of the computer/software. Operational testing and

256

field utilization of the system should not be included even though problems may be uncovered there.

There are at least four general levels at which software testing should be considered. These levels, illustrated in Figure 1, are: module testing, module integration testing, software system testing, and target system integration testing. These levels are discussed in more detail below. However, test planning must cover the full range of testing these levels represent.

Testing Organizations

The development of a computer-based system must include all of the participants, especially the testers, from beginning to end. In order to provide the required lead time and prerequisite activities needed to assure a smooth development and testing, a group which might be called a computer resource working group should be formed early with representatives from the user, tester(s), contractor, and program manager's office. This should be the forum whereby inputs from the various disciplines can be presented, integrated, and (if necessary) traded off to the benefit of the project as a whole.

Usually, the developing contractor's job is to deliver a complete system; so, depending on his facilities and capabilities, he could provide testing at all levels. In the late 1950s the Atlas Missile Program hired an "Independent Software Tester" to provide additional unbiased software test support. This independent software tester concept has since been used on nearly 20 major defense and NASA systems. Now called a Validation and Verification (V&V) contractor, his job extends over the module, functional area, software system, and, in some cases, target system testing.

Regardless of the names of the tester(s), the project manager must assure that the software testing is coherent and flows smoothly through the various hierarchical levels. This means that sufficient information need be transmitted to and among all testing participants *throughout the entire development cycle* and that each tester knows explicitly how he fits into the testing scheme.

Because testing does exist throughout several phases of the life cycle, different organizations institute various types of testing each with differing methodologies and goals. The programmer performs debugging and check-out; quality organizations perform QA testing or V&V testing; other groups are responsible for evaluation testing, while still other groups may do acceptance testing. The point is that since various organizations or activities do perform testing, it is difficult to

FIGURE 1. *Physical software development and testing levels*

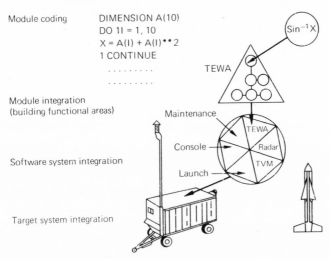

Module coding

```
DIMENSION A(10)
DO 1I = 1, 10
X = A(I) + A(I)**2
1 CONTINUE
    . . . . . . . .
    . . . . . . . .
```

Module integration
(building functional areas)

Software system integration

Target system integration

single out one individual or organization which has the total responsibility for all testing functions.

One word on independence of the testing organizations. As previously mentioned, the early V&V testers were called "independent testers" . . . but, independent of whom? They worked for the acquisition manager, not the contractor. This is not to imply that the contractor would be dishonest. It does imply that the creator of a software product is naturally biased toward the way he produced it. A programmer testing his own product will always show that it meets the requirements (otherwise, nothing would be released). As the development reaches the system integration level, the testing should be even more independent of the developing contractor. However, testing can never be independent of the acquisition manager. To re-emphasize, testing must be an integral part of the development process, not relegated to down-stream, poorly understood circle on a PERT chart that is destined to terminate when the budget runs out. If used wisely, the payoffs of a good testing program are high.

Attitude

A proper attitude toward testing in general must be established. Software problems historically linger beyond deployment. Testing, therefore, *must* be directed toward the identification and eradication of software problems. This direction is inevitably at odds with the idea that a development in which few problems are evident is aesthetically better than a development in which many problems are discovered. In this type of system development the opposite is true. However, from a tester's point of view, he is hated most when he does his job best. Additionally, the tester should never be used to give demonstrations and political shows, especially for computer-based systems. First, this type of system is likely to defeat the purpose of the demonstration by failing in the middle of the performance; second, the tester's time and the developer's usually scarce money can be better spent determining where, when, and how the code "breaks."

Prerequisite Functions

Another basic principle is to assure that testing-related prerequisite functions are done in a timely fashion. When not adequately provided for, testing becomes impossible to perform. The result is that testing is delayed and/or doesn't provide definitive information about encountered problems. Systems reach critical decision points with the software not sufficiently developed. System-level testing too often becomes a software find-and-fix debugging exercise which, for computer-driven systems, is extremely expensive and very time consuming. Testing run-ons and delays, coupled with mounting costs, pressure decision makers into fielding "something" and fixing it later, hopefully.

Just what are some of these test-related prerequisite functions? Probably the single most important prerequisite function is the drafting and verification of system/software requirements and specifications. It is here that the engineering aspects of software are displayed. In this type of system the software must be designed before it is coded. This must be done in a top-down fashion to assure that what is coded satisfies the system's intended goals. Within the Defense community the hierarchy of requirements and specifications is spelled out in MIL-STD-490 and (for software in particular) MIL-STD-483. In these standards each level is an embellishment of the one above it. In software, a high degree of explicitness is needed to assure success in not only testing, but in every facet of the R&D test and evaluation process. Good requirements and specifications are really the development's road map.

Another prerequisite function is the planning for and procuring of test instrumentation and test tools. Many automated tools exist on the open market today. However, molding and modifying them to fit the particular software at hand is not always an easy (or practicable) enterprise. These automated test tools include categorically:

Static analyzers
Code analyzers
Symbolic evaluation systems
Self-metric instrumentation
Dynamic assertion processors
Test data generators
Test file generators
Execution verifiers
Output comparators
Test harnesses
Software monitors
Hardware monitors
System drivers

The testing level that uses the particular category of tools moves from raw code to system testing as per this list. In general, considerable lead time will be required to adapt or build these tools. For example, the system-level driver is often as complex a device as the system being driven. It must be operational and validated by the time the target system is ready for system-level testing.

Another prerequisite function that should be performed is simulation, especially computer/software system system simulation. Computer/software system simulations are discrete event simulations that represent the utilization of hardware resources in time during the operation of program/module code segments. Operating system functioning is also played. These simulations, originally designed and used to study data processing installation hardware and job stream architecture, are extremely helpful throughout the development of these computer-driven systems. Among their uses are:

Sizing studies
Hardware/software trade offs
Timing studies
System parameter interrelationships
Design sensitivities
    Resource utilization
    Time marks and windows
    Computational accuracies
Test scenario design
Failure analysis
Educational tool

This type of simulation can easily be written utilizing several existing macro-language software packages available commercially. These packages allow the user to insert hardware and software architectural, control, and performance parameters plus a dynamic input stream. The simulation outputs can cover a wide range of resource utilization reports in terms of time accumulation and distribution. As the system software (and hardware) parameters become more firmly known, this "table-driven" simulation can be easily updated.

Since this simulation can be used by all participants in all stages of development (plus maintenance), it should be physically located centrally within the developing organization in order to be accessible to all participants.

These prerequisite functions will be addressed later under methodologies.

Additional Axioms

We add to the set of principles discussed above, additional testing axioms given by Meyers [4] which should be considered by management in formulating its software testing strategies. These axioms do not represent a complete list; and we offer them here without explanation.

A good test case is a test case that has a high probability of detecting an undiscovered error, not a test case that shows that the program works correctly.

One of the most difficult problems in testing is knowing when to stop.

It is impossible to test your own program.

A necessary part of every test case is a description of the expected results or output.

Avoid nonreproducible or on-the-fly testing.

Write test cases for invalid as well as valid input conditions.

Thoroughly inspect the results of each test.

As the number of detected errors in a piece of software increases, the probability of the existence of more undetected errors also increases.

Assign your most creative programmers to testing.

Ensure that testability is a key objective in your software design.

The design of a system should be such that each module is integrated into the system only once.

Never alter the program to make testing easier.

Testing must start with objectives.

TEST STRATEGIES

This chapter considers four levels of testing within the development effort — module coding and debugging, module integration or functional area building, software system integration, and target system integration. Figure 1 depicts this graphically. The module coding and debugging level is done mainly by the programmer himself and is highly dependent upon static, syntaxical checks and is highly "answer" oriented (where the exact result is anticipated). The module integration level can be performed by programmer teams and/or by test organizations both within and outside of the developing contractor's organization. Here, the testing is much like module testing plus the problem of module integration on a "local level." Some dynamic testing is usually introduced at this level.

After individual modules and program segments (functional areas) have been tested (debugged and validated), we are faced with two major categories of tests. The first of these is software system integration testing where the various modules and/or functional areas are merged together to form the entire computer program. Several possible approaches can be used to combine the modules, each with various impacts upon testing. Software system integration testing is primarily used to validate proper interface (data flow and control) among the modules that constitute the computer program.

Integration Testing

The process of putting modules together to make functional areas and putting functional areas together to make software systems is known as integration. The testing here is directed at the interfaces and the abilities of mutual coordination and tolerance among the code segments.

Classically, there are two types of integration testing: bottom-up and top-down. However, more recently variations of these strategies have emerged. These variations attempt to utilize the best features of bottom-up and top-down approaches while minimizing the disadvantages.

262

Bottom-up testing: As the name implies, this strategy puts unit testing ahead of everything else. Modules that call or invoke no other modules are tested first, then the modules that call them are tested; and so on up the hierarchy until the software system is completely treated as an entity. However, to get the "calling" module to make the call under interesting data conditions requires "drivers" to be written for each module. There are available commercial tools to assist in doing this for certain languages. One major advantage of bottom-up testing is that it uses proven components in support of the test objective.

Top-down testing: Although the name would imply an exact opposite definition from bottom-up testing, top-down testing usually starts at the top of the hierarchical structure, but first moves down through the levels tracing the paths that get the system's input/output working first. This is done so that the testing can then be driven by user or simulated sensor inputs. The major drawback to top-down testing is that "stubs" or simulations of missing or not-yet-developed modules are required. In very complex and/or real-time software, these can represent quite a formidable and expensive undertaking.

System Testing

Once the software is integrated, one then considers total system testing. System testing is not a comprehensive function test where each function described in the B level software specification is validated. Most software systems are too complex to be subjected to such exhaustive testing after integration. Rather, system testing attempts to expose inconsistencies between the system and its original system-level requirements, while at the same time investigating suspected software weaknesses. It also serves to validate "assumed" or simulated environments or inputs.

One obvious property that each "level" of testing should have is the ability to provide intelligent feed-back to lower levels in case of problems. This means that system-level testing strategy must be more than mechanically putting a system through its paces, even if the test design and instrumentation are well thought out relative to a system-level specification. The system tester must look at the system through the software's "eyes" as being a collection of hardware to be controlled. He, therefore, cannot treat software as a "black box." On the other hand, he does not have time to deal with the code-level problems. He must do "gray box" testing. His test case selection (which is usually limited by time and money) must include scenarios that exercise high problem areas or areas where real-world environment may be quite different from the environment simulated in earlier tests. This means that his monitorship of earlier activities is essential. Further, if he is to provide intelligent feed-back, instrumentation must be provided. This will be discussed later. There may also be a requirement for a system-level driver. The system-level tester should know this by comparing the system performance requirements to his capability to produce inputs at the levels required. When a driver is needed, it should be made known early enough in the program to have it available in a timely fashion. Meyers [4] discusses 14 categories of system-level testing that may be required. All of these point to a general strategy of starting early, assuring that prerequisite functions (requirements/specs validation, instrumentation, drivers, simulations, etc.) are done, and designing tests that not only verify system requirements, but that also fully investigate problem areas.

TESTING METHODOLOGIES

The following discussions cover three of the more important test methodologies: requirements, simulation and instrumentation.

Software Requirements Analysis

For software, as well as for other major components of complex systems, one of the primary activities of the tester/evaluator is to determine whether that major component meets requirements. Whereas the methodologies for this type of activity have been fairly well developed and employed for hardware, the same is not true for software. One of the basic problems with respect to software test and evaluation is the determination of what the software requirements are. A second problem, once the requirements have been identified, is whether they are testable. Experience has shown that software requirements are very often incompletely, vaguely, or qualitatively stated, and thus are not testable. Two additional factors which greatly complicate the problems of developing software are: the attitude that software is not a critical item, but is something to be "poured in" after the hardware is built; and the tendency to change the software to adjust for deficiencies of another system component.

A software requirements analysis involves assuring that software requirements are identified and tested. Steps which can be followed in such an analysis are: the identification of the requirements; the tracing of these requirements, both back to the system requirements and forward to the code; and the demonstration that the requirements were met.

Requirements Identification

The initial problem for the tester/evaluator is to determine what a software requirement is. For most software-supported tactical and weapons systems, a software or data processing system requirements document exists. The problem is that in these documents the "requirements" are not clearly identified; further, information in these documents varies from a general discussion of a system requirement in some cases to a detailed flowchart of how to code a routine (not a requirement) in other cases. This lack of understanding of what the real software requirements are creates problems for the developer as well as for the tester/evaluator—the developer has no more idea of what to build than the tester/evaluator has of what to test and evaluate.

The first matter to be addressed is what constitutes a requirement and how it is to be identified from the maze of documentation. To be implementable and testable, a requirement does not stop with a general statement of what is to be done; it must also contain descriptive information that states its performance attributes (e.g., accuracy, volume, interfaces, etc.). Thus, the identification of requirements should include not only the basic requirement statement, but the descriptors or attributes of each requirement as well. Table 1 lists performance descriptors (PDs) that will provide the minimum information necessary to implement a requirement, along with summary definitions of each PD.

Also included in the identification of requirements is the assessment of the adequacy with which the requirements are stated. This should give an indication of the readiness of the developer to proceed with implementation.* The presence or absence of PD information is indicative of the degree to which the necessary attributes of requirements are stated. This does not imply that the software requirements are responsive to the system requirements or that they are complete; it is an indication of the detail with which software requirements have been stated. Nor must every PD be specified for every requirement. How-

---

*The judgment of the adequacy of the requirements specification is typically developer, not tester, responsibility. The tester's concern with requirements testability is, however, apparent.

TABLE 1. Performance descriptors for software requirements

1. Requirement: A general, but concise, statement of the system or software requirement. The details of the requirement will be presented in supporting columns. The requirements will be structured so that the system-level requirement needing software support will be stated first, followed by the lower level software requirements. The software requirements will be distinguished by placing a dot (°) before each requirement. Additional levels of dots (°° or °°°) can be used to designate breakdown of requirements to even lower-level statements.

2. Source Selection: Document from which each requirement was extracted, followed by the section number (DPSR, FS, DS, MM-3.2.1).

3. Implementing Process: The software unit which is intended to provide the logic needed to satisfy the requirement. For the system requirement, the implementing process will be the major software function(s) which provide overall control.

4. Input: The data (tables, files, or other form) which are necessary to fulfill the requirement. The general guideline is to provide only that information which is required external to the implementing process. Data required in local processing should not be included.

5. Processing Condition: The statement of what conditions, events, system status, etc. (i.e., the software environment) must be present before the implementing process control is provided.

6. Output: Data (tables, files or other form) provided at the completion of the implementing process. See input for additional information.

7. Constraints: Any rules, regulations, etc., which are imposed on the software system as a whole, i.e., priority structure, etc. These are generally determined through review of the supporting information for the requirement.

8. Executing Sequence: The order in which the implementing process is executed relative to other implementing processes can be stated in Boolean form, e.g., (A) (B) (C). Conditions under which control is passed should be noted. No attempt should be made to force several or all implementing processes into a sequence. Processes should be related as specifically stated in the DPSR or as can be determined from related information within the DPSR.

9. Error Response: A statement of what course should be followed in case of an error, such as voids in data, hardware failures, overloads, etc.

10. Processing Volume: The maximum level of processing per unit of time which the system should be capable of, i.e., five tracks, four missiles.

11. Accuracy: The accuracy to which processing should be carried, i.e., tracking of a target within certain boundaries, range to 1 foot, etc.

12. Time: Any constraints on amount of time the implementing process has to complete its function; e.g., time the process should be initiated or time the process should be completed.

13. Sizing: Resource requirements needed in response to the stated implementing process, i.e., memory, tape, I/O channels, etc.

14. Cross Reference: Any reference to any other document, section of a document, or processing unit which will provide supporting information or execution support.

15. Comments: Any additional information needed to fully describe the subject being discussed.

---

ever, the lower the level of documentation which must be reached before open PDs are specified, the more subject to interpretation (and therefore to error) the requirement becomes.

Identifying the software requirements from documentation, such as the type A specification or data processing system requirements, is only the first step in the requirements analysis. Next, it is necessary to determine the traceability of the requirements both from user requirements to code and from code to user requirements. The former will be discussed here. Both are equally important.

Requirements Tracing

As previously stated, the implementation documentation will, in many cases, provide details of the requirement itself in the form of PDs which were not detailed in the requirements document. In this sense, the implementation documentation not only describes how each requirement will be implemented but completes the description and defines additional requirements.* Thus, a first result, or by-product, of this trace is completion of the definition of software requirements. The real products of this trace are information on:

1. Software requirements which are satisfied, totally or partially, by the implementation (including both program structure and function).
2. Software requirements omitted in the implementation.
3. Implemented structures or functions which are not necessary to support the software requirements.

Restated, this downward trace provides information on the completeness and adequacy of the implementation, including requirements which are missing from the implementation, and the exposure of an

---

*This is stated here simply as a matter of fact. The common practice of partial or incomplete statement of PDs in requirements-level documents does not provide for a strong requirements baseline.

extraneous implementation. Such conditions could reflect a misinterpretation of requirements, an expansion or redefinition of the actual requirements, the addition of unrequired "niceties," or a variety of other unauthorized occurrences which would increase the cost and time of development and decrease the quality of the resultant software.

The requirements trace, then, is an analysis conducted early in the development cycle to assess the responsiveness or conformity of the software implementation to the system requirements. The alternative is to rely on test results later in the development cycle, at a point where the cost of detection and elimination of errors has substantially increased. In addition, absolutely complete testing of software for complex tactical and weapon systems is neither physically possible nor cost effective. This does not mean that an acceptable (and in that sense "complete") test program is unattainable; but it does seem to place added emphasis on the necessity for requirements tracing. Software requirements can be traced downward by comparing information from the system, functional, and product documents.

Testing to Requirements

The test design process is much more complex and involved than generally considered. It is not the specification of a few system-level tests to be conducted toward or at the end of the development process; it is a multileveled, multifaceted operation which must be considered throughout the entire development cycle. It involves a detailed knowledge and comprehension of the software and system requirements as well as the design of scenarios to test these requirements. This is of particular significance with large, complex software packages, where complete testing is impossible. The test designer must, based on his knowledge of the requirements, PDs, and implementation, identify a limited number of scenarios or test cases on which to base his evaluation. It would appear that the overall familiarity with requirements and the detailed understanding of the above, equip the analyst for test design.

This leads to another important consideration in test design — that of collecting data from each test. Clearly, the evaluation of any test is dependent not just on the information produced by a test, but on the information collected during that test. Typical of many software controlled or supported military systems, some of which are still being developed, is the inadequacy of or even disregard for information and data collection on software/computer system performance. Collection and recording of data during the operation of a real-time software system does present some problems, in particular the impact of the time required for collection/recording on the real-time process. The seemingly obvious solution lies in the philosophy that the capability for collecting and recording, and the time required for this during real-time operations should be designed into the software/computer system.

Methods or techniques for software testing are more expensive than one might anticipate, and more diverse than a narrow definition of testing might allow. They can be categorized as either static or dynamic: static methods are those which do not involve the execution of (i.e., passing of data through) the target software; dynamic methods are those which do involve execution of the target software. Thus, testing can include not only testing, design and functional requirements in the dynamic sense, but also in the static sense, such as documentation analysis and simulation.* In view of the impossibility of complete dynamic testing, these static methods become necessary forms of testing. This chapter will not discuss each method and its application to dynamic and/or functional requirements; however, it should be noted that there is more than one way to approach the problems of comprehensive software testing.

Role of the System Tester/Evaluator

The role of the tester/evaluator in requirements testing varies from unit through integration and system-level testing. Initially, the role in testing is one of passive involvement, shifting to a more and more active involvement as the test program progresses. At the unit test level, the tester should have a general understanding of the unit test program and philosophy so he can advise the project manager of its adequacy. This involvement by the tester, in keeping with the single integrated development test policy, is necessary for two reasons:

1. Because of the limited amount of system level testing that can be performed, demonstrations of many of the functional re-

---

*Design requirements are those which relate to the program structure or architecture. Included are timing, sequencing, and management and control of the software/computer system. Many of the executive/operating system requirements and the software control (threading) requirements fall into this class. Functional requirements, on the other hand, are those which relate to implementation of math/logic models, accuracies, volumes, and management and control of hardware (e.g., radar, missile). Most of the application software requirements fall into this category. Often it is difficult to distinguish software functional requirements from system functional requirements.

quirements and capabilities of the software which occur during unit testing cannot be repeated in the higher-level tests.

2. Because of the criticality to the tester/evaluator of the data collection and reduction capability during the higher-level tests, evidence of an adequate data collection and recording capability must be demonstrated during unit testing.

At the integration test level, the tester/evaluator's involvement becomes more active. Here many of the top-level requirements relative to software architecture and hardware-software interfaces will be demonstrated. The tester/evaluator should assess the adequacy of the integration test program, identify additional testing needs and assist in the integration of them into the test program, participate in establishing acceptance test criteria, and participate in the evaluation of acceptance test results. At the system test level, the tester/evaluator is again very actively involved. Whereas integration level tests are oriented more toward demonstrating that subsystem (software in this case) level requirements were met, system-level tests are oriented toward demonstrating that the integrated subsystems meet system requirements. The tester/evaluator should assess the adequacy of the system-level test program, identify additional testing needs and assist in the integration of them into the test program, participate in establishing acceptance test criteria, and participate in the evaluation of acceptance test results.

Again, it is not sufficient for the system tester/evaluator to become involved only at system-level testing. Many of the software/system requirements are not demonstrated, or even demonstrable, at this level. Furthermore, if deficiencies are noted (e.g., inadequate testing, insufficient data collection and recording, or even incomplete or inadequate statement of requirements), it is too far into the development cycle to have impact without severe or potentially severe repercussions on schedules and costs.

Software/Computer System Simulation

The application of simulations in the test and evaluation of complex systems and their subsystems is a well-established precedent in both industry and Government. Since any type of testing short of a full-up field test involves some degree of simulation, this is not surprising. All of the software testing during unit- and integration-level and probably during most of the system-level testing would qualify as some form of simulation.

Most test and evaluation techniques are addressed to the functional characteristics of the software/system (e.g., the functional perform-ance of the target tracking filter or the guidance and control laws). Of equal importance, however, is the assessment of the allocation of the data processing resources (both software and hardware) to support these functional operations. It is of little tactical significance to have an ideal tracking filter coded into the software if the program units which contain that filter cannot be enabled and provided with the pro-cessing resources (e.g., CPU time, memory access) necessary to per-form those operations, i.e., if the design of the total software process cannot support the functional operations. The system sensitivities to software design are generally not observable under nonstressing condi-tions; however, under stressing or high-load conditions, where proces-sing resources are at a premium, these sensitivities are observable. Simulation of the software design provides a mechanism for testing and evaluating that design under a variety of load conditions.

Two approaches to software/computer system simulation are the use of a "package" simulator and the use of a "language" simulator:

1. A package simulator provides a generalized algorithmic model of a software/computer system into which a user can put those parameters which define his system. A primary purpose for using a package simulator is that the model itself is prebuilt, and the period for coding, check-out, and validation of the model is avoided.
2. A language simulator, on the other hand, is actually a special-ized programming language tailored to the specification and simulation of software/computer systems.

CONCEPTUAL-LEVEL SIMULATION. Conceptual level simulation is done at a very high level, considering each major software function (or operation) as a single job. This type of modeling would be appropriate early in the software development process. It should be done as soon as the basic software requirements, the type A specifications, are identi-fied, before the code is written. Its basic purpose would be to provide an interactive model of the software requirements, in order to assess initial process designs, and to provide initial timing and sizing esti-mates. (The type of modeling and simulation suggested at this level may well be pencil-and-paper studies not requiring the use of auto-mated or computerized simulation techniques.)

TASK-LEVEL SIMULATION. Task level simulation breaks the software functions into their component tasks. This breakout could be at any of several levels of detail, depending on either information availability or the purpose of the simulation, or both, and would be based on the type B5 computer program development specifications and/or type C5 computer program product specification.

Software/Computer System Instrumentation

One of the most vital prerequisite functions that must be performed is the planning for and procuring of instrumentation and test tools. Many automated tools exist on the open market today. (In fact, one of the most comprehensive glossaries of software tools and techniques is provided in reference 9.) Probably the least understood of the instrumentation is the use of monitors for system-level testing.

A variety of both hardware monitors and software monitors is available in commercial systems. Monitoring problems arise, however, with respect to special-purpose software/computer systems such as those generally associated with military tactical and/or weapon systems.

SOFTWARE MONITORING. A software monitor is usually thought of as a special routine or program incorporated into the executive software which will cause certain data related to the processing which is occurring to be collected. Typical of the data collected are routine processing sequence and processing history, routine start and stop times, executive routine intervention, missed deadlines, and processor idle time.

Although not a software monitor in the purest sense, another type of data collection which is built into a software routine is the collection of data related to the functional performance of that routine. This type of collection is appropriate for applications programs and includes target data, missile data, radar data, etc. Little analysis can be performed without these types of data during maintenance, as well as during the development phase of software acquisition.

A critical feature of data collection is that it must be designed into the software. This is particularly significant for real-time systems operating on a strict data processing budget and for highly interactive systems where the time and point of collection are critical. Tactical and weapon systems qualify on both counts. In order to assure efficiency and appropriate data collection, software monitoring capability must be considered and included in the initial software design, and the resources necessary to provide collection (CPU time, memory, etc.) must be considered when determining the system's data processing requirements. Data collection code added as an afterthought leaves a trail of problems and has several major drawbacks: it affects the overall timing and interaction of the various software modules; it introduces untested code into previously tested code, which now must itself be re-tested; and it is often accompanied by the implicit assumption that it will be removed as soon as the testing it supports is over. The removal of data collection code is a very questionable practice, since modules which have been successfully tested are now being modified by the deletion of this code; this leaves serious doubt as to the validity of the residual code. The axiom "fly what you test" has been demonstrated to be appropriate for both large and small software systems. However, it is not uncommon for a developing contractor to include data collection capabilities in a software package for his own testing, only to remove part or all of them prior to delivery of that package (as part of a tactical/weapon system) to the Government, thus delivering a substantially different set of code than was proven through the test program. This results in greatly reduced visibility into a software package which must be operated and maintained. The next step is obvious: pay "someone" to incorporate a data collection capability into this just-delivered software package.

Hardware Monitoring

A hardware monitor is a probe which, when physically attached to some element of a computer system, is capable of detecting when a signal passes to or through that element. Several such monitors are commercially available. Depending on the sophistication of the monitor, 100 or more such probes can be in operation simultaneously, relying on a minicomputer to process the signals for recording on a storage device (usually magnetic tape). The number of signals to a particular probe can be counted or, in some cases, the content of the signals can be decoded. Further, the characteristics of these probes are such that they produce no distortion, noise, interference, or other side effects which could either negate the validity of the data collected by them or affect the performance of the equipment to which they are attached. Typical measurements made via hardware monitoring include CPU active/wait time, channel activity (channel busy—CPU active, channel busy—CPU wait), peripheral activity (seek in process—CPU active, seek in process—CPU wait), and designated software job activity (number of times enabled, length of time active).

SUMMARY

This chapter has attempted to emphasize, and to some degree inform the reader on, software testing. It is written through the eyes of the system tester, but not (I hope) to the detriment of the other testing levels. There is much literature and general knowledge about the middle ground of software testing, e.g., program structure design, module design, coding, module testing. However, for the very early aspects — requirements, objectives, external specifications, system architecture — and the very late aspects — external function testing, system testing — very little relative knowledge exists. Until such time as the body of knowledge is filled in software testing, the project manager's best policy is to include and seek the input of all the test participants from the beginning.

References

1. *Blown Balloons, Aviation Week,* September 20, 1971, p. 17.
2. Liklider, J. C. R. "Underestimates and Overexpectations," *Computers and Automation,* vol. 18, August 1969, pp. 48-52.
3. *Information Processing/Data Automation Implications of Air Force Command and Control Requirements in the 1980s (CCIP-85): Highlights,* Vol I, SAMSO/SRS-71-1; April 1972.
4. Meyers, Glenford J. *Software Reliability Principles and Practices,* New York: John Wiley and Sons, Inc., 1976.

Epilogue

The preceding chapters explored a broad spectrum of concepts from the rapidly evolving field of software quality management. Each was designed to address one major aspect of this new discipline. The intent was to offer an introductory exposé of software quality management, thereby establishing a foundation upon which the reader could construct his own individual policies for managing quality software. It is felt that the book, if used in this way, will give the manager a practical overview of the field with quick reference to the several concepts and philosophies presented.

While conscious attempts were made to isolate the thoughts and concepts in each of the chapters, several themes or threads continually reappear throughout the book. Highlighted here are several of these themes:

Software quality management is a relatively new and evolving discipline. It will spawn many of its own procedures, processes, tools, techniques, and methodologies. It would be inappropriate to impose upon the software quality management field various practices from previously established fields simply because the word "quality" is common to both.

The sphere of software quality management encompasses numerous functions. In many current organizational structures, these functions transcend existing organizational boundaries. For this reason, many companies and federal agencies find it difficult to assign the responsibilities for software quality management. There is a dangerous tendency to place all these functions under one group — the hardware quality group.

To initiate software quality activities, organizations need a high level of commitment. Without strong management backing, the software quality function is doomed to failure — commencing with the first project manager who refuses to apply good software quality practices.

Good quality practices emphasize front-end loading of projects. That is, resources must be expended at the beginning of a program to assure quality products at the end of the program. Because of its nature, software quality must be designed in. As pointed out many times throughout the book, quality cannot be tested into the software; however, software developments do stress early participation by the test organization.

Emphasis on front-end loading indicates the need for development plans for software and software quality management.

Hardware quality assurance procedures are only partially applicable to software developments. In fact, many of the software quality tools and methodologies presently evolving constitute a discipline unique to software and many foster a reevaluation of some of the traditional hardware quality concepts.

From a software quality management perspective:

Software includes computer programs, data, and very importantly, the associated documentation.

Firmware is a special case of software and should be subject to the same development disciplines as any other software.

Software quality may be characterized by a list of factors and attributes.

Software reliability is a subset and not synonymous with software quality.

Software quality assurance and verification/validation are activities which are subsets of software quality management.

276

Epilogue

The use of hardware metrics such as MTBF cannot be directly applied to software. The physics of software failures and hardware failures are not compatible. Forcing hardware reliability concepts onto software is deleterious to good development practices.